BOTANY BAY

Maria Nugent

Botany Bay is the inaugural winner of the Allan Martin Award, awarded for innovative research which makes a significant contribution to Australian history.

Previous pages:
Selling boomerangs and shell art at The Loop, c. 1950s. Pictured are
Uncle John Timbery (standing), his wife Aunty Marj Timbery (sitting),
Aunty Esme Russell holding her son Bill and Marilyn Russell (the little
girl looking at the camera).
(Photograph of Uncle John Timbery with boomerangs at La Perouse,
1950s, by J.H. Bell. Reproduced by permission of the family and
J.H. Bell. Collection: Powerhouse Museum, Sydney.)

In memory of Clara Mason

BOTANY BAY
WHERE HISTORIES MEET

MARIA NUGENT

ALLEN&UNWIN

This book is published with the assistance of the Australian Academy of Humanities, the Monash University Publications Grants Committee and the Burraga Aboriginal History and Writing Group.

First published in Australia in 2005

Allen & Unwin
83 Alexander Street
Crows Nest NSW 2065
Australia
Phone: (61 2) 8425 0100
Fax: (61 2) 9906 2218
Email: info@allenandunwin.com
Web: www.allenandunwin.com

National Library of Australia
Cataloguing-in-Publication entry:

Nugent, Maria.
Botany Bay: where histories meet.

Bibliography.
Includes index.
ISBN 1 74114 575 9.

1. Botany Bay (N.S.W.) – History. I. Title.

994.41

Typeset in 11.5/13 pt Adobe Garamond by Midland Typesetters, Maryborough
Printed by CMO Image Printing Enterprise, Singapore

10 9 8 7 6 5 4 3 2 1

CONTENTS

LIST OF FIGURES

ACKNOWLEDGMENTS

Gloria Ardler, Beryl Beller, Leslie Davison, Clara Mason, Lee-Anne Mason, Iris Williams and Sharon Williams introduced me to Botany Bay's many-layered meanings and taught me new ways to think about history. This book owes much to them. Gloria, Beryl and Iris, in particular, have supported me over a number of years.

Bain Attwood, Barbara Caine, Ann Curthoys, Tom Griffiths, Paula Hamilton and Marian Quartly were insightful and incisive readers and critics. I benefited greatly from their input at different stages of the writing process.

In 2002, a period of research and writing was made possible by a Nancy Keesing Fellowship at the State Library of New South Wales. Elizabeth Ellis, Mitchell Librarian and Director, Collection Management, provided support during the fellowship and beyond, for which I am especially grateful. Thanks also to Richard Neville, Mark Hildebrand and Linda West for their assistance. I received additional research funding from the Faculty of Arts at Monash University. The original research for the book was supported by a doctoral scholarship from the University of Technology, Sydney. In 2004 I was awarded the inaugural Allan Martin Award, established in memory of the esteemed Australian historian, which enabled me to reproduce the illustrations in the book. I want to express my appreciation to the Australian National University and the Australian Historical Association, which jointly sponsored the Award. I am grateful also to the Australian Academy of Humanities, the Monash University Publications Grants Committee and the Burraga Aboriginal Writing and History Group for support which made the book's publicaiton possible.

The vast Botany Bay archive is spread across many research institutions. For access to those materials, thanks to Ellen Waugh and the Randwick and District Historical Society, Niall Petit-Young and the Bowen Library Local Studies Collection, Stephen Thompson and the Lapérouse Museum, Ann Stephen and the Museum of Applied Arts and Sciences, Bob Percival and the Office of the Board of Studies New South Wales and staff at the State Records Authority of New

South Wales, the Australian Institute of Aboriginal and Torres Strait Islander Studies and the National Library of Australia.

I am grateful to Elizabeth Weiss at Allen & Unwin for her commitment to the book and to Karen Gee for seeing it through the production process.

Many thanks to my colleagues at the School of Historical Studies at Monash University in Melbourne for providing a supportive, enjoyable and intellectually inspiring place within which to work. Barbara Caine, Graeme Davison and David Garrioch in particular generously supported and encouraged me during the preparation of this book.

Finally, I want to thank my family and friends for their generosity in matters big and small.

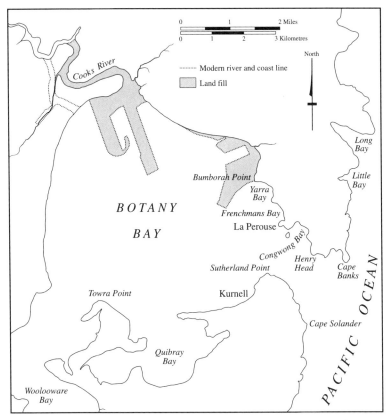

Map of Botany Bay. The shaded areas indicate Sydney (Kingsford Smith) Airport and Port Botany. (Prepared by Gary Swinton)

INTRODUCTION
The road to Botany Bay

When the road to Botany Bay reaches the tip of the north head it circles around in a loop.[1] The looped section is called the Scenic Drive or, as the locals say, 'the Scenic'. And scenic it is. As the road skirts the perimeter of the promontory, a panoramic view over Botany Bay emerges. On a clear day the vista sweeps around from the heads, along the southern shore, across to the runways of Sydney (Kingsford Smith) Airport and over the wharves of Port Botany that poke out from the north shore, until Yarra Bay and Frenchmans Beach complete the scene.

This is not simply a scenic landscape in the sense of being beautiful. It is also scenic in the sense of having been the scene for what are now considered significant historical events. Captain Cook and his crew sailed between the headlands of Botany Bay in the *Endeavour* in April 1770, and Captain Phillip and the First Fleet took the same route in January 1788 followed a few days later by the French expedition under the command of Comte de Galaup de Lapérouse. The southern shore was the site of Cook's first landfall. Yarra Bay was where Phillip made his first landing. And Frenchmans Beach was where Lapérouse established a temporary encampment between January and March 1788. Captain Cook chose the name Botany Bay for this place, and many features of the landscape have since been named for him, Phillip and Lapérouse. Edifices to each of them, as well as to some of their companion travellers, and the history they made can be found there. Because Captain Cook

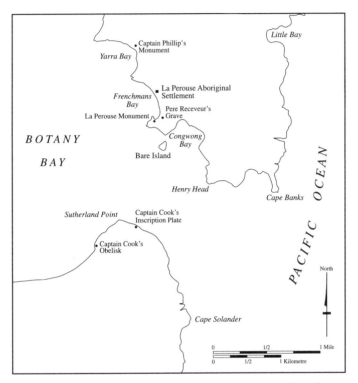

Detail of Botany Bay's north and south heads, showing the Aboriginal settlement behind Frenchmans Beach in relation to various monuments to late eighteenth-century visitors. (Prepared by Gary Swinton)

arrived there in April 1770, Botany Bay is considered a birthplace of the Australian nation. Sometimes it is called the birthplace of Australian history. Nations and histories are often equated.

I first went to Botany Bay in July 1985. My encounter was by no means historic but it was concerned with matters historical. I'd gone there to meet Iris Williams, an Aboriginal woman in her early sixties who lived in the Aboriginal settlement behind Frenchmans Beach on the La Perouse headland. She and some other local Aboriginal people wanted to record their own histories and memories of Botany Bay. They were looking for someone to help with the project and I was being considered for the job.

When our meeting was over, Iris and I stood together on the street in front of her house while she showed me the view. The scene she revealed centred on some scrub on the foreshores of Frenchmans Bay at the bottom of the slope from where we were standing. This was where, in the closing years of the nineteenth century, her mother had been born. She pointed out an oleander tree to indicate the former site of a small Aboriginal settlement, which was known to be in existence in the late 1870s, though perhaps was there earlier. This was Botany Bay as a birthplace of a different kind: a view of an historical landscape preserved in memory rather than monument. For this scene, the panorama of Botany Bay gained from 'the Scenic'—the one that contained a series of monuments to late eighteenth-century landing places—was merely a backdrop.

Iris's intimate introduction to the Botany Bay landscape is the origin of this book in two ways. It was the start of our working together, along with some other local Aboriginal people, on a series of history projects, which ultimately led and enabled me to write this history of Botany Bay;[2] and it provides the theme at the heart of the narrative I tell, that is, the nature of the relationship between

Iris Williams standing near her mother's birthplace at La Perouse, 2000. (Maria Nugent)

local Aboriginal pasts and histories and those that can be described as imperial, colonial and national. The moment Iris showed me the lie of the land—a phrase that I am using in both a topographic and figurative sense—is a metaphor for this history of Botany Bay. Almost from the moment that Captain Cook decided on the name, Botany Bay has been made and imagined through stories of many kinds. Initially many Botany Bay stories were about the origins of the British colony, and subsequently about the Australian nation. Like all foundation stories, they serve to provide an explanation of, and a justification for, the communities, local and national, who tell them. They are fundamentally moral tales, created and reiterated as a means to legitimise past actions in the present. In the case of Botany Bay, these stories are necessarily about discovery, possession and colonisation. Foundation stories—some call them myths—also leave much unsaid but that is a sign of their power. The ones that feature Botany Bay say little about violence towards indigenous people, for instance, or the illegitimacy of the colonisers' claims to a territory occupied by others.

For Aboriginal people who have lived at Botany Bay in the wake of Captain Cook, these stories matter enormously. They matter because they often implicitly, and at times explicitly, say things about the place of Aborigines in the local and national community. Some of these historical stories, especially, though not exclusively, those about Captain Cook and his 'discovery' of Australia, are given physical form at Botany Bay and repeatedly, indeed insistently, told through various modes of commemoration. This serves continually to remind Aboriginal people just which pasts count, and which ones barely register. Local Aboriginal people have responded in different ways to what I am calling Botany Bay stories, at times contesting them, at other times reworking them for their own purposes.[3] By tracing how they interpret and deploy them, my aim is to examine Aboriginal people's efforts to limit the power of colonial storytelling to hurt and dehumanise them. I am concerned moreover to show how they use their own forms of historical storytelling to make a place for themselves within local and national communities, from which they have been, and at times still are, excluded. It is the entanglement of, and interactions between, these various pasts and presences that shapes the narrative that follows. This is what I mean by describing Botany Bay as *where histories meet.*

Throughout the book, well- and lesser-known Botany Bay stories are interrogated, hidden pasts traced, different ways of knowing the past explored and new stories about Botany Bay told. Some consideration is given to the almost legendary historical encounters that occurred at Botany Bay; far more is given to the continuous commemoration of them and to contestations over their contemporary interpretations. The storyline, therefore, constantly moves between past and present. Given that Botany Bay has long been a place of and for historical storytelling, my narrative of it is also structured around both sites and stories. All chapters deal to some extent with how historic events have been imprinted on the landscape. Nomenclature, monuments, suburban development are interpreted as means for preserving, interpreting and telling stories about the past in the present. However, I am aware that a landscape approach sometimes suffers from a propensity to invest the built environment with too much meaning, and also conscious of the related problem that not all pasts produce or leave behind physical remains. So, I am attentive to those pasts that have touched the landscape only lightly.

Memory, or more precisely remembrance, becomes increasingly significant in this respect. Places are not simply history texts to be read through their material and physical forms. They are also 'storehouses for social memory'.[4] In this sense, memory can provide a bridge between the present physical place and its sometimes less visible pasts and historical meanings. Through excavating acts of remembrance, a landscape of absent presences is revealed. But, more than this, I am convinced that remembrance is itself productive of place. French sociologist Maurice Halbwachs is often credited with revealing an integral relationship between memory and place.[5] According to Patrick Hutton, Halbwachs' insight was the way in which 'the memorialist transposes a mental map onto a topographical plane, where it becomes a visible landscape of memory'.[6] Pierre Nora's project on tracing the French past through '*lieux de memoire*' returns to this theme by exploring the ways in which sites (a term which includes localities but is not confined to them) are made into, and function as, repositories of historical memory.[7] Remembrance, which implicitly involves language, therefore makes and remakes place.

The act of appointing myself as yet one more Botany Bay storyteller was in part motivated by a desire to contribute to contemporary discussions in Australia about the role that history-making plays in shaping identities, constructing inequalities, challenging injustices and imagining alternative futures. This seems all the more pressing as Australian historical scholarship, particularly about Aborigines and about relations between blacks and whites in the colonial past, has come under attack in recent years, and as concerted attempts are being made in some quarters to recast the practice of historical inquiry as simply the uncovering of an actual past discoverable through the documentary archive. One of my overriding concerns in writing this book has been to reveal how Aboriginal people especially—but not necessarily exclusively—live daily and intimately with history. The past continually resides in and impinges on their present. By writing a history of this kind, I wanted to remind myself as an historian, and others who read my history of Botany Bay, how some historical stories can have real and sometimes lasting effects. The past, it seems to me, is the stuff of conversations of considerable import. This book is therefore a response and a contribution to the ways in which knowledge about the colonial past, as well as ways of knowing and understanding that past, are being reconsidered and reconceptualised in Australia at the beginning of the twenty-first century.

A PLACE FOR STORIES

*Captain Cook, colonial origins and
hairy wild men*

Botany Bay, Captain Cook, 1770. Place, person, date. The stuff of history. These three elements form a type of triptych in an Australian historical imagination. They became irrevocably joined when, in late April 1770, Captain James Cook sailed into the bay he later named Botany Bay. However, they are code for a much more expansive story—about discoveries, first contact, the founding of a colony and the origins of a nation.

Botany Bay, Captain Cook, 1770. There is sufficient symmetry among the elements—the repeated consonants in each, for instance—to entertain momentarily the conceit that their joining together was, if not destined, then a proper state of affairs. However, much more was required than the encounter that brought them together in the first place for the bond between the three to become seemingly unshakeable. And so, circling the triad are many interpretive possibilities. There are those to illuminate the encounter that entwined Botany Bay, Captain Cook, 1770; there are others to explain how the whole ended up standing for so much more than the sum of its parts.

But, while Botany Bay was literally and figuratively put on the map by Captain Cook in 1770, it soon floated free from his cartography and his history. After the 1770 encounter, Botany Bay became imagined place as much as geographical location, at least from a European point of view. Since Captain Cook, stories of many sorts about Botany Bay have abounded. They often only have a fragile connection to the locale that goes by that name, but they have all contributed to fixing Botany Bay in the mind. Those who have lived at Botany Bay after Captain Cook, and those who call it home, respond in different ways to Botany Bay stories: they take them into their own possession; they add their own interpretations; and they ultimately use them for their own purposes.

Arriving

The *Endeavour* sailed west from New Zealand in early April 1770. On 19 April the southern east coast of New Holland was sighted, and Captain James Cook set his ship's course northwards. As the ship wended its way along the coast, Cook recorded in his journal some names given to remarkable geographic features, mostly according to likeness—for instance, Mount Dromedary because it looked like a one-humped camel and Pigeon House Mountain because, as botanist Joseph Banks explained, it 'much resembled those dove houses which are built four square with a small dome at the top'.[1] In *The Road to Botany Bay*, literary theorist Paul Carter made much of Cook's naming practices to illustrate his thesis that country is colonised by language as well as by settlement, but the renowned Cook scholar J.C. Beaglehole characterised it best when he wryly observed that '[Cook] was not a mere sprinkler of royal dukes'.[2]

While it was ultimately Cook's privilege to decide what to call features on unfamiliar terrain, naming was not a completely solitary activity. Shipboard talk—a constant babble turning observation into conversation—provided some of the raw material from which Cook produced placenames. One can imagine his companions and him playing a maritime version of 'I Spy', a game well suited to relieve the boredom of long trips. The skill in this specific context would have been coming up with a comparison that most suited the feature seen: 'I spy with my little eye something that looks like a . . .' The agreed-upon resemblances were logged by the other journal-writers on board the *Endeavour* who, like Cook, were not content with merely talking in the wind.[3]

From the ship's deck Banks had been familiarising himself with the natives and with nature and he was itching to go ashore to take a closer look. He had seen from the ship '5 people who appeard through our glasses to be enormously black: so far did the prejudices which we had built on Dampiers account influence us that we fancied we could see their Colour when we could scarce distinguish whether or not they were men'.[4] He thus reminded his readers, both then and now, that no observation is ever unmediated. An attempt to go ashore was made near the place now known as Bulli, but it was initially abandoned because of a leaky boat and later because of the big surf. Men with canoes were seen on shore, and Banks and others flattered themselves that the locals were preparing to pay them a shipboard visit. They were wrong. The indigenous people (Dharawal) did not attempt to visit them then, or in fact at all during the next week or so when the opportunities to do so were much greater.

The following day, the *Endeavour* sailed into the place that is the subject of this book. And what happened next—or so the story goes—is history. Or was it? The journal accounts from Botany Bay do not read as though history was being made there and then. Historical is not, one imagines, the word that the voyagers themselves would have used to describe their week-long stopover there. It only later became history. From an Australian viewpoint, this happened after the landfall at Botany Bay was given opening chapter status in a much larger narrative about more singularly historical events, such as the founding of the colony and the formation of the nation. Indeed, on its own and at the time, there was very little to indicate that the *Endeavour*'s encounter in Botany Bay would become heavily laden with historical significance. History is typically dependent on noteworthy events for its sustenance. But Cook's short stay in Botany Bay in late April 1770 was decidedly uneventful—from the point of view of the voyagers, if not for the locals. This is the paradox: it is those on the voyagers' side of the encounter who have gone to such lengths to make history from it.

Remarkable occurrences?

Captain Cook began his journal of his first voyage to the South Seas, which included the sojourn to Botany Bay, with the heading: 'Remarkable Occurences [*sic*] on Board his Majesty's Bark Endeavour, River Thames'.[5] And that captures its contents accurately enough. As he sailed across the South Seas, many remarkable things happened, which he dutifully recorded. Yet, in his account of the eight or so days spent in Botany Bay, the title perhaps ought to have been temporarily changed to 'Remarkable Dearth of Occurrences'. His text records a series of non-events. At one point he writes: 'In the PM I went with a party of Men over to the North shore and while some hands were hauling the Saine a party of us made an excursion of 3 or 4 miles into the Country or rather along the Sea Coast. We met with nothing *remarkable* . . .' (emphasis added).[6]

Throughout the first long voyage, the remarkable often occurred during meetings with local people, but this was not the case at Botany Bay. Even before landing on the shore, those on board the *Endeavour* had observed the way that the locals had all but ignored them and their strange ship. Thus Banks describes people fishing, who 'scarce lifted their eyes' when the *Endeavour* passed 'within a quarter of a mile of them'.[7] A few days after leaving Botany Bay, he describes how twenty or so people, seen walking along a beach, 'pursued their way in all appearance intirely unmovd by the neighbourhood of so *remarkable* an object as a ship must necessarily be to people who have never seen one' (emphasis added).[8] What was worth remarking on here was the locals' nonchalance about the plainly remarkable.

In his journal, Cook repeatedly describes how the 'natives' avoided him and his men, usually 'fleeing' when approached. They showed only scant interest in the trinkets offered to them as Cook and his men attempted to land, and none at all in the boats, water casks and other paraphernalia that the voyagers used as they went about their daily business.

The avoidance Cook describes came after the first landing, which, as is well known, involved shots being fired. When a party attempted to land, they were met with a show of resistance from

Two of the Natives of New Holland Advancing to Combat from Sydney Parkinson's *A Journal of a Voyage to the Seas in History Majesty's ship* Endeavour, first published in 1773. (Mitchell Library, State Library of New South Wales)

two local men brandishing spears. Cook ordered a musket to be fired. One local was injured. The two men retreated and the landing was made.

The voyage's artist, Sydney Parkinson, preserved two 'warriors' in image, with bodies painted, weapons raised and physical strength displayed. They are portrayed as impressive specimens, against a bare background, devoid of setting and without a target. These two men are not necessarily the ones on the beach at the moment of the landing. Banks describes a scene a few hours prior to the landing in which a few:

> Indians ... remain on the rocks opposite the ship, threatening and menacing with their pikes and swords—two in particular who were painted with white, their faces seemingly dusted over with it, their bodies painted with broad strokes drawn over their breasts and backs resembling much a soldiers cross belts, and their legs and thighs also with such broad strokes drawn round them which imitated broad garters or bracelets.[9]

Parkinson's rendition of the two men has been repeated, in modified form, in many images depicting the landing of Captain Cook at Botany Bay. For example, a lithograph published in a supplement with the *Town and Country Journal* in 1872 Christmas edition

This lithograph *Captain Cook's landing at Botany, A.D. 1770* was presented as a supplement with the Christmas edition of *Town and Country Journal*, 21 December 1872. The model for the two men on the beach is clearly Parkinson's sketch. In this image, Cook is depicted in a conciliatory pose, standing at the bow of the boat with arms outstretched. He has not yet given the order to fire the musket and there is no indication that this was to happen. Indeed all the firearms held by the sailors are pointing away from the direction of the men on the shore. The 'aggression' in this image belongs to the 'native warriors'. With this vision of history, the readers of *Town and Country Journal* could enjoy Christmas with an easy conscience. (National Library of Australia)

depicts the two 'warriors' opposing the landing. Similar images appear over and over again in the popular press and in multiple volumes about Cook and Australia's history. It is in this defiant stance that the two men on the beach, their names unknown, entered a colonial imagination and a local Aboriginal one too.

In the presence of strangers

The combination of resistance and avoidance on the part of the local indigenous people caused Cook to comment in his journal that 'all they seem'd to want was for us to be gone'.[10] It's an oft-repeated line, used alternatively as evidence for Cook's ethnographic sensibilities and for Aborigines' resistance from the very outset to the incursion of Europeans into their lives and on to their lands. But the encounter is obviously more complex than either of these interpretations of Cook's one-liner. The local indigenous people no doubt did want the strangers to go, but it is also worth entertaining the idea that the display of force and the cold shoulder treatment were a type of protocol to be followed when in the presence of strangers. They were perhaps designed to pave the way for some form of exchange to occur. Later ethnographic accounts (albeit belonging to different times and different places), documenting what happened when Aborigines and strangers (both indigenous and non-indigenous) met, suggest as much.

The classic ethnographic text on this matter is one by Baldwin Spencer and Frank Gillen, produced, according to the archaeologist, Sylvia Hallam, when they 'were with an Arunta community near Alice Springs in 1901'.[11] Hallam has used Spencer and Gillen's description as a model for illuminating the fragmentary evidence of other meetings between strangers in the south-west of the continent in the early nineteenth century, arguing that similar patterns seem to have been followed across Australia and that, in general (and when both sides knew the rules), they were 'highly structured affairs, with elements of ceremonial preparedness for conflict, formal peace-making, reciprocal exchange of gifts and sometimes actual conflict and resolution of conflict'.[12] Some of the elements that Spencer and Gillen, and Hallam, describe are evident in the encounter at Botany Bay. For example, the practice of taking no notice of the strangers when they first arrive is common, as is the stylised display of strength, particularly by two men. Based on this evidence, the locals at Botany Bay in 1770 were not only already playing their part by the time the *Endeavour* came into view, but they also remained in role for as long as the situation demanded. The voyagers had entered a staged event.

The initial display of nonchalance, followed by animated resistance when an attempt to land was made, presumably was performed to enable a meeting of sorts to occur. But that meeting, as the record of the voyage tells us, did not take place. This was not, as is often implied, because the locals were (by nature) resistant to the shock of the new, nor essentially apathetic, charges that have been repeatedly made against Aborigines throughout the colonial period. The animated show of resistance by the pair of armed indigenous men on the beach was part of a repertoire of responses covering encounters with strangers, not an invitation for retaliation. It did not require a counter-display of force, which is how events proceeded when Cook ordered the musket to be fired after Banks had suggested that their spears might have poisoned tips. If the description given by Spencer and Gillen can be taken as a model, then what should have happened next, had the strangers held their fire, is that the other local men waiting out of view behind the two 'warriors' would have come out to accompany the strangers into an open space. And there they would have been met by more local people, including women and children. With shots fired and a man wounded, this did not happen. In this situation, various options were now available to the locals. They might have agreed to give the strangers another chance. Or not. The course they seemed to have decided upon was to have nothing more to do with them. And so ensued some more days of evasiveness—whenever the strangers approached, the locals 'fled' or 'hid'.

But why does suggesting this alternative mode of interpretation matter? This event (and others like it) has become historically significant, particularly at a national level. As such, the conventional and popular lines of interpretation of it have far-reaching and enduring effects. They create meanings that stick. The apparent habit of fleeing, both at Botany Bay in 1770 and at other places at other times, has been used against Aborigines generally to suggest that they did not defend their land and therefore that the arrival of the British, whether as voyagers searching for territory or as settlers, did not amount to invasion. From the opposite direction, the singling out of the two men brandishing their spears as Cook attempted to land ascribes to Aborigines a somewhat simplistic and unchanging reputation as 'resistors'. Local Aboriginal people in the post-1770 period have not themselves been immune to this, often deploying the two men opposing the landing as the first in a long line of Aboriginal fighters. These somewhat diametrically opposed and overly simplistic interpretations, drawing from the best-known and concomitantly most rehearsed and reiterated elements of what was a messy and confusing encounter, mask the complexity and ambiguity involved.

The paradox at the heart of this encounter in Botany Bay in 1770 is that the much commented upon lack of interest in the visitors on the part of the locals may be evidence for just how actively and deeply engaged they were in this drama, behaving in concert with each other in ways that the situation demanded. It was neither simply ambivalence nor apathy, but a ceremony of sorts—perhaps a prelude to the main act. In the end, by leaving rather than staying, the strangers may have managed to redeem themselves. And maybe it was this that allowed the next cargo of strangers brought from the sea in January 1788 to begin their stay with an encounter of a closer kind.

When Captain Arthur Phillip and a few of his men first landed on the north shore of Botany Bay in January 1788, they exchanged signs and words with the locals, who led them to water. It was a good start for Phillip, who fashioned himself as the friendly coloniser. Historian Keith Willey argues that for local indigenous people, by 1788, the encounter in 1770 'would have already been fading into legend'.[13] But transformation into legend ought not suggest fading from memory. Just as the Dharawal and other local indigenous groups had no doubt deliberated at length about what to do when the strangers arrived in 1770, there was more than likely a considerable amount of analysis after they left. It would have been something to talk about and perhaps to make ceremony from.[14] In ways that are pertinent to this discussion, anthropologist Deborah Bird Rose canvasses the possibilities for the remembrance or otherwise of collectively considered events among the Aboriginal people she has lived with in the Victoria Downs region of the Northern Territory:

> The event might be forgotten . . . and thus would be 'washed away' with the debris of what does not endure. Alternatively, it might be coded into

a form of remembrance that would hold it as a story or song for those who come behind . . . It would become part of the past that endures and is kept alive within social memory.[15]

In a mode akin to the way that Cook's 'discovery' is commonly perceived as an inevitable precursor to British 'settlement', it is equally feasible to argue that the encounters at Botany Bay in 1770 and in 1788 are connected in some way. The 1770 encounter ought to be considered germane to the process by which relations between colonisers and locals were clumsily established from 1788 onwards. Such an approach would add an extra element to Inge Clendinnen's evocative metaphor 'dancing with strangers' which she uses in her re-examination of the nature of cross-cultural relations in the first four years of the British settlement at Sydney Cove. She argues that 'the Australians [by which she means indigenous people] and the British began their relationship by dancing together'.[16] But I think a step has been missed. One could perhaps say that the 'Australians' began by playing hard to get and only later agreed to dance.

From Sting-ray Bay to Botany Bay

The more enduring legacy of the 1770 encounter in Botany Bay was not knowledge about natives but about natural science, a fact nicely encapsulated in the name given to this place. Given that the locals turned out to be such frustratingly evasive specimens, Banks had to satisfy himself almost exclusively with the plants. He noted in his journal that he was 'botanising as usual'.[17] Anthropologist Nicholas Thomas notes that 'it was not quite compensation [for the absence of encounters with the locals], but Banks gathered a staggering range of plants—more here, more quickly and more that were new than he and Solander [the other naturalist on board the expedition] had found anywhere else'.[18] The place was eventually named to reflect that this 'botanising as usual' had been the most remarkable feature of the visit. For a time, however, Banks' botanising was overshadowed by the only other *remarkable* event—the killing of a quantity of large and heavy stingrays. Immediately after his observation that an excursion into the country had met with 'nothing remarkable', Cook describes how the yawl that had gone out in the morning to fish for stingrays had 'return'd in the evening with upwards of 4 hundred weight; one single one wieghd 240 lb exclusive of the entrails'.[19] This apparently was remarkable indeed. And so, in the absence of any other obvious name for this seemingly unremarkable place, it came to be known as Sting-ray Bay. (Without any dialogue with the locals, what they called it was not recorded.)[20]

In a scale of significance influential for bestowing naming rights, picking flowers appears to have been no competition for catching a big one—at least not initially. But after leaving the bay the significance of Banks' botanising—perhaps unclear even to him at the time—became impossible to ignore. And so it was that, some months, perhaps as many as five, after leaving what Cook had dubbed Sting-ray Bay, the Captain decided to alter its name: first to Botanist Bay and then finally to Botany Bay. Sorting through the paper trail which tells the story of the name change, Beaglehole informs us that in one account 'we have partly deleted, the words "The great number of these . . . fish found at this place occasioned my naming it Sting Ray Bay", with the substitution of "The great number of New Plants &c" our Gentlemen Botanist [sic] have collected in this place occasion'd my giving in [sic] the name of Botanist Bay.'[21] Thus the logic behind the name remained the same—quantity mattered. But the value given to the respective product had changed: the once-remarkable stingrays had become less significant under the shadow of the botanical collection. These shifting contours of significance seemed sufficient for Cook to change his mind about his original choice, Sting-ray Bay. Or, perhaps, the more likely scenario is that Banks pressed him for the name change.

The change from 'Botanist' to 'Botany' was purely stylistic: it looked better on paper. There is a nice symmetry between the words 'botany' and 'bay', having as they do the same first and last letters. As Beaglehole first, and Nicholas Thomas after him, argue, on his first voyage Captain Cook was not only feeling his way in a navigational sense but also as a writer.[22] If nothing more, the change from

Botanist to Botany is evidence for this. It not only looked better; it sounded better too. Botany Bay is melodic, euphonious and alliteratively appealing.[23] That might not have mattered if the only historic thing to happen in Botany Bay was Banks' botanising or Cook's landing. But its melody became useful once 'history' took another course. With the subsequent selection of Botany Bay as the site for the penal colony, it was soon occupying a prominent place in the English popular imagination of the 1780s and beyond. That it remained fixed in it, even after Botany Bay was rejected for Port Jackson as a suitable site for the convict settlement in 1788, might best be explained through reference to the qualities of the name itself.

Its literary merits have well served, and perhaps even substantially contributed to, Botany Bay's prominent place in the popular and historical imagination, both in Britain and New South Wales, particularly in the late eighteenth century and for most of the nineteenth century. In relation to its enduring association with convictism, functioning as a familiar term for the convict settlement, despite playing only a minor and momentary role in that entire history, the historian Lloyd Robson suggested that 'it may have been kept in currency by ballads because it was a much more useful rhyme than New South Wales or Sydney Cove, and of course had the advantage of alliteration'.[24] Sting-ray Bay rhymes too, although one suspects that this would probably not have been sufficient to fix it as firmly in the imagination as Botany Bay. This is because, while significant, the quality of the sound was not all that mattered. The associations were important. Stingray, then as now, means just one thing; Botany, by comparison, oozed—and oozes still—with associations. It means both the subject-matter and the scientific study of that matter. And, in the late eighteenth century, this was science on the frontiers of new knowledge. Indeed, as a profession, a pursuit and a puzzle, botany was at the very centre of the eighteenth-century voyaging enterprise that had caused the bay that now goes by the name of Botany Bay to acquire, even require, a new name. Taking this into account, the appellation can therefore be read as a type of acknowledgment that one of the deeply desired aims of some on board the *Endeavour*, not least of whom was

Banks, had been realised. If Possession Island represents the accom-
plishment of one item on Captain Cook's list of things to do while
coasting around New Holland, then Botany Bay remembers the
achievement of aims formulated by his gentlemen companions. The
botany collected at Botany Bay by the naturalists was set to turn on
its head the taxonomy that had been hitherto used to organise the
plant world. This was no ordinary botany: it was unique, exotic,
perplexing and wild. As news of Banks' quarry circulated, Botany
Bay soon gained a reputation for the bizarre in nature, at least
among the educated classes in Europe interested in the new science.

   With the decision in the late 1780s to send convicts to the new
colony, Botany Bay's almost decade-old reputation for inversion
and for wildness was put to new use and into overdrive, so much so
that its association with nature gone mad was sometimes (paradoxically) strengthened rather than diluted. 'The colony,' observes the
historian John Hirst, 'lived up to its name as a place where the usual
order of things was completely reversed.'[25] The placename, Botany
Bay, proved to be accommodating rather than anachronistic as the
actual site's fortunes took a new turn. That it never was actually the
site for the penal settlement mattered not. By then Botany Bay had
already burst its geographical moorings: it was now simply a name
that floated free, seemingly soaking up any association thrown at it.

The 'wild man' from Botany Bay

Synonymous with convicts and with bizarre nature, Botany Bay was
woven into fabulous tales that circulated among a British audience
hungry for stories from faraway lands. Classic examples in this
genre of storytelling involving Botany Bay are the accounts of 'wild
men'. In the late 1780s or perhaps early 1790s, a cheap broadsheet
was published announcing the arrival in England of 'a wonderful
large WILD MAN, or monstrous GIANT, BROUGHT FROM
BOTANY-BAY'. The broadsheet describes 'various Reports concerning this most surprising WILD MAN or huge savage GIANT,
that was brought from Botany-Bay to England, numbers of People
arguing and disputing his enormous Size'.[26] The monstrous giant,

it was claimed, had arrived in Plymouth on board the *Rover* on 29 November 1789. A copy of this particular broadsheet is held by the Mitchell Library in Sydney. The library also has another version, with similar text but a different image. This second version claims the 'beast' arrived in Plymouth on 24 April 1790. And there are others still.

The inspiration for the broadsheets may have derived from an actual event: it is known that two Aboriginal men, Bennelong and Yemmerrawanie, were taken from the British colony in Sydney (which was commonly referred to as Botany Bay) to England in

Detail from the broadsheet *A DESCRIPTION of a wonderful large WILD MAN, or monstrous GIANT, BROUGHT FROM BOTANY-BAY,* c.1790. (Mitchell Library, State Library of New South Wales)

1792. Given that the exact date of the publication of the broadsheet is not known, perhaps the arrival of these two Aboriginal
men in England was the catalyst for the production and circulation
of exaggerated, popularised and fabulous accounts about 'savages'
from Botany Bay. But it is equally likely that these stories were not
inspired by any particular event: there was already a well-estab-
lished belief that faraway places were inhabited by far-out
creatures. Whatever the case, the wild man nonetheless ought to be
interpreted as a comment on antipodean 'natives'. He belongs to
the tradition whereby 'native others' in new world colonies were
characterised as, Michael Taussig notes, 'the cruel, lascivious, bes-
tially hirsute and deformed savages or wild men of medieval and
Renaissance legend'.[27]

The figure of the wild man existed in European thought long
before the colonisation of New Holland, and even before the
Medieval and Renaissance periods to which Taussig refers. But
while stories about hairy wild men did not originate in the imperial
age when distant lands were encountered for the first time, they did
re-emerge and gain new currency in this period, feeding popular
fears about the unknown and the radically different. Wild men were
half-man, half-beast. It is now common to interpret this phenomenon psychologically and symbolically as an anxiety about or
commentary on the bestial side of human nature. In the late eighteenth century, however, such figures were believed by some to be
literally true, and they played into popular ideas about the edges
of empire as a world upside down. Botany Bay, with its wild reputation already well established, and popularly believed to be
populated by strange 'natives' and by 'deviant' convict men, was the
perfect habitat from which such a creature should emerge. 'European folklore and superstition,' historian Robert Holden argues:

> had populated the Antipodes with a bizarre menagerie of creatures as well
> as fantastic races of people. Imagine all this within the context of a
> heightened awareness of Botany Bay. The result was a heady opportunity
> for the even further imaginative excesses—the timely arrival in the
> English provinces of the 'wonderful large wild man . . . brought from
> Botany-Bay.[28]

This reputation for wildness, where the divide between nature and culture is blurred, was at the core of Botany Bay's popular meanings. Indeed, the Botany Bay enigma arguably derives from its in-between quality, situated as it is at the nexus between geography and history, between place and time.

National origins and founding myths

But this was not yet the full extent of the role Botany Bay would play in various forms of storytelling, both British and Australian. During the nineteenth and twentieth centuries, it acquired further valency. After the initial phase, when it figured more in the minds of the English than it did for those who were actually living in the colony, Botany Bay assumed a central place in the persistent local search for colonial and later national origins.

Australia has had at least two contenders for its founding myth—discovery and convictism—and, as already shown, Botany Bay is associated, however tenuously, with each. (Both myths eclipse the dispossession of Aborigines, but have never succeeded in completely burying that knowledge.) Histories of discovery and histories of convictism emphasise different pasts, but they often seek to fulfil similar purposes by claiming to offer an explanation of Australia's beginnings. Each, in different ways, offers an alternative starting point, and thus an explanatory frame, for the story of the nation. As part of this continuing search for the nation's origins, Botany Bay's enduring place in the Australian imagination was, from time to time, reiterated, although historical monographs, journal articles and school textbooks gradually came to take the place of cheap chap-books, broadsides and pamphlets as the purveyors of its meanings.

In Australian historiography, discovery-as-origin was long preferred to convictism-as-origin. Obviously, the first landing of Captain Cook at Botany Bay in 1770 is pivotal in the discovery foundational myth. By setting eyes and feet upon land, Captain Cook was credited as bringing the future colony into being. This depiction of the event and its meaning was particularly popular in the late nineteenth and early twentieth century, and is encapsulated by E. Phillip Fox's 1902 painting *Landing of Captain Cook at Botany Bay, 1770*. The discovery origin story served nation-building by stressing that twentieth-century Australia had been envisaged from the outset, and had become the very thing—even better—than the soothsayer discoverers could have imagined.

If the discovery narrative evoked pre-ordained destiny, then the appeal of the convict narrative was achievement by overcoming

Although diminutive in the distance, the two 'warriors' make an appearance in E. Phillip Fox's history painting, *Landing of Captain Cook at Botany Bay 1770*, which was commissioned to mark Federation. The image is ambiguous in its depiction of the force used by the British against the locals. One officer has his weapon trained on the two indigenous men, but Cook appears to be ordering other crew members not to take aim. Cook and the man next to him, Banks, point in opposite directions, suggesting some discord between them. The most central element in this tableau is the flag, which symbolises possession. (E. Phillips Fox, *Landing of Captain Cook at Botany Bay 1770*, 1902, oil of canvas, Gilbee Bequest, 1902, National Gallery of Victoria, Melbourne)

humble origins. The convict past as foundational myth marked how far the nation had outstripped its beginnings. Convictism was imagined as a first hurdle, which necessarily had to be overcome to achieve greatness, thus making twentieth-century Australia even more impressive than it might otherwise have been. This in part explains the appeal of the convict story in national histories produced in the early twentieth century. By the 1920s, for instance, Australian historian George Arnold Wood was of the view, according to Julian Thomas, that 'the origins and the consequences of the convict system constituted the central subject of colonial history',[29] a view not shared by his nineteenth-century predecessors. Alan Frost dates this development slightly later, identifying 'such twentieth-century historians as Manning Clark, A.G.L. Shaw and Lloyd Robson [as] the first to face squarely the fact of our convict beginnings, to examine it dispassionately and in detail'.[30]

Botany Bay inevitably appears in the convict historiography: it features in discussions about what led the British government to select it as a site for a penal colony,[31] or as part of the discussion about how the penal colony was perceived and featured in a British imagination. For instance, in 1939, L.R. McIntyre began his chapter-length account about the convict system in Australian history with ruminations about how the mere mention of Botany Bay could scare small English children into obedience.[32] And, given that Botany Bay subsequently had very little to do with the actual penal colony, in some historical scholarship it is briefly discussed as enigma.

By the 1960s, Julian Thomas suggests, Australian historians had 'lost interest in colonial beginnings', or at least the ones that had been widely touted, such as convicts and discovery.[33] Revisionist historians working in this period were dissatisfied with the conventional stories about Australia's origins, and in their place proposed some new ones. For instance, there was a move to acknowledge 'feminist foundations': foremothers in place of forefathers.[34] And Henry Reynolds, among others, was claiming that Aboriginal land rights were there from the beginning,[35] and he also focused attention on the racial violence foundational to colonisation. Accompanying, or at least running parallel with, the effort to replace conventional national birth stories with others was another historical tradition. Exemplified by Richard White's *Inventing Australia*, published in 1981, this scholarship reconceptualised the nation as invented and imagined. This was a more self-conscious form of writing national history. In this mode, birth stories, or foundation narratives, were exposed as contrivances by nature, serving the interests of those with the power to define what the nation ought to be at any particular time. With the nation thought about in these terms, there could be *no* moment of birth because nations were not born, but invented and then manufactured through representations. Botany Bay had a place in this historical scholarship, but not as the stage for, or as synonymous with, actual historical events or processes. Its interest to historians working within this tradition was in terms of how it had been the subject of, and deployed in, diverse forms of storytelling about Australia and Australian-ness. Thus, during this post-1960s period in the writing of national Australian history, two approaches to the problem of origins can be broadly detected: one advocating new origins, the other none at all.

A view of history

While many nineteenth- and twentieth-century Australian historical narratives evoked Botany Bay, only the Captain Cook discovery story, distilled in the formulation Botany Bay, Captain Cook, 1770, was implicitly interested in the actual place itself. In this historical tradition, the geographical place Botany Bay mattered (and matters still). Those who made history from Cook's landing—in both the nineteenth and the twentieth centuries—were as interested in Botany Bay's place in history as they were in the history that could be found in the place.

Both James Martin and Charles H. Bertie, separated by nearly a hundred years, belong to this tradition. James Martin, author of *The Australian Sketch Book* published in 1838, provides one of the first 'intellectual' studies of Botany Bay.[36] Martin perceives Botany Bay as a place infused with the memory, the spirit and the physical traces of the founding historic event for the young colony: the landing of Captain Cook in 1770. He tells his readers:

> I had long been anxious to visit Botany Bay, as much on account of the magnificence of its scenery as in consequence of its being the place where the immortal Cook first landed on our southern shores . . . when some historical incident is intimately connected with a beautiful and romantic spot, the surrounding scenery acquires additional interest in my estimation, and, when it is in my power, I never fail to gratify my curiosity at the earliest opportunity.
>
> [. . .]
>
> But in no place throughout this Colony, save Botany Bay, is there a single spot hallowed by the memorable incidents of by-gone days, and rendered sacred by the transactions of illustrious men.[37]

At the time Martin was writing, this was a country perceived as lacking historical depth and in which the sacred belonged to the historic rather than the 'pre-historic'.

Martin was not alone in his desire to visit Botany Bay to view history. It was a popular site for visitors wanting to see for themselves the place where their history supposedly began. They could read the terrain as history book: see the rocks where Cook landed and the stream from which the crew collected water. In contrast to other historic sites in and around nineteenth-century Sydney, what was especially attractive about Botany Bay was that little had physically changed since the *Endeavour* had been there. The stream that the crew used to replenish water supplies apparently continued to flow for almost a hundred years after 1770. The claim that the landscape had changed little since those momentous events took place is significant. Here at Botany Bay one could not only see where events of historic import happened, but also see it as it was when Captain Cook first viewed it. Visitors could imagine themselves in Cook's shoes. This was a historic site that had the verisimilitude that living museums can now only crave. And, whereas the landscape of Port Jackson functioned as a memorial to progress, the historical significance of Botany Bay was the complete opposite: a place frozen in time, caught forever in some original moment. As such, Botany Bay functioned as a counterpoint to Sydney Cove, representing the 'before' in a before and after shot, its purpose to provide the baseline against which to measure the magnitude of the change that had occurred since (and because of) that original moment. Together Sydney Cove and Botany Bay told a complete story, one with a beginning and an end.[38]

Almost a century after Martin's piece on Botany Bay was published, Bertie's article, 'Captain Cook and Botany Bay', appeared in print.[39] Like Martin, he began by evoking the sacred qualities of the landscape by virtue of it having been a stage for and a witness to historically momentous deeds. Bertie quotes Dr Johnson from *A Tour of the Hebrides or Western Isles*, in which Johnson claims that he and his friends do not subscribe to 'such frigid philosophy as may conduct us indifferent and unmoved over any ground which has been dignified by wisdom, bravery, or virtue'.[40] Taking this as his cue, Bertie writes: 'Amongst the spots in Australia which have been "dignified by bravery" and over which one would have to be a "frigid philosopher" to pass "indifferent and unmoved" is Botany Bay.'[41] The bravery that dignified Botany Bay belonged to Captain Cook.

Indigenous witnesses to history

One might argue, along with many late twentieth-century Australian historians, that making national history from the bare bones of Botany Bay, Captain Cook, 1770 and other supposedly foundational events is 'about establishing the white history and identity of the nation'.[42] If so, that poses the problem for those telling the story of how to deal with the indigenous people there at the time of the landing. In the narratives woven in the nineteenth and early twentieth centuries from Captain Cook, Botany Bay, 1770, it was not a simple matter of completely ignoring Aborigines. That strategy is more evident from the 1930s onwards, when Australian history became more professionalised and institutionalised. Some historians argue that this was when the veil of silence in Australian historiography about the nature of relations between Aborigines and colonisers descended. By comparison, Chris Healy has argued that some early nineteenth-century history-making about Captain Cook, Botany Bay, 1770 fundamentally depended upon the inclusion of indigenous people to validate what would otherwise have been an unwitnessed event. Healy discusses the Philosophical Society of Australasia erecting a brass plaque on a cliff face at Botany Bay in 1822, to mark the spot where Cook had stepped ashore. On Healy's reading, this memorial gesture depended on an old local Aboriginal man who was found to identify the specific spot where the landing occurred, although Bertie argues that little store was given to the 'native's' testimony.[43] At one level, then, the commemorative gesture can be interpreted as acknowledging an indigenous presence because it relied on indigenous knowledge. But Healy argues that it simultaneously disavowed such a presence, given that the plaque marked only the historical deeds of Cook and Banks and made no reference to those who occupied the land when the pair arrived. The Aboriginal eyewitness played only a bit part. The absent presence on the plaque was local indigenous people, both at the time of Cook and as contributors to his historical remembrance.

That unnamed Aboriginal witness made his contribution to historical remembrance in 1822. One hundred years later, in 1924, Bertie drew upon the evidence of some other Aboriginal witnesses which he found in the archive. In his paper on Captain Cook at Botany Bay, he discusses what Aboriginal people living around Sydney in the 1830s—half a century or so after Cook had actually been at Botany Bay—knew or believed about the arrival of the *Endeavour*. His information comes from a letter that had been written in 1863 by a priest. It included details of a conversation that the priest reportedly had in 1833, when based at St Mary's Cathedral, with an Aboriginal man from Botany Bay, whose father had allegedly witnessed Captain Cook's arrival. While the Aboriginal man's account confused, and indeed conflated, known details about Cook with the various other voyagers who sailed into Botany Bay in the late eighteenth century, he claimed that the men and women on shore thought the *Endeavour* was a big bird.[44] After providing this view from the beach, Bertie provides his own gloss, claiming that the encounter had been 'the death knell of the aboriginal race'.[45] He does not embellish. By making this statement, he relegates Aborigines to the status of 'historical transients'[46]—there one minute, gone the next—and proceeds with his detailed reassessment of the evidence about Captain Cook's sojourn in Botany Bay.

Aboriginal people only enter Bertie's account as historical sources. Another example is an old woman named Sally Mettymong who he presents as the authority for the location of the grave of Forby Sutherland, the young man who died while the *Endeavour* was at Botany Bay. She had passed her knowledge on to a young white boy living at Kurnell in the 1850s, when she was about 80 years old, which made it possible that she had been in the area at the moment of Captain Cook. In 1923, the memories of the young boy—by then an old man—were retold:

> the old woman was accustomed to pass up and down the beach, accompanied by him, during the period that the property was in his father's possession . . . On several occasions as they were traversing the little beach immediately below the Solander monument, the aboriginal woman pointed up the slope and state[d] 'white man buried there'. She had vivid collections when she was a little girl of seeing Captain Cook's ship come in and a party land at Kurnell.[47]

Like the priest's informant, Mettymong was perceived as belonging to an era that was continuous with Cook's time, which made her a witness worth citing. But she was also implicitly cast as the last link to that historical period.

During the period when Bertie was writing there was a relatively large and quite permanent Aboriginal population living at Botany Bay. None of these people feature in Bertie's account, presumably because he regarded them as unconnected to—or, perhaps more precisely, disconnected from—the subject of his paper. Bertie was by no means being original by drawing a line between the Aborigines at Botany Bay in 1770 and those living there over 150 years later. It was commonplace to represent Aboriginal people as stranded in time, completely cut off from an earlier past and, moreover, without a future. Yet, this comprehensive division between the past and the present was one that local Aboriginal people regularly unsettled in their own historical storytelling. Certainly by the late nineteenth and early twentieth century, but possibly earlier, many local Aboriginal people were claiming to be the direct descendants of those who had been on the beach when

Captain Cook arrived in 1770. For instance, a missionary who lived with Aboriginal people in the settlement at La Perouse on Botany Bay's north head in the 1890s recalled in her memoirs that:

> I was destined to become acquainted, nearly a century and a quarter later, with a son of one who witnessed the landing of Captain Cook. Old Jimmy, who was near the century mark, was grandfather of the camp where I began my missionary service . . . Jimmy's 'old people' had graphically rehearsed, again and again, the story, which he passed on, of their scare of 'Moomiga', and what he told was verified by others, whose grandparents were amongst those who looked from the shore, at the oncoming vessel—the forerunner of a civilisation which has well nigh destroyed a branch of the oldest stock of the human race.[48]

Old Jimmy and others were in many respects making an audacious claim, and one that was contrary to some other historical evidence, including the testimony given by an Aboriginal man known as Mahroot to a parliamentary select committee in 1845.[49] Mahroot claimed that he was the last male survivor of the original people from around Botany Bay at the time of Cook. As his people had diminished in number after British settlement, blacks from other neighbouring groups, mainly from Liverpool and the Five Islands, had moved in. Mahroot had a small piece of land on the north shore given to him by Governor Richard Bourke. But, at another level, the claim Old Jimmy and others were making was accurate. This was a story in which all Aboriginal people associated with Botany Bay were involved. They were descendants of those who had seen it, although that descent was not strictly biological or genealogical. This was a form of descent akin to the way that imagined communities—national and local—claim descent from a common forefather.

These types of claims have been preserved over time in texts compiled by the white interlocutors who heard them. And, in turn, they have been excavated from the archives to be used as sources in new histories of Botany Bay. For instance, a recently published history of Sutherland Shire, which includes Botany Bay's south shore where Captain Cook landed, begins with this epigraph: 'They all run away; two fellows stand; Cook shot them in the legs; and they run away too.' This is presented as a 'rare eye-witness account by an Aboriginal observer'.[50] But this highly abbreviated version has much in common with Cook's own account, putting a question mark over just how rare it is. The conduit between the witness and the present was a well-known Aboriginal woman, Biddy Giles, who had lived at Kurnell on Botany Bay's southern shore in the 1840s. The witness was apparently her uncle. She had in turn passed the story on to R. Longfield, who told it to W. Houston, who wrote it down. It ended up in the 'archives of the Captain Cook's Landing Place Trust', Box 12, Item 141. In this narrative, the standoff between Cook and the 'two fellows' remains a central element in the story of Botany Bay but, by having an Aboriginal person describe the scene, the author addresses in part the cultural politics of the late twentieth century when the book was published. In the pages that follow, however, Aboriginal people continue to appear predominantly as the recipients of 'the history' that Cook's arrival inaugurated. Yet within the eyewitness statement that begins the book lies evidence of something else. That the view from the beach borrows so heavily from Cook's own account, much popularised since 1770, suggests that local Aboriginal people did not simply find themselves in 'a new era in the history of the Australian continent' which was ushered in by the arrival of the Europeans.[51] Rather, it suggests that they were also seriously engaging with the stories that the new settlers and their descendants told about that new era.

Almost 90 years earlier, a history of the local shire on Botany Bay's north shore had also began with an account of Cook's landing from 'descendants' of eyewitnesses to it: 'Descendants of King "Timbury" in the Aborigines' Mission station at La Perouse, relate the story of their ancestors witnessing Captain Cook's "Endeavour" making the coast under full sail at Botany Heads. They assert that instead of the aborigines spearing the visitors, they took fright and fled headlong from the coast.'[52] This version of the encounter is well suited to the author's purposes because, with the Aborigines making their departure, he could continue with his account about local white settlement and progress that was at the heart of his historical narrative. While an Aboriginal presence at the moment of contact is given some prominence, it is simultaneously quarantined. It is placed outside the historical narrative, either by reference to Aborigines' apparent voluntary absence from the scene or as a later consequence of the colonisation to which the event gave rise. This is a reading of the extant sources that turns 'fleeing' as a response to a specific situation into an autonomous decision not to participate in the history then being made. The legacy of this form of historical interpretation has been that the story of Aboriginal people living at Botany Bay in the post-colonial period is almost completely divorced from the story of Captain Cook at Botany Bay and from the indigenous people who were present when he arrived. In this respect, post-1770 indigenous (local) history and non-indigenous (local and national) history are depicted as though they belong to parallel universes. But one might argue that the story of Aboriginal people across Australia, let alone at Botany Bay, is never totally unconnected to the stories that colonisers tell about Botany Bay, Captain Cook, 1770. Deborah Bird Rose's interpretation of Captain Cook stories told by Aboriginal people from the Wave Hill area in the Northern Territory is evidence for this, although it is worth pointing out that Captain Cook probably only assumed prominence in indigenous historical storytelling in that region as a result of the considerable nationwide commemoration on the occasion of his bicentenary in 1970. The Aborigines who lived at Botany Bay were aware of the symbolic power of Captain Cook for a considerably longer period of time because they lived in a landscape of his memory.

By the time the claim of direct descent from those who saw Cook arrive in 1770 was being made public by local Aboriginal people, which, according to archival traces, was in the late nineteenth century (although this was not necessarily when the claim *originated*), Captain Cook had become the focus for more visible commemoration at Botany Bay, in part because he had begun to achieve national forefather status (discussed in detail in Chapter 3). Local Aboriginal people's status in the national story and in the national community was, in contrast, peripheral and precarious. This claim of direct descent from the eyewitnesses to Captain Cook in Botany Bay in 1770 functioned to firmly bind the two pasts together—the local indigenous and the national non-indigenous. By claiming descent from eyewitnesses to the event that supposedly inaugurated the nation, these local Aboriginal 'historians' were insisting that they too were part of the nation's never-ending story. Their mode for doing so was familial and localised, making it all the more compelling. When Captain Cook, Botany Bay, 1770 is used to tell stories about Aboriginal discontinuity—once there were Aborigines but now there are none—this local indigenous claim of kinship provides a thread from which to weave an alternative narrative of continuity. But to characterise this local Aboriginal history-making as astutely national, and as particularly political, in its focus is probably to overstate the case. In many instances, the claim became especially pronounced when local Aboriginal people's right to remain resident at Botany Bay was threatened, and thus was central to their efforts to hold on to the little piece of land they occupied. Moreover, it circulated more widely when local Aboriginal people told it as they sold the souvenirs they made to non-Aboriginal tourists (as I discuss in Chapter 3) and so its function in that context was partly economic.

Reclaiming history

Art historian Joan Kerr has suggested that the National Library of Australia's large collection of Captain Cook memorabilia has provided a 'provocative context for indigenous interpretations of the [Captain Cook] legend'.[53] Botany Bay has too. There the arrival and landing of Captain Cook has been the most popular and persistent subject for such interpretations. In more recent times, however, other stories attached to Botany Bay have had their meanings reworked by local Aboriginal people in ways which make sense to them and which communicate some powerful messages to those who hear these alternative interpretations. The 'wonderful large wild man from Botany Bay', discussed above, has been a subject for local 'indigenous interpretation'.

In 1997, the broadsheet about a 'wonderful, large wild man' taken from Botany Bay to England was put on public display at the

State Library of New South Wales as part of an exhibition evocatively titled 'A Rage for Curiosity', the theme of which was the collecting culture of the early colonists, focusing on the period from 1788 to the 1830s. Richard Neville, the exhibition's curator, was keen to show that there were two types of curiosity at play in early colonial society: the learned and the popular. The wild man broadsheet belonged to the latter. 'If the curious was not present,' Neville notes in the exhibition's catalogue, 'then it was invented, known in the trade as a "cock", and so it was with the broadside, *A description of a wonderful large wild man, or monstrous giant, brought from Botany-Bay.*'[54]

I saw the broadsheet on display at the State Library in company with Aboriginal women from Botany Bay. We had been visiting the library together regularly since the mid-1980s, when we were working on a project to make the Aboriginal history of Botany Bay public (described in more detail in Chapter 7). I am not sure what we had gone to the library in search of that day, but we were drawn from our researches to the exhibition and, when we encountered the wild man broadsheet, whatever it was we had hoped to find was immediately overshadowed by this discovery. When my friends came upon the broadsheet describing a wonderful large wild man, they did not see a 'cock', but rather a confirmation of their own local stories about the existence of wild hairy men. They interpreted the broadsheet as evidence for their own, not necessarily unique, local tradition about wild men, who they believed lived in their local landscape on the foreshores of Botany Bay. And their immediate response was to request copies of the broadsheet for their own research collections. The public display of the broadsheet provided an occasion for it to be reclaimed by local Aboriginal people from Botany Bay for purposes quite different from the function it was performing in the State Library's exhibition.

Aboriginal people from Botany Bay are not the only ones to believe in hairy wild men (also known as 'yahoos' or 'yowies'). There is ample evidence from the nineteenth century that the wild men existed in folklore in both Aboriginal and non-Aboriginal communities. Robert Holden wonders whether the figure moved from Aboriginal society into colonial society or vice versa. He concludes

that 'opinion is divided as to whether indigenous apes were originally part of Aboriginal legend and then crossed over . . . or whether
they were part of imported European imaginings incorporated into
Aboriginal story telling.'[55]

The encounter between local Botany Bay Aboriginal people
and the wild man from Botany Bay broadsheet at the Mitchell
Library centres on a different issue. The substance of the issue is
not the wild man *per se*, but rather how a particular broadsheet that
describes one purportedly from Botany Bay—an item which has
been acquired by the State Library of New South Wales and
displayed by it as an illustration of how late eighteenth century
English society imagined the antipodes—acquires a new layer of
meaning through a process which I am calling indigenous interpretation. This is not an isolated incident. It is occurring in libraries
and museums across Australia (and indeed across the globe) as part
of a broader project in which indigenous people are drawing on
colonial collections for their own storytelling, weaving new narratives from documents and objects produced by others.[56] In many
instances of indigenous interpretation, there is something undeni-
ably powerful in the act of taking into one's possession a material
trace, such as the broadsheet, that has its origins in the history of
one's *dis*possession.

The process by which material traces from the past find their
way into the collections of libraries is often one of de-privatisation.
They move from private hands into a public institution. In the case
of indigenous interpretation, the reverse process can be seen. Items
in public collections are in the process of being *re*-privatised. The
wild man of the late eighteenth-century broadsheet is being claimed
in intimate ways by Aboriginal people for whom Botany Bay is
home, rather than a metaphor or shorthand for something else altogether. In the process, they not only turn an imaginary Botany Bay
into a known locality, but also reject a representation that implicitly
dehumanised indigenous people. As a result of this contemporary
reworking of the meanings of an historical trace, a new layer of
significance is added to an item in the library's vast collection. The
value of the wild man from Botany Bay broadsheet does not now
simply derive from its very own history, but also from the type

of history-making that it inspires and currently makes possible. Following Peter Cochrane's formulation, it is a 'treasure', both by virtue of its own provenance and the 'multitude associations' that now surround it.[57]

SYDNEY'S BACKDOOR

Isolating the city's unwanted at Botany Bay

For most of the first hundred years of British settlement in the colony, Botany Bay languished, living up to its reputation as a wild, unruly, untamed place. Restrictions on settlement upon its north headland in the early nineteenth century, imposed by Governor Lachlan Macquarie to discourage smuggling into the colony, were one among many obstacles to its progress. Yet, had restrictions not been applied, one suspects that Botany Bay would still have struggled to attract settlers. It already had a reputation as unsuitable for human habitation, acquired when Captain Arthur Phillip rejected it the moment he arrived in 1788. 'The openness of this bay, and the dampness of the soil, by which the people would probably be rendered unhealthy, had already determined the Governor to seek another situation,' explained the official record of his voyage.[1] This set the tone for subsequent scorn of this spot.

'Barren' and 'wild' were among the adjectives most commonly used for late eighteenth- and nineteenth-century Botany Bay. It compared poorly with other parts of the larger Sydney landscape, such as along the Hawkesbury and Nepean rivers where the soil was more fertile for agricultural uses. And, although Botany Bay continued to be acclaimed for its abundant native flora, this only added to its reputation as uncultivable and unproductive. French navigator Hyacinthe de Bougainville, visiting Sydney in 1825, noted that 'the marshes [between Port Jackson and Botany Bay] are very deep and perilous for cattle, which inevitably perish once they are bogged down. These marshes stretch all the way along the coast from Port Jackson to the bay, which owes its name to its treacherous nature.'[2] Botany Bay's native nature, its pre-colonial plentifulness preserved in its name, had come to be seen as something of a curse.

Throughout the nineteenth century, little happened to improve its fortunes or its reputation. The few settlers who had ventured to parts of Botany Bay had by all accounts made little impact; some were accused of only contributing further to its undesirable reputation. By the 1880s, Botany Bay's foreshores were regretfully described as having been 'left so long in their natural wildness, [and] used so badly by their few tenants'.[3] Not only had it failed to thrive, but it could not shake a reputation for being impervious to improvement. Its miserable state was used as evidence that Governor Phillip's original decision to settle at Port Jackson had been prescient. And so, within the intensely colonised landscape of greater Sydney, Botany Bay functioned as a stubborn reminder that there were perhaps some limits to what the newcomers could achieve. Some wild places simply refused to be tamed.

But progressive cities eventually find themselves in need of their apparently useless margins, and this was to become Botany Bay's fate by the closing decades of the nineteenth century. Precisely because of its physical and symbolic peripheralness, in the early 1880s Botany Bay—the northern peninsula especially—was chosen by the colonial government of New South Wales as a place of exile for people and functions considered incompatible with and undesirable in a progressively cosmopolitan city. The people least wanted were those considered most threatening to the city's health, which was understood in both moral and material terms. The victims of a smallpox epidemic, mendicant Aborigines and the dead interred in an inner-city cemetery were especially targeted for removal to Botany Bay's north head. Hitherto a place geographically and symbolically isolated, Botany Bay was to be transformed into a place of isolation.

The removal of particular types of citizens or, in some cases, non-citizens from the metropolis was an increasingly popular form of government control in the late nineteenth century, one that sought to serve two seemingly opposite purposes. On the one hand, spatial segregation was advocated as a means by which to protect colonial bourgeois society from the potentially degenerating influence of those deemed deviant, such as Aborigines or the insane. On the other hand, it was purportedly a means by which to protect supposedly vulnerable types, like Aboriginal people living on the edges of colonial society, from potential demoralisation caused by succumbing to temptations associated with urban life. Hence a contradictory logic was at work in late nineteenth-century practices of spatial exclusion—the source of degeneration was simultaneously perceived as both those expelled from the city and as the city itself.[4]

The choice of Botany Bay as a site for the dumping of social outcasts was, it seems, a case of history repeating itself. A hundred years earlier, Botany Bay had been on the very precipice of receiving a cargo of convicts as new residents. Now it was somewhat belatedly preparing to receive the abject again. It is curious that, by this time, Botany Bay had still not been able to shake completely its association with convicts even though it had never been home to them, whereas Sydney Cove had by and large cast that aspersion aside and was basking in its own prosperity. While not directly contributing to its selection as a segregation site, the fact that Botany Bay was still burdened by this (misplaced) stain made it appear an obvious choice. And so it gradually became to Sydney what Sydney had once been to Britain, and a new layer was added to Botany Bay's already layered reputation for 'wildness'.

The Coast Hospital

In 1881, a smallpox epidemic broke out in Sydney. While describing the spread of the disease as an epidemic was at the time (and certainly is now) alarmist, nonetheless the presence of smallpox did cause dread within the city because it allegedly 'threatened to spread human suffering, disfigurement, and death amongst the community and to inflict grave injury upon the shipping interests of the port'.[5] The immediate response of the colonial secretary to the crisis was to set up a board of inquiry charged with, among other things, responsibility for the establishment of an isolation hospital. The function of the hospital was to preserve the public health of the city by 'cutting off all communication between any persons infected with the said disease and the rest of Her Majesty's subjects'.[6] This was a public health measure aimed at the control of bodies in space, separating sick from healthy, infected from uninfected.[7] An area of 500 acres was selected for the hospital at Little Bay on the stretch of coast leading to Botany Bay's north head, which was considered 'sufficient distance from the metropolis to ensure safety and confidence' but still relatively accessible.[8] It was situated on a peninsula, and so possessed many of the qualities of an island, the pre-eminent isolation site. The considerable amount of land set aside for the isolation hospital was deemed necessary in case the epidemic spread rapidly through the domestic population, and in order to deal with the potentially large numbers of passengers and crew on board infected ships that might call at Sydney.[9]

Isolation for the infectious. Coast Hospital at Little Bay, c. 1890s. (Government Printing Office collection, State Library of New South Wales)

Apparently this was not the first time that the land in question had been used as an isolation site for smallpox victims. A local tradition claimed that Little Bay had been one of the places which indigenous people had used to isolate the sick when in 1789, a year after British settlement, a smallpox epidemic had spread rapidly through the indigenous population living around Sydney. David Collins, who arrived in the colony with the First Fleet and held the office of judge advocate, described reports of the devastation that had been witnessed on beaches around Sydney Cove as a result of the disease:

> Early in the month [April 1789], and throughout its continuance, the people whose business called them down the harbour daily reported, that they found, either in excavations of the rock, or lying upon the beaches and points of the different coves which they had been in, the bodies of many of the wretched natives of this country. The cause of this mortality remained unknown until a family was brought up, and the disorder pronounced to have been the small-pox.[10]

In the southern portion of the colony, a cave at Little Bay, immediately below the new isolation hospital site, had been used as an isolation place for infected indigenous people—or so claimed Obed West in his regular newspaper column, which reported:

> By peculiar coincidence, the native hospital for blacks who were afflicted with smallpox was in the immediate vicinity of the site selected by the Government for a Sanatorium for our own people . . . On the south side of the bay, about 200 yards back from the beach, there is a large over-hanging rock, forming a cave. This was shown to me by the blacks as the place where all who had the disease went.[11]

The local blacks who had shown West the cave reportedly told him that the infected would isolate themselves there and that their kin would leave food for them at its entrance. Accordingly, the caves became known as the 'Blacks' Hospital'.

There is no evidence that those charged with the responsibility for establishing the isolation hospital at Little Bay in the early 1880s were aware that the site had been used for the same purpose almost a hundred years earlier. The hint of continuity between how the area had been used in the late eighteenth century and how it was to be used in the late nineteenth is, in my view, extremely evocative. This was a landscape already marked by epidemic. The Blacks' Hospital was a reminder about the effects of epidemic. The site was a prophetic witness to the potential decimation of a healthy society from introduced disease. The story about the past uses of the new hospital site served as a parable about the perils of contact between locals and foreigners. Yet, whereas in 1789 the locals were indigenous people, by the 1880s the foreigners, British colonists, had assumed the status of locals. They feared epidemic introduced by other foreigners, in this instance, Chinese people.

The authorities repeatedly justified the need for an isolation hospital in terms of protecting healthy subjects from infected ones. However, it is clear from the extensive correspondence and reports generated by the epidemic, and produced by the new public health authority established in response to it, that the definition of health and sickness was highly racialised. In the government reports made at the time, and in subsequent histories based on them, the origin of the smallpox epidemic is commonly blamed on a Chinese boy. Singling out this boy as the carrier and the culprit reinforced the already close association drawn between smallpox and Chinese people. The Chinese were blamed for its introduction and for its spread, and inner-city Chinese neighbourhoods were the primary focus for public health campaigns aimed at ending the epidemic. Although the main focus was on Chinese neighbourhoods, there was at the same time a more general concern about the condition of inner-city Sydney and its apparent vulnerability to epidemic. During the 1870s, the local council in Sydney and the New South Wales colonial government had become increasingly concerned about the health of the metropolis and its citizens. In this period, the population in Sydney had rapidly expanded and was more settled than it had been previously. Where boarding houses for itinerant workers had hitherto dominated the inner-city area, by the 1880s these same areas, close to factories and wharves, had become places of permanent residence for labourers and other workers. As urban historian Shirley Fitzgerald has convincingly shown, the infrastructural development of the city did not keep pace with its expanding population. She contends that a relaxed administrative and legislative response to the creation of public amenities directly contributed to the development of crowded and substandard living conditions in many parts of the city.[12]

In 1875, the colonial secretary, concerned with evidence of increased public health risks, had appointed the Sydney City and Suburban Sewage and Health Board to conduct an inquiry into sewage disposal and the measures required to protect the health of the city's inhabitants. The picture created by the twelve detailed reports produced by the inquiry was of a city without the means to dispose of waste or to ensure a clean water supply. This is pertinent to the subsequent smallpox epidemic because, in the reports produced by the New South Wales Board of Health to explain why the epidemic had occurred, a repeated association was drawn between stagnation and disease. 'Many months had passed,' the board's report stated, 'without the occurrence of rain sufficient to cleanse the ground surface and flush the sewers, the structural sanitary condition of the city was in many points faulty.'[13] Overcrowding, lack of ventilation, absence of light and stale air were added to the list of problems in the inner city, making epidemic possible. The conditions, it seemed, were ideal for the heightened levels of anxiety—hysteria even—that accompanied the notification of smallpox cases. A relatively small number of smallpox cases was transformed into an epidemic, requiring extensive and excessive public health measures, like the large isolation hospital on Sydney's fringe.

The human body was a commonly used analogy for the city in the nineteenth century. Like human organisms, cities were often represented as being vulnerable to disease, whether introduced from outside sources or contracted through miasmic processes. A city's constitution was sometimes pathologised, a breakdown in its health explained through reference to a pre-existing physical condition or an inherent susceptibility. But the analogy of body to city extended beyond the order of literary comparison. The city was also 'made and made over into the simulacrum of the body'.[14] It was designed to function along anatomical and physiological principles, and its development was managed according to these. This included the application of the medical principle of containing infection to limit its spread and, when possible, the removal of the disease-causing agent. Applied to the metropolitan landscape, this entailed creating places on the periphery as isolation sites for the impurities expelled. In turn, this expulsion was believed to facilitate improved circulation, which was probably the most important principle in medical discourse of the Victorian era. Just as the human body depended for proper functioning upon proper circulation (of blood, of fluids, of air), so too did the city (of goods, of people, of waste). This highly valued trope of circulation explains in large part the preoccupation with stagnation and overcrowding as a cause of disease, and with spatial segregation as a necessary response once infectious disease had taken hold. Not only would the removal of the infected facilitate restored circulation within the city, but it would guarantee proper circulation around the expunged entities themselves. This explains the practice of locating, or sometimes relocating, infectious diseases hospitals and cemeteries to the edges of a city, where sufficient space, light, clean air and exposure to the elements would guard against stagnation.

The large isolation hospital for smallpox patients established at Little Bay in 1881, known aptly as the Coast Hospital, was on a site that maximised circulation and minimised stagnation. It was nestled in the coastal heath, facing the sea, on an exposed and windswept site. The site was so vast that the logic behind it seemed to be not simply the control of bodies in space, but the prospect that patients would become lost in space, at least figuratively. They were expected to use the site's natural facilities: the bush for walking, the beaches for sauntering and the sea for bathing.[15] This was a period in which the perceived salubriousness of the sea was at its height.

But, despite the government's promotion of the supposedly health-giving qualities of the littoral landscape, its aim to exclude and contain those infected with smallpox was not achieved without considerable contestation and resistance. Many of those diagnosed resisted enforced removal to the Coast Hospital, and absconded to avoid isolation. In response, the government health authority sought greater powers to forcibly detain and isolate, which were eventually granted under the *Infectious Diseases Supervision Act* 1881.

While some patients and their contacts had been temporarily housed in tents at the site, the Coast Hospital proper was ready to receive its first smallpox patients in December 1881; two months later, the 'epidemic' was over. Despite government fears about the possibility of future epidemics and their potential threat to the city, the hospital was only used again for quarantine purposes on two other occasions. Although rarely used for large-scale isolation purposes, the Coast Hospital nonetheless became a treatment centre for other infectious diseases. For instance, in 1883 it began receiving typhoid patients from metropolitan hospitals where committees believed that 'the presence of an undue proportion of fever cases in their wards [was] prejudicial to the other patients therein'.[16] By the late 1880s, it had become the colony's treatment centre for a small number of leprosy patients. But no matter what its specific uses were, the Coast Hospital had already served its most enduring function: inscribing this part of the outer metropolitan landscape as a wasteland.

Relocation and isolation

As efforts were underway to remove smallpox sufferers from the city to the coastal periphery, similar attempts were being made to remove and relocate Aboriginal people. Their respective destinations—Little Bay for the infected and La Perouse for the indigenous people—were within a short distance of each other, Little Bay on the coastal side of Botany Bay's northern peninsula and La Perouse on the bay side.

By the closing decades of the nineteenth century, an Aboriginal presence in the city had become much more visible, and at the same time was considered increasingly out of place. The 1870s had witnessed growing concern about the condition of Aboriginal people generally: there was growing apprehension not only about the continued existence of an Aboriginal population within the colony, but also about their emergence as a pauper class. At this time, many Aboriginal people faced a situation in which they were less able to provide for themselves through their own labour because of changes from pastoral to agricultural modes of production, the latter much less dependent upon Aboriginal workers. This was certainly the experience of Aboriginal people living on the south coast of New South Wales. Some historians have suggested that this directly led to an increase in the number of Aborigines living in Sydney in the 1870s and 1880s, when they were forced to migrate to the city in the hope of gaining employment or, failing that, of qualifying for government and/or charitable assistance. The Aborigines Protection Association, a committee made up of private citizens, had begun distributing rations to some metropolitan Aboriginal camps in 1880, and in the following years this aid was sometimes supplemented by government assistance.

The conspicuous Aboriginal presence within Sydney, including reported displays of vulgar behaviour, was a cause of concern for private citizens and politicians alike. Historian Ann Curthoys noted: 'Their public flaunting of the values and standards of civilised life was found painful and offensive by the towns and a city [that is, Sydney] which were increasingly concerned with stability, prosperity, and respectability.'[17] Reports were tabled in parliament and made in the local press about the apparent nuisance that Aborigines were causing to the city's citizenry, and about concerns regarding their alleged bad influence upon the 'morally weaker of the colonists'.[18] Some prominent men, parliamentarians among them, strongly argued that the best course of action was to prevent Aboriginal people from taking up residence within the city. In pursuit of this, they opposed rations being given to Aboriginal people who set up camp in Sydney.

At the same time, there was a strong push to remove those already living in the city. George Thornton, a member of the New South Wales Legislative Assembly at the time, and twice previously mayor of Sydney, was one of the most prominent advocates of their complete removal from Sydney. A camp at the government boat-sheds at Circular Quay was the main focus of his ire. The boatshed had become notorious for drinking, fighting and riotous behaviour.

The campers' behaviour was apparently bad enough to warrant repeated rebuke. It was not simply the fighting and drinking that worried Thornton and his colleagues: it was that the spectacle of it attracted so many onlookers, sometimes, according to one report, two or three hundred people, enough to block the public thoroughfare. This was a form of cross-cultural exchange requiring censure. The camp had to go. In July 1881, the police forcibly closed it down and dispersed its residents. While some apparently left for the South Coast of New South Wales, most reportedly went across Sydney Harbour to the north shore of Sydney.

The Circular Quay camp was by no means the only one in the city at this time, although it was amongst the largest and was the one that attracted most attention. There were many others dotted throughout the Sydney landscape, some more permanent than others. For instance, there is evidence that Aboriginal people were living at Manly, Neutral Bay and Double Bay. Curthoys describes a letter printed in the *Sydney Morning Herald* in 1878 complaining about the annoyance caused by the North Shore camp of Aborigines to residents of the area around Blues' Point.[19] There were also relatively large numbers of Aboriginal people living around Botany Bay, mainly on the north shore at Botany and La Perouse, as well as some living at Kurnell on the south shore and a small camp at Sans Souci on Botany Bay's western shore.

An official report about the camps on Botany Bay's north shore tells us:

> In the year 1881 there were about fifty (50) aboriginals all told, in the district. They had two (2) camps—one (1) at La Perouse, the other on the reserve at Botany. The chief camp was at La Perouse where there were about thirty-five (35); the remainder about fifteen (15) camped on the reserve [at Botany]. They were continually going to and fro from one camp to the other, and were occasionally visited by aboriginals from Wollongong, Georges River, and Burragorang.[20]

These numbers tally with the estimate made by Daniel Matthews, the missionary, who recorded in his diary that at the La Perouse camp there were 31 adults and children, made up of five families.[21]

It is worth noting that the reference to connections with Wollongong, Georges River and Burragorang is consistent with Mahroot's evidence of 1845. He had explained to a parliamentary inquiry that the Aboriginal people living at Botany Bay at that time were originally from these areas, specifically the Five Islands, which is near Wollongong, and Liverpool, which is on the Georges River. This was 35 years earlier, which suggests that the country around Botany Bay, including its north shore, had continued to be occupied by people from these regions, probably on a semi-permanent basis, over much of the middle period of the nineteenth century.

By the early 1880s, the reserve for Aborigines at Botany, 'between the high road and the beach', had become 'equally useful to the colonists, to whom,' one commentator predicted, 'it will ultimately revert, and who, sooner or later, will greatly improve it.'[22] The township of Botany was developing rapidly in this period, in part because its wharves serviced an expanding shipping industry. When the Botany Aboriginal camp was shut down, probably in late 1881, some of its residents took up an offer made to them by Daniel Matthews to relocate to the private mission he had established for Aborigines at Maloga on the Murray River. But others chose to remain in the vicinity, shifting to the other local Aboriginal camp at La Perouse. Describing this state of affairs, the local police constable reported that 'during the whole of 1882 there was but one (1) camp, viz., at La Perouse, and the average number of aboriginals there has been about twenty-six (26) all told. They still occasionally have been visited by their countrymen from Wollongong, Georges River and Burragorang.'[23] Among the 30 or so Aboriginal people living at La Perouse in 1882 were five men: William Foot, Wm [William] Rowley, Charles Edwards, Joseph Dixon and Timberly. We know their names because they signed a letter addressed to George Thornton in January 1883.[24] Some appear to have had links with the area over a long time. A William Rowley was reportedly born in 1831 at Towra Point on Botany Bay's southern shore and, after its establishment in the 1860s, was an employee on the Holt Estate at Kurnell.[25] The men owned some boats between them, which they used for fishing or sometimes rented to visitors. The fish they caught were either used as food for their families, or sold at markets in

Sydney. La Perouse, like other places on the Botany Bay shoreline, supported a small fishing industry serviced mainly by professional non-Aboriginal fishermen. The 1882 *Sand's Sydney and NSW Directory* lists the names of some of these resident fishermen. Among them are two Aboriginal fishermen, George Timberley (also spelt Timbrey or Timbery) and Bundong, suggesting that they were part of a local industry.[26] Aboriginal women living at the La Perouse camp at this time contributed to the livelihood of their families by making shell baskets, which they sold in the city and the suburbs.[27]

In the closing years of the 1870s and the opening years of the 1880s, the camp of Aboriginal people at La Perouse was probably little different from other Aboriginal camps in the vicinity of Sydney. It was on Crown land, its residents supported themselves through subsistence fishing and casual labour (for instance, some local men had worked on the construction of the Coast Hospital), and they continued to move about following the fish and visiting kin in other camps further afield, in this case, south along the coast and west to the ranges. The settlement supported no more than a handful of families. A newspaper report in early 1883 explained that 'the camp at La Perouse is in a somewhat out-of-the-way position'. Describing the camp's origins, the correspondent from the *Sydney Morning Herald* claimed that it had long been used as a 'halting place for aborigines since Captain Cook's time, and probably before', but that 'about four years ago, George [Timbrey] had found the camp deserted and settled down there with his wife and somewhat numerous family'. He built a hut, got use of a boat for fishing, was joined by some other families and 'now they form a little village'. By this means, 'the place seems to have become a permanent settlement'.[28] Two points are worth stressing about this potted history: the site chosen by Timbrey was a known campsite with a long history of use, and he, not the government, had selected it as a suitable site for him and his family as a permanent dwelling place.

However, during the 1880s this camp on Botany Bay's north head underwent considerable change in ways that distinguished it from others around Sydney that existed in the same period.[29] It became entangled in the process whereby Aboriginal people were both being removed from Sydney proper or being prevented from taking up residence there. As the Aboriginal camp closest to the city that the government would tolerate, the small settlement became both a relocation site for those expelled and a stopping place for those hoping to get to the city. By this means, the camp became part of Sydney's fringe of isolation-style 'institutions': a place to which the unwanted in the city were removed and a place relatively close to the city where it was permissible for them to be.

Like the Coast Hospital, once it became used for isolation purposes, the camp became more enmeshed within the city. But it was also separate from it: it had to be, otherwise it could not properly serve its purpose of isolation or segregation. And so, depending on one's standpoint, the Aborigines' camp on Botany Bay's north head was either just outside the city's gates or right on its doorstep.

'Protecting' the camp

The story about how the camp on Botany Bay's north shore became a key location for the relocation of Aborigines has George Thornton at its centre. In December 1881, Thornton, who had previously agitated for the closure of the Aboriginal camp in the government boatsheds at Circular Quay, was officially appointed Protector of Aborigines for the colony. In this role he was to inquire into the status of Aboriginal people and make recommendations regarding government assistance. In this position, he pursued his campaign to remove Aboriginal people from Sydney. 'One of my first anxieties on assuming the duties of Protector,' he reported, 'was to endeavour to get all the aborigines away from Sydney and suburbs and back into their own districts, and I took such steps as would attain that object.'[30] Those steps, as I have already described, were forcibly closing down the metropolitan Aboriginal camps and prohibiting the provision of rations to city-dwelling Aborigines. The latter measure was designed to discourage those living in the city from remaining there and as a disincentive against newcomers moving in. Yet, despite his apparent zeal for turning the city into a no-go area for Aborigines, Thornton tolerated the Aboriginal camp at La Perouse. By his own account, he conceded to a request from the five

Aboriginal men named above to remain with their families in their camp on the northern foreshores of Botany Bay. Moreover, Thornton arranged for them to be provided with rations and with building materials. These allowances seemed, on the surface at least, somewhat aberrant.

Thornton detailed his actions in regard to this camp in a report to parliament. That report was made not because he had deviated from stated policy; rather it was because he had been accused by two fellow parliamentarians of having failed in his duty of care to ensure that rations were provided to the Aboriginal people there over the Christmas period in 1882—a failure that had apparently resulted in their going hungry. His accusers were John McElhone and Richard Hill, both members of the Aborigines Protection Association. Through these charges, they put Thornton in an unenviable position as Curthoys notes: 'appointed to rid Sydney of its Aboriginal nuisance he now found himself trying to prove that he had freely given rations to Aborigines in Sydney'.[31] But, from Thornton's perspective, the Aborigines' camp on Botany Bay's north head was

Isolation for Aborigines. The Aboriginal settlement at La Perouse, c. 1910s. (Government Printing Office collection, State Library of New South Wales)

located outside city limits at a sufficient distance not to pose a threat or cause a nuisance. Perhaps more importantly, in his report he presented the camp as different from other metropolitan camps. He described the people as settled: 'I found some of them *settled* at La Perouse, and [they] were anxious to remain there' (emphasis added). He continued: 'The men are all young, strong, intelligent (some able to read and write), able and willing to work—they are nearly all half-castes, with half-caste wives and a number of children.'[32] This image of domesticity and potential productivity contrasts with descriptions of the camps in the city proper, including the one that had been at the government boatsheds at Circular Quay. By describing the men as industrious, Thornton cast their request to remain resident on the Botany Bay headland as a valid one, and justified his own actions in helping them to establish further their small settlement there.

It is worth noting that by no means did George Thornton concede to their request to remain at Botany Bay on the basis that the Aborigines he 'found there' had any genuine tribal affiliation with the place. He repeatedly claimed that there were no Aborigines left from the Botany Bay or Sydney tribes. Indeed, Thornton's stated preference upon assuming the position of Protector was that all Aborigines found in and around Sydney be returned to their own districts. That he was giving assistance to Aborigines at Botany Bay, even though he did not believe there were any Botany Bay Aborigines left, contradicted his stated policy.

The question about whether the blacks at Botany Bay had any 'own district' to which to return was a contested one. Was not Botany Bay now, and had it not perhaps for some time been (albeit not permanently), their district? Thornton's detractors repeatedly and publicly challenged him on this point about Aborigines needing to be in their own districts to qualify for government assistance. They argued that many Aborigines had no district to return to because all the land had been taken. Missionary John B. Gribble posed the question in relation to the 'blacks at Botany': 'Where, I ask, is their "own district"? Does not New South Wales belong to them?' On a more practical level, and in a less rhetorical mode, a Presbyterian minister, Reverend Curtis, who had been visiting the blacks at La Perouse in this period to conduct monthly church services, claimed that they came from many districts, and often a man from one, his wife from another and their children born in yet others, which made it 'practically impossible, or, to say the least, harsh and unjust' to require them to return to those districts in order to qualify for assistance.[33]

There were two lasting effects of this moment in the history of the small Aboriginal camp on Botany Bay's north head, then known as Currewol (also spelt as Curriwul or Cooriwal and, in the twentieth century, as Guriwal or Gooriwal),[34] when the newly appointed government Protector of Aborigines, George Thornton, allowed it to remain. The first effect was that this little piece of Botany Bay came to be seen as the camp residents' 'own district', and the second was that from this time onwards they were forever within the government's orbit.

'Blacks' Camp'

In 1883, the single office of Protector of Aborigines was replaced by a board known as the Aborigines Protection Board (APB). During the 1880s and 1890s, the approach taken by the Protection Board became more explicitly isolationist and protectionist than earlier colonial responses to Aborigines had been. It is in this slightly later policy context that the making of Botany Bay's north head as the *main* site for the settlement, and for the segregation, of Aborigines within Sydney is firmly embedded. In this period, the existing Aboriginal camp at La Perouse became permanent and was the place to which many Aboriginal people who were no longer tolerated in the city were relocated, forcibly or otherwise. Peter Wandy's Christian testimonial illustrates the pattern. In a transcription of his life story—a witness to his Christian conversion—Wandy, an Aboriginal man originally from Western Australia, described how he had ended up sleeping in the Sydney Domain after being abandoned by his employer some time in the 1890s:

> One night . . . I just get to sleep and big fat policemen get hold of me, and shake me and say 'What you doing there?' I say 'Can't you see what I am

doing?' He pulled me out and send me away. I watch him till he get out of sight, and then I go back and have another sleep. One day I meet a policemen and he talk kind to me, and tell me to go to La Perouse.[35]

Once it became enmeshed in the colonial government's practice of segregating Aborigines, the small settlement on Botany Bay's north shore, which had predated Thornton's personal project as well as the one implemented by his successors on the board, changed in composition, function and meaning. Physically, it became a more permanent presence on the local landscape as huts continued to be built and a fence was eventually erected around the settlement. In the 1890s, missionaries moved in and asserted their presence by building a small church. The settlement was fixed cartographically too. A place variously labelled 'Blacks' Camp' or 'Aboriginal Quarters' began to appear on maps of the locality from 1884 onwards. This cartographic acknowledgment of the Aboriginal presence on the north head of Botany Bay occurred more than a decade before a reserve was formally gazetted for the 'exclusive use of Aborigines' in 1895. The mark on the map was a powerful acknowledgment that this was a site of Aboriginal occupation. By these means and others, the headland became known in Sydney as the place where Aborigines (or 'the blacks') lived.

In turn, as the place was increasingly occupied by Aborigines and explicitly used for their segregation, other pre-existing and potential future uses of the north head of Botany Bay became matters of contestation. For instance, some speculators who had hoped to cash in on the increasing popularity of the seaside were thwarted in their attempts to erect a hotel on the headland, mainly because it would have compromised its function of racial segregation.[36]

Whitewashing the historical landscape

The purging of an Aboriginal presence from Sydney during this period was not only bodily. It was also representational. Along with being physically removed, Aborigines were increasingly excised from colonial images and stories about Sydney. The physical erasure

of the presence of Aboriginal people from the metropolitan landscape was made more permanent, both at the time and later,
through a type of historical amnesia. The histories of Sydney
written from the late nineteenth century until quite recently largely
failed to account for an Aboriginal presence throughout the city in
the nineteenth century, apart from a handful of well-known identities. This helped to create and reinforce their absence. The effect on
collective memory was well articulated by a Mr Trescoe Rowe, a
long-time Sydney resident, in 1966. In a letter to the Aborigines
Welfare Board (AWB) (which replaced the APB in 1940), in which
he requested information about a camp of Aboriginal people that
had existed at Darling Point in Sydney's inner east in the early
1890s, Rowe explained: 'I am having considerable trouble with my
friends who live in Darling Point believing that I remember these
Aborigines being situated on or near the Mona Estate.'[37] Rowe
recalled that the Aboriginal people living on the estate had been
removed to La Perouse in the late 1890s and that his governess,
Miss Baker, had gone with them.[38] This example illustrates how the
practice of racial segregation cannot be achieved purely on physical
grounds: it is accompanied by and reinforces structures of forgetting.[39] As the past is represented in ways that make indigenous
presence in the landscape largely invisible, that presence becomes
almost impossible to remember, let alone imagine. Yet, through
archival fragments like Rowe's inquiring letter—perhaps sent to
confirm that his own memory was not failing him—Sydney in the
late nineteenth century and earlier can be re-envisioned as a place
peopled with Aborigines. These memories reinsert an Aboriginal
presence into a metropolitan landscape largely imagined as devoid
of one. Rowe's childhood memory is a poignant reminder that the
development of Sydney, even in the late colonial period, entailed
the displacement of Aboriginal people. While the dispossession of
Aboriginal people from land around Sydney in the early colonial
period is well known, it is clear that the dispersal of Aborigines from
the metropolitan landscape a hundred or more years later is not so
prominent in Sydney's historical imagination. But by far the most
curious aspect concerning the whitewashing of the Sydney landscape is that it was Botany Bay—soon to become inscribed as yet

another birthplace of the nation in the lead-up to Federation—
which became the receiving dock for the Aborigines expunged.

While Trescoe Rowe struggled with the historical amnesia to
which his friends had fallen prey, local Aboriginal people living in
the settlement at Botany Bay have wrestled with another aspect of
this same phenomenon. They reject historical representations that
overlook, or play down, an Aboriginal presence at Botany Bay in
the period between the late eighteenth century and the late
nineteenth century. And they seek to challenge accounts that the
Aboriginal settlement was almost completely the product of a shift
in government practice, or which mistakenly conflate the camp's
origins with the removal of Aborigines from Sydney. In these types
of historical analyses, government practice is privileged, which
obscures Aborigines' own efforts to make a place for themselves in
the colonised landscape. The historical accounts that local Aboriginal people themselves give about the La Perouse Aboriginal
settlement perhaps not surprisingly give comparatively short shrift
to governmental influence, while giving credence to connections
that allow them to tie their own present to a pre-1880 past. What
is especially striking about the forms of historical remembrance and
the historical narratives that Aboriginal people from Botany Bay
produced and made public in the 1980s and 1990s is this explicit
effort to fill the historiographical gap between the late eighteenth
century and the late nineteenth century with an Aboriginal presence. Aboriginal people's own historical narratives suggest that the
year 1880, 1881 or 1882 is not the *origin* point for the settlement,
or for a post-contact Aboriginal presence at Botany Bay, but rather
just a *flash* point.[40]

Local Aboriginal people push back the conventional starting
point in the history of their settlement in two main ways. First,
rather than position the place where their settlement is located primarily as an outpost of Sydney, they emphasise that it is a node in
a geographical area that extends from the north shore of Botany Bay
southwards along the coast. They point out that Aboriginal people
have long followed the fish up and down this coastal 'beat'.[41]
By emphasising how the Aboriginal settlement on the northern
foreshores of Botany Bay was (is) situated in this alternative geo-

graphy, they reinforce the idea that it has been continually used, if not permanently settled, for the whole period of white settlement. This is an historical perspective that acknowledges that there are forces other than the vagaries of government influencing Aboriginal people's experiences, in this case the seasons for fish.

Second, some local Aboriginal people emphasise how Botany Bay was part of the larger landscape claimed by some Sydney Aborigines during the earlier part of the nineteenth century. This is a geographical pull in a slightly different direction. One example is Queen Gooseberry, who was the second wife of Bungaree. She was described on one breastplate made for her as 'Queen of Sydney and Botany'. Her relatively recent incorporation into local Botany Bay Aboriginal histories is in part facilitated by the fact she is buried in the cemetery that overlooks the Aboriginal settlement at La Perouse (discussed below). She, along with some other Aboriginal figures who were known to be associated with Botany Bay in the nineteenth century such as Mahroot, have become integral to a broader Aboriginal history of Botany Bay, one which importantly predates the interventions made by the government in the closing two decades of that century.

The desired effect of these local Aboriginal histories is to impress a sense of historical continuity and of temporal depth. This challenges other historical claims, and a somewhat common perception, that in the post-contact period local Aboriginal people's association with the place is only relatively recent, and therefore discontinuous with the earlier historical period. At the same time, the purpose is to bring into the picture an Aboriginal historical presence which is perceived as being at risk of being forgotten or misrepresented if not claimed and championed by present-day Aborigines connected with the same general locality.

The arrival of the dead

By the turn of the century, a cemetery in the inner city had been relocated to Botany Bay, occupying the same thin strip of land as the Coast Hospital and the Aboriginal settlement. The arrival of the dead further marked Botany Bay generally and its northern peninsula particularly as a wilderness and a wasteland. The removal of the cemetery from the city centre to the margins was symptomatic of the same logic that had governed the establishment of the nearby isolation hospital and the 'Blacks' Camp' which the cemetery overlooked. The hospital, the Aboriginal settlement and the cemetery each accommodated a presence that had hitherto existed in the city, but which had come to be considered a hindrance to metropolitan progress. That in part explained their place on the periphery.

The graves that were eventually moved to the hillside on Botany Bay's north shore had previously been in what was known as the Devonshire Street Cemetery. This cemetery had been in existence since 1820. It was completely closed in 1888, although, due to overcrowding and attendant fears about the health risks that crowded cemeteries in cities posed, restrictions had been placed on the number of burials there in 1867. While the cemetery was closed in 1888, it was another twelve years before the interred were transferred. In the interim, the cemetery simply fell into disrepair while the city continued to expand around it.

By 1900, the land still occupied by the discarded Devonshire Street cemetery was wanted for the extension of the railway line. To free up the space needed for the circulation of goods and people within the city, the permanently sedentary had to go. The decision was taken that the government would bear the cost of the removal of the remains and their monuments to any other cemetery that relatives of the deceased nominated. The unclaimed went to Botany Bay.[42]

The unclaimed bodies (among them Queen Gooseberry) and their burial markers were transported from the old cemetery to the new by tram. An extra section of tramline from the Botany terminus to the cemetery was specially built for the purpose which, paradoxically, compromised the isolation of the site by making it easily accessible to the city. Indeed, after carrying tramloads of dead people, the new section of the tramline was more likely to bring people in pursuit of health and long life. In this same period, Botany Bay's north shore came to be valued for its reputed salubrious qualities and, like other seaside locations throughout Sydney, it

Isolation for the interred. *Cemetery Botany Bay,* from the photographic series 'Bound', 1992. (Ian Provest)

progressively developed into a pleasure ground. In terms of this development, the extension of the tramline was a significant boon. Crowds came to swim in the sea under the lee of a hillside, which in time would be covered in headstones.

If the cemetery was not the last nail in the coffin for Botany Bay's already troubled reputation, then the construction of a women's penitentiary between 1900 and 1909, later known as Long Bay Gaol (and now a prison for men), perhaps was.[43] The gaol was situated next door to the Coast Hospital, making the incarcerated and the infected close neighbours. Situated side by side, the two institutions heralded the very outer limits of turn-of-the-century Sydney.

The 'abject' suburb

Cursed with a poor reputation in the late eighteenth century, one that was reactivated and reinforced in the late nineteenth century, Botany Bay (and especially some sections of it) has ever since failed

to rid itself of its marginal status in the Sydney landscape—a fact
perceptively observed by travel writer Jan Morris. When describing
the cultural classification of Sydney suburbs, she noted:

> Others . . . maintain their social reputations more or less inviolate down
> the generations. La Perouse, down on Botany Bay, has never been able to
> escape its multiple social disadvantages (an Aboriginal settlement, a
> prison, toxic inductions and unlovely setting) while any Sydney citizen
> has a mental image of the kind person you are likely to be, if you say you
> live in Double Bay, St Ives or Granville.[44]

In some twentieth-century histories of Sydney, the north head of
Botany Bay and La Perouse in particular, has been cast in the role
of the pariah suburb. For instance, in 1987 the Sydney History
Group produced *Sydney—A City of Suburbs*, edited by Max Kelly,
which told the story of Sydney from the perspective of its
suburbs.[45] This was a departure from other urban histories, which
had often bypassed suburbs altogether, considering them unwor-
thy of serious study. In the collection, particular suburbs were
presented as exemplars—'the garden suburb, the leisure suburb,
the railway suburb, the owner-builders' suburb'.[46] La Perouse was
included as the 'abject' suburb, the one most antithetical to the
'attractive' suburb, which in the book was Manly on the north side
of the Harbour.

Journalist and social commentator John Pilger also uses La
Perouse as an exemplar of abjectness in his polemic on Australia's
shameful past, *A Secret Country*. A childhood memory of a trans-
gressive moment when he ventured into the Aboriginal settlement
on Botany Bay's north head nicely serves his rhetorical intent. He
presents La Perouse as epitomising the 'dark side' of the nation by
providing a particularly pathetic image of the Aboriginal settlement, in which he describes the houses as 'fruit boxes'. He recalls
the stench, the flies and the rubbish. Pilger also casts his boyhood
escapade in the out-of-bounds space of the La Perouse Aboriginal
settlement as a personal epiphany, one in which he seems to have
become almost instantly cognisant of the gap between national
myth and everyday reality:

La Perouse, 1951 It was one of those moments in childhood when you stand outside yourself, outside 'normal' experience. The silhouettes related to no one. They were not meant to exist. They were meant to have 'died off'. Certainly few adults spoke of them as if they existed and, anyway, they were not counted, unlike the nation's sheep.[47]

Here La Perouse is not merely outside the city: it is beyond the imagined bounds of the national community.

The common thread in these twentieth-century commentaries on Botany Bay's northern headland is its apparent 'otherness': the repeated suggestion is that this was a place that civilisation had bypassed. It is primarily the presence of Aborigines that makes it 'other' to the city and 'other' to the nation.

One can see in the writing of one other late-twentieth century observer why the Botany Bay landscape has been so resistant to domestication. 'The land has flattened out into a wilderness that one feels is but shallowly marked with mankind's small scratchings and scribblings,' Ruth Park tells her guidebook readers in 1973 as she takes them to Botany Bay from Sydney:

> The place is very wild, bright, slightly mad, with everything tossing and glittering before a fresh wind which stitches the shirt to the ribs. Sand oozes up between the grass roots, trees have a permanent cant before the wind, seagulls rise and fall above the rough water like willywillies of torn white paper. You can feel very strongly the aboriginal character of Australia, the profound indifference to the stranger which gave the early settlers psychic unease. Give Botany Bay half a chance, one feels, and it would blow down the factories, submerge the rows of demure mousy houses, steal back the reclamations, and flood the droplet lakes that curve in a chain through the Lakes golf course until the whole bayside became a water meadow once more.[48]

Botany Bay does have a cruel wind, but here Park is giving far more than an account of its climate. Her reading of Botany Bay's landscape serves to give expression to an enduring uncertainty which lies at the heart of a settler society like Australia. Her response to Botany Bay is inseparable from the moment when Aborigine and stranger first met. That original encounter was characterised by 'profound indifference' and it is this that continues to haunt. This is Botany Bay as unsettling place—where 'civilisation' has only the most fragile hold.

BOOMERANGS FOR SALE

Tourism in the birthplace
of the nation

In 1895, the New South Wales Aborigines Protection Board reserved seven or so acres on Botany Bay's north shore for the exclusive use of Aboriginal people.[1] This portion of land was where a handful of Aboriginal families had already permanently established themselves, certainly since the late 1870s but perhaps earlier; where the newly appointed Protector of Aborigines had by his own account allowed them to remain when he found them there in 1881; and where Aboriginal people from other metropolitan camps had relocated in the 1880s and 1890s when forced out of the city. Formally creating Aboriginal reserves, typically pieces of land already occupied by Aboriginal people, was a common practice of the Protection Board at this time. The reserves were for the exclusive use of Aborigines 'where useful employment, education and resting place for the old and sick would be offered'.[2]

In 1899, four years later, a much larger portion of Botany Bay's foreshore was formally reserved. On the south shore, 248 acres, including the spot where Captain Cook had first landed in 1770, was resumed by the government from private ownership and set aside as a public reserve with the intention of preserving it as an historic site. The land in question had been held in private hands since the early 1800s, and during that time had been used relatively unsuccessfully for grazing and farming. In the years leading to Federation, its value was reappraised in historical terms.

The creation of the two reserves within a few years of each other resulted in an odd, albeit unplanned, arrangement whereby Aboriginal people occupied and even possessed one headland while the memory of an historical figure and an historical event implicitly associated with the dispossession of Aborigines imbued the other. This arrangement was, it seems, a case of one headland not knowing what the other was doing.

The two reserves faced each other across the bay. The view from the Aboriginal reserve on the north shore took in Captain Cook's Landing Place reserve on the south shore, including an obelisk erected to Cook in 1870. And the vista from Cook's obelisk back across the bay incorporated the Aboriginal settlement nestled in the sandy heath behind Frenchmans Beach. With this spatial arrangement, the Botany Bay landscape was simultaneously a parchment for the story of the nation and a witness to what had been excised from the national story. A visible Aboriginal presence in a landscape being inscribed as a birthplace of the nation made the act of historical forgetting, if not impossible, then at least less straightforward. Yet, the coexistence of the two reserves at Botany Bay was in important respects less oppositional than appears to be the case.

In the years leading up to and immediately following Federation, the historical figure of Captain Cook underwent a renaissance of sorts. As the colonies moved to nationhood, he was cast anew as national founding father. And, as part of a revived search for national origins at this time, Botany Bay, a landscape that remained intimately associated with him and his deeds, acquired renewed and new historical significance. Popular curiosity about Captain Cook and the part he had played in the story of the nation attracted increased numbers of excursionists to Botany Bay, contributing to a local tourist industry. From this point on, Botany Bay's local future would largely lie in its national past. Local Aboriginal people played a considerable role in the tourist industry developing at Botany Bay in this period. They positioned themselves as one of the tourist attractions on offer at Botany Bay and as tourist traders, making and selling souvenirs. In this respect, the making of Botany Bay into a national historic site was a crucial means for their local economic survival. For Aboriginal people, the national past had its local uses too. It was a means to a future, however uncertain that future might be.

Commemorating Cook and Banks

Intermittently throughout the nineteenth century Captain Cook had been given monumental form at Botany Bay. It began in 1822 with a plaque attached to a cliff face on the southern shore, a gesture sponsored by the Philosophical Society of Australasia. The plaque memorialised the arrival in 1770 of the *Endeavour* in Botany Bay. On it, James Cook and Joseph Banks had equal weighting, their names listed on the same line and credited as jointly responsible for the deed of discovery. Cook was described as the Columbus and Banks as the Mæcenas of their time. Of much, if not most, prominence in this abbreviated historical text engraved on brass was British science: it was this that had made their discovery possible, even necessary. In 1822, this was not yet a spot for celebrating the colony, or the nation, but rather the 'ardent pursuit of knowledge'. As a monument to scientific endeavour, the brass plaque should be read in part as a commemoration of the Philosophical Society of Australasia, which was then only recently established. As a monument to science, it attracted those in 'pursuit of knowledge'. One of the earliest and best-known images of the plaque was by the Ukrainian-born naturalist Johann Lhotsky. He had visited the site to pay homage to those in whose shoes he now metaphorically walked. The memorial was perhaps more likely to be a place of pilgrimage for explorer-scientists than local colonists in the first half of the nineteenth century because of its obscure and rugged location, which was in keeping with the naturalist enterprise.

In 1870, on the centenary of Captain Cook's arrival in Botany Bay, local landowner and then member of parliament Thomas Holt erected an obelisk marking what was believed to be Cook's first landing place. This monument was a more individual commemorative gesture than the 1822 plaque in two ways: it was erected by one man for one man. The inscription makes this clear:

Captain Cook landed here on 28th April, A.D., 1770. This monument was erected by the Hon. Thomas Holt, M.L.C., 1870, Victoria, Regina. The Earl of Belmore, Governor.

The imagined line of descent that Captain Cook was deployed to serve this time was not science's, but Holt's. It was a decidedly British pedigree that Holt was celebrating in this somewhat private, although also public, memorial gesture. Through the obelisk, Holt positions himself in British time: Cook lands and a hundred years later Victoria reigns. The Earl of Belmore is her local representative in the colony and Holt the local parliamentary representative for the people who now live where Cook first landed. It is an impressive lineage.

The obelisk was private in another way: it was situated on land that Holt owned. Beginning in 1861, he acquired much of the south shore of Botany Bay which Cook and others had traversed in 1770. By 1875, five years after the obelisk was built, he had acquired about 13 000 acres, which covered almost all the peninsula from Kurnell

Johann Lhotsky's *Captain Cook's tablet at Cape Solander, Botany Bay, 1839.* (Heritage Collections, State Library of Tasmania)

to Cronulla.[3] Holt experimented with various agricultural and pastoral enterprises, none of them particularly successful. By 1881, the Holt–Sutherland Estate Land Company Limited had been formed, the objective of which was to 'lease from Holt his Sutherland Estate'.[4] Once formed, 1000 acres of the estate was subdivided for sale. It was a portent of things to come: subdivision created and indeed characterises that part of Sydney now affectionately and parochially known as the 'Shire'. It was partly due to the estate's subdivision at the end of the nineteenth century that the land surrounding the obelisk erected by Thomas Holt in 1870 could be set apart in 1899, and turned into a public reserve to preserve its past.

This commemorative project was driven by another historically minded parliamentarian, Joseph Carruthers, who at the time was Minister for Lands, and later became premier of New South Wales. His historical sensibility was more public-minded than Holt's had been, and his use of Captain Cook more motivated by nationalist sentiment. The creation in 1899 of the Captain Cook Landing Place reserve was part of a broader process that accompanied a move to nationhood. This required the iteration and reiteration of myths of origin. These types of public historical gestures both acknowledged national foundations and aimed to instil historical sensibility in 'the people'. Most newspaper reports about the dedication of Captain Cook's Landing Place reserve, and about subsequent commemorative events held there to mark historical anniversaries, include lamentations about how apparently little valued by the general population were Captain Cook, this spot where he first landed and the history he embodied. The ceremonies that accompanied the original gazettal of the historic reserve, and those held later, drew only small, although reportedly 'enthusiastic', crowds. They tended to be made up of officials, mainly public servants and politicians who considered it important to mark historical events and historical sites. This is not to say that the Landing Place reserve was not a popular site; rather, it is simply evidence that public participation in historical commemorations was minimal.

From the outset, Carruthers had conceived this as a public reserve: a place where the masses could come to pay homage to Cook and his deeds, and through him the nation. To make it appealing

Frank Hurley, 'Monument at Captain Cook's landing place Kurnell',
c.1950s. The obelisk erected by Thomas Holt is at the centre of the
image. The pines amid the eucalypts are ceremonial plantings by
various visiting dignitaries over a century or so. At the beginning
of the twenty-first century their future is threatened as plans have
been proposed to return the reserve to its 'original vegetation'.
(National Library of Australia)

and accessible to the public, the meanings implicitly embedded in
the landscape needed to be made explicit. Whereas, in the early
nineteenth century, visitors to Botany Bay had apparently needed no
assistance to interpret the site's historical significance because they
could read its natural landscape for meaning or because the landscape itself (as sacred ground) spoke directly to them, in the closing
years of the nineteenth century this was less the case. To compensate,
the landscape was overlaid with monumental texts which instructed
visitors about what to look for and made clear the messages about
the past and its significance they were to take from it.

    Moreover, the site became a stage for many commemorative
events: tree plantings, historical re-enactments, dignitary visits,
monument unveilings, anniversary celebrations. These various

commemorative ceremonies, and the reports about them published in the press, can be read primarily as history lessons. The lesson to be imbibed was that Cook's deeds at this spot had been a necessary precursor to the act of colonial foundation. His deeds, most importantly discovery, were consciously linked to settlement and he was depicted as a visionary as well as a voyager. In popular historical imagery, Cook did not step ashore at Botany Bay only to survey it; as he stepped ashore, he also envisioned the nation that would grow up on this land. His 'discovery' of Botany Bay was progressively reinterpreted as consciously directed toward the founding of the nation.

Yet it was not only his actual deeds, however they might be interpreted, that were mobilised for storytelling about the new nation. It was Captain Cook himself who functioned as a model and inspiration for its citizens. The story of his life was rendered that of a young man who overcame humble beginnings to achieve greatness through strength of character, single-mindedness, resourcefulness and discipline. In this, Cook was an exemplar for a young nation 'compelled . . . to carve our own fortunes'.[5]

In the context of this more explicitly nationalist vision, and within the inscription of Botany Bay as a birthplace of the nation, Joseph Banks' role and significance in the history of Australia became more layered, and more independent of Captain Cook, Botany Bay, 1770. The part that Banks had played in the subsequent selection of Botany Bay as the site for a British penal colony gave him a prominent place in the more deliberately nationalistic rhetoric of the late nineteenth and early twentieth centuries. As an historic figure, he straddled the dual national historic themes of 'discovery' and 'colonisation'. 'Banks and Botany Bay are inseparable terms,' noted a newspaper report commemorating the 135th anniversary of 1770, 'and his good offices did not end with the assistance he afforded Captain Cook':

> Long after that he continued to take an active interest in the first efforts at colonisation, as our 'Historical Records' bear ample testimony. His wise counsel made its influence felt in many ways, and the early settlement at the head of Sydney Cove owed a great deal to his advice and influence.[6]

In this way, Banks was elevated from imperial voyager to a type of national foundational figure, much like Captain Cook had been in the same period, although in ways that drew upon different historical material.

Although Joseph Banks was always referred to in the various commemorative events staged at the Landing Place reserve after its gazettal, his individual historical memory was not given concrete form there until 1947. By this time, the explanation of his multi-layered historical significance was well rehearsed as evident in the inscription on his monument:

> In grateful memory of
> Sir Joseph Banks
> 1743–1820
> Famous British Scientist
> who visited these shores with
> Captain James Cook, R.N.,
> In 1770.
> His advocacy of British settlement in
> New South Wales, his beneficial influence
> on its early administration, his comprehensive
> researches into its flora, his vigorous
> personality and breadth of vision, merit
> his recognition as
> THE PATRON OF AUSTRALIA

Not quite founding father, but patron nonetheless.

Seeking 'native essence'

When first created at the close of the nineteenth century, Captain Cook's Landing Place reserve was difficult to get to. There was no road linking the historic site to the city. One was not built until the 1950s, when an oil refinery was established nearby, primarily servicing it rather than the public reserve. Without a direct overland route, visitors approached Cook's landing place in the most authentic way

possible: by sea. Early excursionists travelled from the city to settlements along Botany Bay's shore, such as Sans Souci, Botany and La
Perouse, where they either hired a boat to row themselves across the
bay, or caught a steamer to the historic site. Improved transport in
the early twentieth century made the route via La Perouse one of the
most popular approaches to Captain Cook's Landing Place reserve.
In 1902, La Perouse was linked to the city by tram, and by 1906
excursion steamers were carrying passengers across the bay. A tourist
ferry was plying between the two sites, at least by the 1920s and
perhaps earlier.

Those taking the tram to La Perouse could not help but get a
glimpse of the Aboriginal settlement that was located there, or its
residents as they went about their day-to-day lives on the headland.
For some visitors, the sight of Aborigines so close to Sydney was
something of a surprise. Annie Starr had arrived in Sydney as a
domestic servant from England in the early part of the twentieth
century. In about 1917 she caught the tram with a male friend to La
Perouse and her memory of that day stuck firmly in her mind. When
interviewed for the New South Wales Bicentennial Oral History
Project, she recalled how she had become an accidental tourist at La
Perouse and described her impressions of what she saw there:

Oh, and then one afternoon we went out, it was Sunday afternoon see.
Went out to Maroubra and he was as bad as I was. We went as far as the
tram went and there was a lot of black people [laughing] about, and we
were scared stiff to move. We sat in the . . . tram shelter shed until the
tram come back again and took us back [laughing]. I'll never forget that.
We were both scared stiff.

Interviewer: It must have been out at La Perouse . . .

La Perouse, that's right. And it went as far as the tram line. We thought
we'd go for a run to see what it was like out there. And we never moved
off the [laughing] shelter shed, the two of us. I was scared stiff. There was
some black kiddies running around and some black men walking
around. We weren't used to that. And he wasn't either, because he only
just come down to Sydney. I remember that trip.[7]

But for others, and increasingly so in this early twentieth-century period and beyond, the expectation of seeing Aboriginal people was a substantial part of the attraction of a trip to Botany Bay's north head. La Perouse had by then become known as the 'home of the blacks' in Sydney, and people went there in order to see Aborigines.

The curiosity about Aborigines derived both from the way in which they were perceived as embodying the native essence of the new nation and, paradoxically, from the presumption that they were passing away. A Californian visitor to La Perouse reportedly once asked:

> How is it that Australians make so much of their kangaroo, and have so little interest in the man who represents the holders of the continent before Captain Cook's time? I made many enquiries before I could find an aboriginal. I have been told of caves and mountains that visitors ought to see, and all kinds of interesting things, but I want to see the living anthropological representative of old Australia.[8]

This Californian visitor found what he was looking for at La Perouse: it was a place where 'the man who represents the holders of the continent before Captain Cook's time' could be found in close proximity to the city.

But the Aborigines living on Botany Bay's north shore did not satisfy everyone's desire for native essence. For some, they were not sufficiently native. They were considered too contaminated by the influence of white society, and indeed too metropolitan, to qualify. But they were the closest thing the city could offer to those in pursuit of 'primitivism', and the thing closest to the city for those unable to travel to where presumably real or more essentially native Aborigines lived. This, it must be remembered, was in the period before the Red Centre emerged as the essential, in both meanings of that word, tourist destination in Australia.

As more and more visitors, domestic and foreign, came to Botany Bay's north head, either specifically to see Aborigines or on their way to Captain Cook's Landing Place reserve on the other side of the bay, local Aborigines turned the situation to their advantage by satisfying, as best they could, the expectations and wants of visitors. They were geographically well placed to do so as Botany Bay's attractions assumed some prominence on Sydney's tourist itinerary. Moreover, they already had some experience in providing for visitors: reports from the 1880s and 1890s indicate that Aboriginal men living in the settlement at La Perouse earned some money by renting their fishing boats to visitors and selling honey and 'native weapons' that they had made, while Aboriginal women and girls sold wildflowers and shell baskets.[9] From the closing years of the nineteenth century, and through to the 1950s at least, Aboriginal people found a place for themselves as tourist traders within a local amusement precinct that developed on the headland as tourist traffic to the area increased.

A journey back in time

As the seaside became a more popular place for leisure in the late nineteenth century, amusement quarters that had hitherto been located in the centres of cities followed the crowds to the coastal periphery, either setting up permanently at a particular beach or travelling around from destination to destination. On the La Perouse headland, the tram terminus—known as The Loop because the tramline circled around to enable the trams to make the return journey—was the site for a local amusement precinct. Upon alighting from the tram, visitors were greeted with a scene of noisy entertainments and delights. The amusements on offer were typically bizarre and spectacular.

One of the earliest, and most enduring, acts on the headland was a snake show, which had begun business in 1897.[10] By 1919 it had been taken over by a local resident, George Cann, and has been operated by the Cann family ever since. Reptile shows were a fixture in popular entertainments in this period. Their appeal stemmed from their position in the nexus between science and entertainment which was characteristic of many forms of popular culture. Reptile shows combined science with spectacle, providing information about the risks of handling reptiles while at the same time playing on age-old cultural fears about serpents.

By the 1920s and 1930s, the snake show was only one of many spectacles vying for the attention of visitors to Botany Bay's north head. 'As you approached La Perouse down Anzac Parade,' the snake man's son, George Cann (Jnr), told me:

> Dad was the first show there. On the other side of the kiosk, where Rogers had the shop, they used to have performing dogs. Or when they'd go away another bloke would come in—old Tomahawk Joe I think they used to call him. He was a bow and arrow act, and knife throwing and tomahawk throwing.[11]

This is the scene of the fair, of carnival, where the world is momentarily turned upside down. Here dogs behave like humans, 'pushing dolls' strollers with each other in it',[12] an inversion of animal (nature) and human (culture). The archetypal exotic 'other', in the guise of Tomahawk Joe, is from another time and another place.

Unlike other seaside resorts around Sydney in the same period, Botany Bay's north head did not boast a grand amusement pavilion modelled on exotic oriental architecture. Visitors were, nevertheless, provided with opportunities to imagine themselves transported from the here and now to the there and then. In the absence of architectural exoticism, tourist traders working the La Perouse headland relied on the natural landscape to evoke a fantastic world, such as the 'sheik' who took people for camel rides along the beach as if it were the deserts of Arabia. At Botany Bay, the use of the natural landscape as a backdrop for the spectacle was possible because the area had been little developed. This was different from other Sydney seaside resorts which appealed precisely because they had been modernised and remodelled. Rather than manufactured, Botany Bay's exotic appeal was somewhat homegrown. Its attraction was its enduring associations with things 'primitive', 'native' and 'prehistoric'. In the first half of the twentieth century, much was still made of the fact that parts of Botany Bay, including the north head, had remained as they were when Cook and Banks had been there. Here some very old nature had survived, remnants from a deep prehistorical time.

It was within this local, exotic, natural landscape that some Aboriginal people, Australia's own 'primitives', lived. Aborigines, like the native flora, were commonly perceived as relics or remnants, if not from another place then certainly from another time. The exotic appeal of Botany Bay was therefore temporal. There one could apparently find what modern Australia had sprung from, but also what it had left behind. Ironically, what made Botany Bay all the more appealing to tourists in this period was its geographical proximity to Sydney: one did not have to travel far through space in order to go back in time.

Imagining Botany Bay as an exotic, prehistoric landscape was not completely contrary to its inscription as a birthplace of the nation. It was, rather, appropriate and affirming. Relatively recent settler societies like Australia tend to have multiple birthplaces to mark almost every possible phase in the birth process. Each captures a slightly different aspect of the sometimes protracted birth, which makes one birthplace seem insufficient. As a national birthplace associated primarily with discovery, rather than settlement, Botany Bay can be understood as evoking a phase prior to the actual birth—the first birth pangs rather than delivery, perhaps. As such, it was fitting that the landscape contained signs of what life and landscape were like pre-colonisation, pre-birth.

Promotional material advertising the tourist tram ride to Botany Bay's north head presented the journey as time travel. As excursionists went south from the city, they moved from modernity, suburbs boasting modern villas, to the pre-modernity of the scrubby coastal heath of Botany Bay's north head. But, rather than the final destination being heralded as the end-point of the journey, it was frequently described as an origin point. One commentator wrote in 1909:

> It is surely fitting that the longest tramline in the metropolitan area, unfolding in its journey matchless and ever-changing land and seascapes, should terminate at a vantage point from whence the visitor may look out across the waters to the landing place of the intrepid navigator, who, after battling through many unknown seas, lifted up a lonely voice on Kurnell Beach, announcing to posterity the nationality of this great island continent of the Pacific.[13]

This vision of Botany Bay, as a place caught in time, provided the setting for the spectacle of Aboriginality, or Aborigines, found there. To satisfy a general desire for native-ness, local Aboriginal people performed 'being Aboriginal' for visitors in quite stylised ways that emphasised the exotic, the primitive and the traditional. The most popular performance they staged for tourists was boomerang throwing. Alongside Tomahawk Joe, that archetypal, almost universal primitive figure, could be found a more local version, one that might be called Boomerang Joe. The boomerang itself, and boomerang throwing, conformed to the popular versions of Aboriginality at the time. The boomerang as the pre-eminent marker of Aboriginality is evident in the almost ubiquitous representation of the figure of the Aboriginal man as hunter. This archetypal image of Aboriginality, or Australian primitiveness, was certainly what overseas visitors came in search of when they made the trip to Botany Bay's north head in order to see some living Aborigines. Rather than desiring the metropolitan, almost suburban, version that the La Perouse Aborigines were often accused of being, what they wanted was tradition and native essence. And this is what they got via the boomerang.

The La Perouse Aborigines were accustomed to entertaining people in search of what might be called the 'domestic primitive'. Among the more celebrated visitors they received in the early part of the twentieth century was the British Admiral, Lord Jellicoe, in 1919, and nine years later the Prince of Japan.[14] Each was entertained with displays of boomerang throwing. These notables were followed by a steady stream of American tourists in the 1930s, when La Perouse was placed on the tourist itinerary for cruise ships in Sydney. Throughout the 1940s and 1950s, it became a regular whistle-stop for celebrities, including Hollywood actresses, dancers and singers and international sportsmen on tour in Australia. Pam Koeneman, an Aboriginal woman who grew up at La Perouse, recalled that in the 1940s and 1950s 'we used to get a lot of entertainers—overseas entertainers. People used to come from everywhere.'[15] 'Oh, look I tell you now,' Ruth Simms confirmed, 'Bill Hayley, Harry Belafonte, all the top American singers, they'd come out to Lapa [La Perouse]. Katharine Hepburn came out to

Lapa.'[16] Paul Robeson came too, but as a black rights activist as well as an entertainer, his interest in the Aboriginal settlement and its residents was in important respects different from his counterparts.

The boomerang throwing staged for visitors, sometimes in highly choreographed ways, was not simply a display to watch but also something to participate in. It provided an opportunity for the visitors to imitate the Aboriginality staged for their consumption. It was a performance in which conventional relations were momentarily suspended and inverted. In the first instance, an Aboriginal man, removed in time from precolonial indigenous society, mimicked popular notions of traditional Aboriginality. He left his own temporality and entered another. In turn, the spectator assumed the pose of Aboriginal man as hunter as he, or indeed, sometimes she, attempted to master the action of throwing a boomerang. This momentary inversion in which a white man or woman imitates a black man is captured in the many visual images taken of these staged events. For instance, the report describing Lord Jellicoe's visit, printed on the

'Admiral Jellicoe and the Boomerang', *Sydney Mail*, 1919. In the background a group of Aboriginal people from the La Perouse Aboriginal settlement look on. (State Reference Library, State Library of New South Wales)

Local boomerang makers and sellers Wes Simms (left) and Joseph (Joby) Simms (right) pose for a photograph with a visitor to La Perouse c. 1930s. (Randwick and District Historical Society)

front page of the *Sydney Mail*, included a photograph of him in full naval uniform in the archetypal stance of Aboriginal man as hunter with the boomerang raised above his head. Aboriginal people are shown merely as onlookers. The image's power derives from an expert in modern combat mastering the skill of 'primitive' weaponry. Once the skill is mastered, Aboriginal people are left to look on admiringly. The caption informs readers: 'he also did some throwing, and after a little practice succeeded in bringing the boomerang almost to his feet'.[17]

This same trope features in publicity shots of celebrities in the 1940s and 1950s. Men and women alike were depicted in the stance of Aboriginal-man-as-hunter. The whole cast of Broadway actresses from the musical *Guys and Dolls* was pictured in the pose of Aboriginal man as hunter flanking an Aboriginal man, Bob Simms.[18] In this instance, the inversion of relations had a gendered dimension to it whereby the prototypical Aboriginal hunter could be re-envisioned as both white and female.

Botany Bay souvenirs

The performances of Aboriginality staged for visiting dignitaries and celebrities were not the scene that more ordinary, everyday visitors witnessed when they alighted from the tram on Botany Bay's north head and walked down the hill on their way to the jetty to take the tourist ferry to Captain Cook's Landing Place reserve at Kurnell. The more common sight that greeted them was Aboriginal people standing at their stalls at The Loop, alongside various other traders, selling souvenirs.

One of the earliest accounts of Aboriginal men at Botany Bay selling 'native implements' to visitors was an 1890 report of the New South Wales Aborigines Protection Board in which it was noted that '[the men at the La Perouse settlement] are generally employed fishing; some also make native weapons for sale'.[19] But with a steady decline in fishing, mainly due to competition from whites, the production and sale of native implements was to become a progressively more valuable means of making a living. It was certainly less vulnerable to competition: unlike fishing, the

Albert Shepherd and Charlie Ahoy selling boomerangs and shell art at The Loop, c. 1930s. (Courtesy Gloria Ardler (nee Hoskins), Albert Shepherd's grand-daughter)

trade in Aboriginal curios was an Aboriginal-only industry. The demand for, and the value of, the objects were precisely due to the fact that they were produced by local Aborigines.

The market for traditional Aboriginal objects, particularly boomerangs, as souvenirs was spurred by the growing popularity of Botany Bay as a tourist site. With the growth in the number of visitors coming to the see the sights—historic, ethnographic and natural—sales of objects produced locally by Aborigines increased. These objects were now being purchased primarily as mementoes, something tangible that held the memory of the buyer's visit to the place where the souvenir had itself been produced. Like all souvenirs, the La Perouse objects enabled visitors to take home with them some of the experience of visiting that place. For the objects to work as souvenirs, they needed to capture for the tourist the experience of a trip to Botany Bay. La Perouse, imagined as an Aboriginal place and popularly known as the 'home of the blacks' in Sydney, it seemed obvious that archetypal Aboriginal objects like the boomerang would appeal most to tourists.

The decoration of the boomerang was also used to convey Aboriginality and to capture the tourist experience of a trip to Botany Bay. Like those made elsewhere across New South Wales and Victoria, the souvenir boomerangs were decorated with burnt-on designs using a piece of heated wire. The most common designs were native fauna, especially emus, kangaroos and koalas, and native flora, such as wattle, banksias and waratahs. Each boomerang-maker could apparently be distinguished by his designs, whether, for instance, his kangaroo's ears pointed forwards or backwards. The use of native fauna and flora designs on the boomerangs worked at a number of levels: it captured a popular association of Botany Bay as native landscape; it played on the popular idea that Aborigines were close to nature; and it expressed Australianness by using the country's unique flora and fauna, which was increasingly expressive of national identity in the early twentieth century. On the Botany Bay boomerangs, kangaroos, emus and koalas typically framed the inscription 'Greetings from Sydney'. (Indeed, they performed a similar framing function as the emu and the kangaroo on the Australian coat of arms.) This inscription tapped into the way in which a trip to

Botany Bay was for many part of a Sydney holiday. The tram ride to La Perouse and the ferry ride to Kurnell provided an outing that many visitors to Sydney included on their itinerary, along with a train ride to the Blue Mountains and a ferry ride to Manly. It also explains why the Sydney Harbour Bridge became, somewhat curiously, a popular design on the boomerangs made and sold by Aborigines at Botany Bay. This reinforced that the boomerangs were a Sydney souvenir. From a design point of view, the Sydney Harbour Bridge was the perfect decorative image for a souvenir-boomerang because it fitted so snuggly into the boomerang's shape.

Shell art made by Aboriginal women was also sold to tourists at The Loop at La Perouse. Like 'native weapons', shell art had been refashioned by local producers to satisfy a more explicitly tourist market. Aboriginal women making and selling shell baskets was first recorded in the early 1880s. In that period, the baskets were mainly sold to white suburban women, among whom there was a fashion for shell art. However, the designs were remodelled in the early part of the twentieth century as the local tourist trade grew. This included the introduction of shell boomerangs, which do not seem to have been part of the original portfolio of designs. The process of the transformation of shell art from Victorian-era curio to a Sydney souvenir was complete when a shell Sydney Harbour Bridge hit the stalls. While popular, the problem with shell art-as-souvenir was that it was neither sufficiently nor unambiguously Aboriginal. It was not a definite marker of Aboriginality like the wooden boomerang.

Had the drawcard for tourists to Botany Bay only been Aboriginal people, it is arguable that the souvenir trade may not have lasted as long as it did, or provided a source of income for as many people. That it did was paradoxically due to Botany Bay's inscription as an historic site celebrating the birth of the nation—a nation that did not have a place for Aborigines. The proximity of the Aboriginal settlement to Captain Cook's Landing Place reserve meant that a local Aboriginal tourist trade was viable for much longer than in other places where a similar industry had relied more exclusively on an interest in Aborigines, such as at Corranderrk near Melbourne. Moreover, La Perouse, where the Aborigines lived, became increasingly accessible due to improved transportation from the city

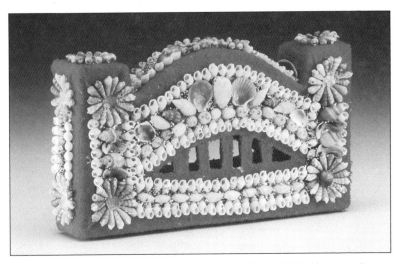

After the Sydney Harbour Bridge was opened in 1932, Aboriginal people at La Perouse incorporated it into the designs of the souvenirs they made. Aboriginal women made, and continue to make, shell art bridges like this one from the collection of the Powerhouse Museum in Sydney. Aboriginal men also used the Sydney Harbour Bridge in the designs they burnt onto their boomerangs. They were popular mementoes bought by tourists. My grandfather bought my grandmother a boomerang engraved with the Sydney Harbour Bridge, when they visited La Perouse in 1935 while on their honeymoon in Sydney. She treasured it for 60 years before passing it on to me. (Mavis Longbottom and Lola Ryan, La Perouse, 1986. Collection: Powerhouse Museum, Sydney)

during the twentieth century, which ensured a steady stream of excursionists. Confirming the importance of these factors, Ruth B. Phillips, in her discussion of the fortunes of Native American communities involved in tourist object-production, states that 'the importance of trade ware [that is, souvenir] production was greatest in communities with easy access to cities and tourist sites'.[20]

The economic significance of the trade features prominently in local Aboriginal people's rich historical remembrance about it. During the first half of the twentieth century, it became one of the main sources of income for local Aboriginal people and proved to be vital to their survival. To earn a living or to supplement income from other sources is how the practice of making and selling boomerangs is commonly described in oral history recordings with Aboriginal people from La Perouse.[21] An Aboriginal woman, Gladys Ardler (nee Ryan) remembered that in the 1930s her stepfather 'used to make a few boomerangs . . . on the side and sell them and my mother used to make shell work and sell that. That supplemented the living.'[22] The objects were cheap to produce, made as they were from local, natural materials. The mangroves around Weeny Bay near Captain Cook's Landing Place reserve supplied timber for boomerangs and other wooden objects. Seashells for shell art were gathered from beaches around Botany Bay, Sydney and the South Coast, and the cardboard and fabric required were collected as scraps and off-cuts from local shops and factories. The labour involved in making the objects was shared among family members, both young and old, and the entire production process was rarely considered a burden but rather an enjoyable form of sociality, involving as it did camping trips to collect raw materials and groups sitting around kitchen tables or out in the open manufacturing the items.

The trade contributed to Aboriginal families' ability to resist repeated pressure to be moved from their settlement. Dispersal was a constant threat during the first half of the twentieth century, particularly as the city progressively encroached on this once-isolated settlement and as the area became more attractive to speculators as a site for residential and recreational development. Because they could support themselves to some extent, Aboriginal people at Botany Bay had some leverage against outside pressure, contesting their right to remain resident there.

Telling Captain Cook stories

As already noted, the process by which souvenirs were made was a very social one. For instance, groups of young girls would assist their mothers, aunties and grandmothers in collecting shells along the beach; young boys learnt how to burn designs on to boomerangs under the tutelage of their uncles, fathers and grandfathers. People would sit around in groups to manufacture the objects and they would yarn as they worked. This process has been remembered as a time when knowledge about the place in which they lived was passed down from one generation to the next. The souvenir production process provided a context for some oral traditions to continue and for some new ones to be made.

Not surprisingly, one of the stories that younger children, particularly those growing up in the 1930s and 1940s, were told was the 'Captain Cook story', which as I noted in Chapter 1 was in circulation at least by the closing years of the nineteenth century. Gladys Ardler vividly remembered that particular story from her childhood. The version she had been told was that her mother's grandmother:

> was here when Captain Cook landed and she [Gladys' mother] told us about that and they still talk about that today. She'd tell us how they was on the beach at Kurnell on the ridge and Captain Cook came in and landed and how they shot a couple of them on the ridge. She'd tell us about grandfather and her great grandmother and that's all history down Botany Bay. But that's what we was just told that our [great] grandparents saw Captain Cook landing.[23]

Like earlier versions, this story still clearly drew on the most popularised elements of the historical account of Captain Cook in Botany Bay in 1770.

In the same period, the Captain Cook story was often told to tourists. They typically heard it when they bought a souvenir boomerang. It was used as a spiel to encourage buyers, or as an element in the actual sale.[24] In this way, having purchased a souvenir boomerang, a buyer did not only get the object itself but this local Aboriginal story about Botany Bay too. The story was one that the tourist perhaps added to his or her own repertoire about the day the object had been bought. At one level, the Captain Cook descent story operated like a certificate of authenticity: it told the buyer that this was the real thing because it had been produced by the real thing, that is, by an Aborigine with an almost perfect pedigree. The need to authenticate their wares in this way was sometimes necessary at La Perouse where, as I discussed above, the local Aborigines were not always seen to be sufficiently authentic themselves. They were not, ethnographically speaking, 'pure products' because they had apparently been too corrupted by the modern life.[25] And because they were not themselves considered truly traditional, it naturally followed that their merchandise was commonly considered to be of an inferior quality. Indeed, W.E.H. Stanner, the eminent anthropologist, was rather dismissive of the wares on sale at La Perouse in the 1930s. He wrote, in a piece about Aborigines in Australia published in 1939, that 'spurious boomerangs are still made for tourists, and others only slightly less spurious for innocents who visit the encampment at La Perouse, but most of these artifacts are so inferior that even tourists pass them by'.[26] Stanner was certainly not alone in this assessment, as this possibly apocryphal story, printed in a Sydney metropolitan daily, attests:

> One La Perouse aboriginal tells the story of a visitor who seemed to doubt the genuineness of the article. 'A real Australian boomerang for three shillings,' the aboriginal remarked, but the lady turned to her male escort and said, 'Don't waste your money on imitations, dear. Anyone can see that he made it himself'.[27]

It is in this context that Aborigines perhaps felt a need to assert direct descent from eyewitnesses to Captain Cook's arrival in Botany Bay.

Yet local Aboriginal people's intention for telling the story, or indeed the effect it might have had on those to whom they told it, was not always about authentication. Through reciting the story among themselves (that is, between one generation and the next) as well as with others (that is, tourists), the narrators are explaining and to some extent producing their own historical attachment to Botany Bay. It is worth noting that in this period they drew on an historical event to explain the relationship between themselves and the place in which they lived, rather than making reference to a Dreaming story, for instance. It is also the case that those selling the boomerangs and telling the descent story were making an historical point. This indigenous interpretation of Captain Cook at Botany

Bay reminded those who listened or, perhaps more precisely, those who could hear, that Aborigines had been there when Cook arrived and more importantly that they were still there. Perhaps, for some tourists, the experience was disorienting. They might have been perturbed that on their way to pay homage to the founder of the nation—a nation whose imagined future had no Aborigines in it— that they met Aborigines who seemed to be claiming a central place in the history of the nation, or at least one that was continuous with it. For other visitors, it was no doubt simply part of the entertainment on offer, and the Aborigines making the claim were seen as more to be pitied or ridiculed than seriously believed.

It is worth pointing out that local Aboriginal people were not the only ones making this claim public. The claim of continuous lineage from eyewitnesses to Captain Cook was incorporated into material about Botany Bay produced by the imagined descendants of the voyagers too. Such a claim was useful to those promoting Botany Bay's historical significance. That the Aboriginal people who lived there now were descended from those who were there in 1770 contributed to Botany Bay's claims to be a unique and valuable historic site. 'Other points of interest at La Perouse,' a 1928 tourist guide explained, 'are a war veterans' home and an aborigines' settlement. The latter is of particular interest to visitors, as here, quite close to the city, may be seen the descendants of the natives of Australia at the time of Cook's landing.'[28] While the statement is a little ambiguous because it is not clear whether the notion of descent is being used in specific or general terms, the point is nonetheless made: what adds to Botany Bay's interest is that the visitor can still see the types of people who Captain Cook himself saw.

More than simply speaking about it, some local Aboriginal people also gave lasting form to their version of Captain Cook's landing at Botany Bay in 1770 on the objects they made. These objects, usually boomerangs, can be thought of as history texts. One such boomerang-as-historical-tableau was made by Joe Timbery in 1936. The graphic burnt on to the boomerang presents a birds' eye view of Botany Bay and shows the complete shoreline from the heads to the western perimeter. The *Endeavour* floats in the middle of the miniature blue bay. Cook and his men are shown approaching the southern shore in their longboat. A handful of local people carrying spears anticipate its arrival. One is on the lookout at the top of a tree. The country on both sides of the bay is covered in trees, burnt stumps and tussocks of native grasses. It is a busy scene: the black figures are animated. One or two are running. Almost all have their arms raised.

The illustration has some superficial elements in common with various popular images depicting the landing of Captain Cook. For instance, Timbery has etched 'Landing of Captain Cook 1770' under the image—a common title. He also has depicted the *Endeavour* plus the longboat, which is in keeping with some other images. These parallels suggest that, just as Aboriginal oral accounts found their way into non-Aboriginal written texts, colonial visual culture was the inspiration for Aboriginal-produced historical texts.

Joe Timbery's boomerang is particularly interesting for the way in which it focuses on the drama on shore prior to the landing. It is concerned with the moment when Cook and his men make their approach in the longboat, although they are still a short distance from shore. The locals—eight are shown—are preparing themselves. They are clearly focused on the approaching boat. The two 'warriors' are yet

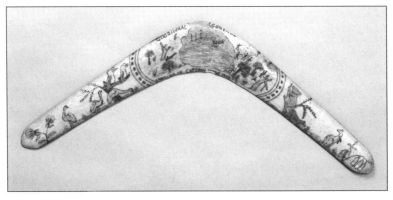

Joe Timbery's boomerang showing his version of the landing of Captain Cook at Botany Bay in 1770. (Joe Timbery, La Perouse Aboriginal Reserve, Sydney, 1936. Collection: Powerhouse Museum, Sydney)

to take their position on the beach. In this respect, it is an image that sits between ones that show indigenous people still simply going about their everyday business while the *Endeavour* passes through the headlands and ones in which the only locals shown are the two 'warriors' on the beach who resist Cook and his men as they prepare to land. Joe Timbery's boomerang pulls the curtain back on a scene that had largely dropped out of popular storytelling about Captain Cook's landing in Botany Bay.

Above the image, Joe Timbery has etched the word 'Gooriwaal' and another word beginning with the letters 'gun' but which cannot be deciphered because part of the boomerang has broken off. Gooriwaal is the word that local Aboriginal people use for the north head of Botany Bay.[29] The inclusion of Gooriwaal reinstates the meaning of the country before Captain Cook made history by coming ashore. While Cook and his men are still stranded on their boat in a watery no-place, the land all around the bay remains unambiguously indigenous. It is Gooriwaal, not yet Botany Bay.

Yet Joe Timbery's boomerang is more than simply a representation of the state of affairs when Cook made his landfall. It is also implicitly a statement about how things were understood, and the demands that Aboriginal people in and around Sydney were making, in the period in which it was produced, that is, the 1930s. During this period, there was a considerable amount of activism among Aboriginal people in the area on land matters, as historian Heather Goodall has clearly shown. Repeated calls were being made by Aboriginal people for some form of rights to land. For instance, Joe Anderson, who sometimes called himself King Burraga, and who was no doubt well known to Joe Timbery, was agitating for land rights. Joe Anderson was living at the Salt Pan Creek camp on the Georges River during this period, a camp that had strong links to the settlement at La Perouse. Like so many other local Aborigines, he publicly claimed direct descent from the eyewitnesses to Captain Cook. For instance, in a letter to anthropologist A.P. Elkin written in 1936, he described himself as the '3rd direct descendant of the Challengers of Captain Cook, when he Landed [*sic*] in Botany Bay, In [*sic*] 1770'.[30] Anderson strongly believed that Aboriginal people had a right to land on the basis of being the original owners of the country. On a Cinesound news film made of him in 1933, he said that 'it quite amuses me to hear people say they don't like the Black man . . . but he's damned glad to live in a Black man's country all the same.'[31] Joe Timbery's boomerang captures something of this politics. Timbery's image shows that the country was the 'black man's country' at the time of the landing of Captain Cook, and more importantly that it was understood to have continued to be so since. The act of making the boomerang itself, and inscribing it with the word 'Gooriwaal', is testament to this.

About seven years before Joe Timbery made his boomerang, the Aboriginal reserve on the north shore of Botany Bay was relocated from its original position to a new one. It is a long story involving a local government push to have Aboriginal people removed from the area altogether and a compromise negotiated by the Aborigines Protection Board whereby the Aboriginal settlement was shifted a little way up the hill, back from the foreshore of Botany Bay, to allow for greater public access to the beach. Today, local Aboriginal people explain the move as necessary because their huts on the beach had been sinking in the sand. Presumably this was an argument that the board used to convince them that the move was warranted.

In 1929, during the demolition of huts on the old reserve, a brass breastplate was found. It was engraved: 'Joe Timbrey, Chief of the Five Islands'.[32] The excavation of the breastplate, which probably dated from the first half of the nineteenth century, was a poignant reminder that local Aboriginal people's historical presence was literally in the place. The breastplate had possibly been buried with Joe Timbrey, or with one of his descendants. It is perhaps evidence that the original reserve had included a burial ground.

Although the spelling of their last names is slightly different, Joe Timbery, the boomerang maker, and Joe Timbrey, the chief of the Five Islands, are kin. However, the exact relationship between the two is not clear. It is possible that the latter was the great-grandfather of the former. Through their personal objects, which have been preserved over time, and are now held in cultural institutions in Sydney (the breastplate at the Australian Museum; the boomerang at the Powerhouse Museum), the two men are forever bound

Joe Timbrey's breastplate, n.d. (Australian Museum)

together. Joe Timbrey's breastplate and Joe Timbery's boomerang are material evidence of their historical presence in and their historical attachment to Botany Bay. Together they act as reminders of the depth of local Aboriginal people's historical roots at Botany Bay since Captain Cook. In this way they are monuments of a sort. They are not as solidly or permanently fixed to the ground as the imperial markers—Captain Cook's obelisk or Joseph Banks' memorial. But, in a deeper and more subtle way, they tell a story about people's connection to place, and so provide an important form of historical remembrance.

A LITTLE PIECE OF FRANCE

Commemorating the French at Botany Bay

Although primarily associated with James Cook, historic Botany Bay was never his alone. For most of the nineteenth century, it was that other imperial navigator, the Frenchman Jean-Françoise Lapérouse, who was more majestically memorialised there. So much so that to turn Botany Bay into a national Australian historic site, it had to be wrested from the French who had first possessed it with their penchant for making *lieux de memoire* wherever they went.[1] The Lapérouse expedition had arrived at Botany Bay in January 1788 within a handful of days of Captain Phillip and his cargo of convicts, and ever since then what to do with the French presence at the very moment of the colony's founding has posed something of a conundrum. But it was neither Lapérouse's presence at the founding of the colony, nor his navigational achievements—often compared favourably with those of Captain Cook—that caused him and his expedition to be memorialised at Botany Bay in the first place. His memory was preserved there because he lost his way soon after leaving the bay and was tragically and mysteriously never heard from again. As memorial landscape, Botany Bay, initially at least, commemorated disappearance, not discovery.

When Lapérouse's two ships followed the eleven British transports into Botany Bay in 1788, local indigenous people could have been forgiven for thinking that reinforcements had arrived. With the coincidental arrival of the British and the French, they temporarily faced what seemed like a dual assault. Aboriginal people who have lived at Botany Bay after 1788, particularly those occupying its north head where the Lapérouse expedition established a temporary camp, have subsequently and consequently dealt with a memorial advance from two sides.

Lapérouse's landing

On 26 January 1788, two French ships, the *Astrolabe* and the *Boussole*, under the command of Lapérouse, sailed into Botany Bay. They had been attempting to enter for two days, but had been unable to round the point because of strong headwinds. By the time they entered, Captain Arthur Phillip had already left for Port Jackson, and the other ships in what is now known as the First Fleet were preparing to join him there. The First Fleet had arrived in Botany Bay only a week or so before the French, but Phillip had quickly deemed it unsuitable for settlement, and had chosen a place he named Sydney Cove at Port Jackson instead. Captain Hunter, commander of the *Sirius*, had sent a man to the French ships with an offer of limited assistance before proceeding with the others to Sydney Cove. The French, in the meantime, continued into Botany Bay and, after anchoring, set up a small camp on the northern headland. There they spent about six weeks preparing for the next and indeed final leg of their voyage. 'As the English have established their settlement at Port Jackson,' wrote Lapérouse to a friend in Paris, 'they have left this entire bay to us.'[2] The entire bay was not exclusively occupied by the French, of course. There was a large indigenous population living around Botany Bay, who in time the French were to encounter.

The Lapérouse expedition had left France in 1786, burdened with extraordinarily high expectations about what it might achieve. The expedition is sometimes characterised as one that aimed to complete the work that Cook had left unfinished at his untimely death a decade earlier. By the time Lapérouse received instructions from Paris to drop down to Botany Bay to check on the British, much had already been accomplished by his expedition: coastlines mapped, discoveries made, knowledge accrued. The expedition was on its home stretch but, just prior to their arrival in Botany Bay, the French had been involved in a violent altercation in Samoa, in which twelve of the crew, including Lapérouse's second-in-command, de Langle, had been killed, and 20 others wounded. 'Many more Samoans than French died that day,' notes historian Jocelyn Linnekan.[3] With the memory of this affray still fresh in his mind, Lapérouse was in no mood for giving the 'natives' the benefit of the doubt. He had his men erect a stockade around their encampment on Botany Bay's north head, presumably as protection against the natives. Behind it they built two strong boats to replace ones lost in Samoa. Lapérouse's tolerance for indigenous people was low, and he was also out of patience with those among his men who accepted Rousseau's idea of the 'noble savage'. He blamed this philosophy for the clash at Samoa, which he believed could have been avoided had his own men been less trusting.

Given that this was a predominantly scientific voyage, Lapérouse's men at Botany Bay continued with their scientific pursuits, collecting flora and fauna, observing the natives and watching the stars. Among the expedition's naturalists was the priest Pere Receveur. Receveur died at Botany Bay and is buried on the north head, near where the French had their camp. It has long been believed that he died from wounds received in Samoa, an explanation provided in Governor Phillip's own official journal, although in recent times considerable doubt has been cast on this version of events. The eminent Lapérouse scholar, John Dunmore, has raised the possibility that Receveur died from wounds inflicted by local indigenous people at Botany Bay.[4]

The French and the locals had clashed violently at Botany Bay in the opening weeks of 1788. Almost all the journals produced by the British make reference to this violence, noting, sometimes in detail, sometimes in passing, that the French had 'some quarrel with the inhabitants', which 'obliged' them to shoot at them.[5] This situation was a potential diplomatic nightmare for Governor Phillip, who seemed intent on establishing good relations between his contingent and the local people. However, it was only a matter of weeks before there was violence between Phillip's men and the local indigenous people, a circumstance that David Collins attributed in part to the French. After describing how convicts stealing locals' belongings had aggravated the situation, he noted:

> we also had the mortification to learn, that M. De la Perouse had been compelled to fire upon the natives at Botany Bay, where they frequently annoyed his people who were employed on shore. This circumstance materially affected us, as those who had rendered this violence [the locals] necessary could not discriminate between us and them [the French].[6]

If nothing more, the violence between the French and the Botany Bay people raises an interpretive issue about whether Phillip's own encounters with Aborigines during the early days and years of settlement—encounters that continue to receive considerable attention—can be treated in complete isolation. I have already suggested in Chapter 1 that Phillip's encounters in the opening weeks of 1788 ought to be interpreted with reference to Captain Cook's earlier encounter there in 1770; I am proposing here that they ought also be interpreted through reference to the French, who momentarily shared the zone of cross-cultural encounter with the British and who perhaps were responsible for throwing the first punch.

While the British and the French went to considerable lengths to mark out and to respect each other's national boundaries while they coexisted for a short time on New Holland's coast, David Collins was no doubt right when he said that the locals 'could not discriminate between us and them'. They were probably not deciphering the language, symbols and signs of national difference. They might have noticed some distinctions, but presumably there was sufficient in common between the British and the French for this to be interpreted by the local indigenous people as a single assault. For those who ranged the country between Sydney Cove and Botany Bay, the coincidental arrival of the British and the French, and the establishment of their respective camps, would have felt like an assault advanced from two sides. They might have thought the strangers were purposefully trying to hem them in. But, even had the differences in the respective camps of strangers been sufficiently pronounced for the locals to know that they were dealing with two intrusions rather than one, then this must have caused considerably more confusion and alarm in what was already a deeply troubling state of affairs.

And so, while the British and the French went about their respective business with only minimal and occasional reference to each other, the local indigenous people were no doubt observing them all with equal interest and, when the opportunity allowed, comparing notes among themselves about the two camps. Considered from this standpoint, with an eye on each camp, it is not too fanciful to suggest that the local people's interactions with the British, in those opening weeks of 1788 and subsequently, must have been to some degree influenced by the nature of their encounters with Lapérouse and his men and, indeed, vice versa. And as such, the French—often given short shrift in early colonial Australian histories about the establishment of the colony—must have had some, perhaps even much, influence on the very earliest cross-cultural encounters. But unfortunately this line of analysis is thwarted by the absence of the French expedition's records about its time in Botany Bay. After staying in Botany Bay for about six weeks, the two French ships set sail. The British at Sydney Cove presumed they were heading north, with the intention of returning to France in a matter of months. They were never heard from again. Forty or so years later, it was established that the ships had been wrecked off the coast of Vanikoro not long after leaving Botany Bay. Their records went to the bottom of the ocean with them.

The French Garden

When it became clear that something terrible had happened to the French expedition, the site of its camp on Botany Bay's north head almost instantly, and somewhat organically, became a memorial to its loss. This was a natural place to preserve the lost expedition's memory because it was here that it had last been seen.

In this respect, what happened after rather than what had happened during the short period when Lapérouse and his men had camped there imbues this particular spot with special significance. In fact, the details of those six weeks in early 1788 when the north head of Botany Bay was a temporary home to the French expedition are somewhat incidental to its subsequent history as a memorial site. In the 200 or so years that Lapérouse has been commemorated at Botany Bay, the stuff of history has not necessarily derived from the 1788 encounter, but from other places and from other times. The material that sustained and nourished this *lieu de memoire* has pursued trajectories and meanings distant from, and often tangential to, anything that occurred there.

In a mode similar to history-making about Captain Cook at Botany Bay in 1770, the stories told about and the histories made through the historical encounters of the French at Botany Bay service a far more expansive vision of the past. It is one that can simultaneously incorporate a history of this particular voyage, others that followed it, eighteenth- and nineteenth-century exploration in the Pacific region more generally, the making of modern France, and even an Australian and French alliance in World War I. As a result of its almost accidental association with, and the subsequent repeated inscription on the landscape of the memory and meaning of the fateful French imperial expedition, this local spot became a parchment for telling stories about national, international and global pasts, presents and futures. In the process, the more troubling aspects of what actually happened there, particularly between the Frenchmen and local indigenous people and the legacies of that specific encounter, have been elided.

Standing on the north head of Botany Bay it is now impossible to forget that Frenchmen were once at this place. That passing presence is retained in the names of various features on this landscape—Frenchmans Bay, Frenchmans Beach, Frenchmans Road, for instance. Some of these names probably emerged while the Lapérouse expedition was at Botany Bay, given that its presence was clearly the most distinguishing and noteworthy feature in this new and unfamiliar landscape. The British colonists called the actual encampment site the 'French Garden', although this name has not endured, in part because it was replaced by a presumably better name: La Perouse, after the expedition's commander.[7]

The original name, French Garden, represents a spontaneous rather than an official act of naming. Unlike the later La Perouse, it was certainly not honorific, which was the more common pattern in nomenclature, such as Sydney Cove, that the British colonists were using for their new home. As a placename, French Garden was more straightforwardly descriptive, marking the site through a recent and palpable association.[8] The French Garden described the place where the Lapérouse expedition had established its temporary camp in 1788, and so in this sense it was a name that functioned both geographically and historically: it was a marker of place that also marked time.

The French Garden presumably referred to a garden, which is the assumption made in most nineteenth- and twentieth-century accounts about it. Yet there is some doubt about whether a garden was indeed sown by the French expedition.[9] That doubt stems from the fact that there is no mention of a cultivated plot in any of the First Fleet journals, even though most refer to the other material traces left behind by the expedition such as the stockade and the priest's grave. But perhaps that matters little. The French were generally in the habit of planting a garden in places where they stayed, as an experiment in the transportability of Europe. The Lapérouse expedition's horticulturist had planted European vegetables and other plant species elsewhere, and it is also the case that during later French voyages around Australia, such as D'Entrecasteaux's, garden plots were established. Whether the name French Garden was a precise label or not, a marker of a real garden or merely a figurative description, it turned out to be a useful, even suggestive, description for this place, particularly in the wake of the French expedition's disappearance. The name performed a significant symbolic function in the memory work at Botany Bay about the Lapérouse expedition.

At one level, the garden functioned as a reminder of death. For members of a French expedition aboard the *Coquille*, who visited the site in 1824, this was its predominant meaning. A description of it in the expedition's published journal explained:

This garden to-day, partly uncultivated, formed in the sandy scrub, provides some vegetables for the soldiers who are quartered in a small tower built a short distance away on one of the points of the bay. The fruit trees are dead and could not take root there, shaken as they are by the winds from the sea. Quickly growing weeds have taken possession of the greater portion of its surface, like a symbol of the vain toil of man.[10]

In this description, an overgrown, run-down, half-dead garden on the lonely headland, believed to be the original handiwork of the Lapérouse expedition, symbolises failure and futility. A lingering sense of the national disappointment that shrouded the expedition after it failed to complete its voyage can be detected here. For the company of the *Coquille*, the garden and the landscape surrounding it were mainly experienced as a *memento mori*.

But, at another level, the garden was sometimes used to symbolise endurance despite death. A garden is perfect for this role, given that it can live on after the demise of those who planted it. And in a landscape as sandy and barren as Botany Bay's north head reportedly was, if the putative garden had in fact survived then this was a small marvel, making its presence all the more poignant. A garden symbolised in some small way the purpose of the Lapérouse expedition and others like it. The transplantation of European culture and nature to the antipodes had occurred, despite the voyage foundering before it had finished its work. The putative garden was then testament to this larger truth about the fruits of imperial voyaging.

The crew of the *Coquille* made a pilgrimage to the French Garden in 1824 as a commemorative gesture. 'As Frenchmen, as travellers,' they noted in their official account, 'we wished to pay our tribute by visiting the spot on which the illustrious and unfortunate La Perouse [*sic*] wrote the last dispatches which had arrived in Europe, the encampment which he formed at the north point of Botany Bay.'[11] As a memorial, the spot was significant not simply as the expedition's former encampment, but also because it had been its very last postal drop. 'A voyage begun is a voyage to be ended,' observes Greg Dening.[12] This spot, by default, was the end-point for Lapérouse's voyage.

Viewed as end-point, the grave of the priest, Receveur, who had died and was buried on Botany Bay's north head, assumed greater significance than might otherwise have been the case. While his death was not directly associated with the ultimate loss of the rest of the expedition, it was nonetheless fitting that there should be a grave belonging to one who had been on board that expedition here. The humble tomb soon became a substitute mausoleum for the entire voyage. Like the putative remnant garden, it functioned as a sign on the landscape that the expedition's history had been cut tragically short. And, also like the garden, by the time Frenchmen began visiting this natural memorial site, it was barely visible on the landscape. It had to be restored if it were to assume a more expansive monumental function.

In keeping with what seemed to be general practice among imperial travellers when they came across the gravesite of a European buried a long way from home, the early British colonists, under the direction of Governor Phillip, made an effort to maintain the French priest's lonely gravesite. The French themselves had modestly marked it with a rough mound of stones and an epitaph painted on a piece of wood, according to the First Fleet officers who stumbled across the grave soon after the French ships had sailed. Upon learning of the grave, Governor Phillip arranged for an engraved copper plate to be attached to a nearby tree, although, as David Collins noted, 'rain, and the oozing of the gum from the tree, soon rendered . . . that illegible'.[13] After this, nothing more appears to have been done to preserve the grave, and so it languished on the exposed headland. But, when various French expeditions in Sydney began to make pilgrimages to Botany Bay to honour their hero-navigator, Lapérouse, the grave was rescued from threatening oblivion. The *Coquille*'s record-keeper wrote:

> A soldier who had been for a long time stationed at the spot took us at our request to the place where tradition assigns the grave of Father Le Receveur . . . He showed us a mound under which is buried this companion of La Perouse [*sic*], and which for a long time bore [an] epitaph graven on copper by order of Governor Phillip and fastened to a tree which we found there still.[14]

He means the tree, not the copper plate. The crew of the *Coquille* spent the day engraving the tree with the inscription (in French): 'Near this tree lie the remains of Pere Le Receveur: visited in March, 1824',[15] thus marking the grave and their own pilgrimage to it.

A later account claims that the source for the exact location of the priest's grave was an Aboriginal man, Cruwee. Obed West recollected, many years later:

> seeing the tree which marked the spot [of the grave] before the present monument [to Lapérouse] was erected, a few days after the inscription was placed upon it by the French officers who came in search of the Admiral . . . When I first saw the inscription I made enquiries about it and was informed that a person named Richards took the party of French officers to the spot, and then got a blackfellow called Cruwee to point out the spot where the men [*sic*] of La Perouse's [*sic*] ships who died were buried. Cruwee pointed out the spot and it was [on] his information that the tree was marked so that the site should not be lost.[16]

Once again it is a local Aboriginal man who points the way. As had been the case in 1822 with determining James Cook's and Joseph Banks' first landing place, so it was in 1824 with Pere Receveur's last resting place. In efforts to determine the exact spot where some historic event on 'virgin' territory happened, as Chris Healy has argued, the Aboriginal eyewitness assumes special status.[17] But the moment a permanent marker replete with text is affixed to the place hitherto held in memory, local, indigenous and orally transmitted knowledge becomes redundant. It is a European monument, not an Aboriginal man, which becomes the supposedly faithful witness to the past from then on.

The tree near the grave was described in the *Coquille*'s journal as 'a witness of the mournful scene', a phrase that yet again depicts the landscape as one associated with loss and death. The tree was a witness to the grave but, with the addition of the inscription that the Frenchmen had spent the day carving on its trunk, it also became a witness to their own pilgrimage. By engraving 'visited in March, 1824', the crew of the *Coquille* began a tradition that has continued to the present. Every time a French expedition visited the site throughout the nineteenth and twentieth centuries, they left a 'we wuz 'ere' message. In the twentieth century, brass plaques replaced the tree trunk as the parchment for memorial graffiti. The plaques were attached to the base of the monument built on the headland in 1828 to the Lapérouse expedition. These mini-monuments, attached to the larger monument, amounted to a continuous and composite record about French voyaging in the Pacific region. While the Lapérouse expedition itself occupied a pivotal place in that larger and longer history, these little plaques demonstrated that its work was continually being added to, even completed, by subsequent French expeditions. Each new plaque represented another chapter in the historical narrative about the imperial and colonial French presence in the antipodean region. So, while at one level the site was imagined as the symbolic end-point of Lapérouse's voyage, at another it was conceived as an origin point for a new, and seemingly never-ending, story about French naval presence in the Pacific.

In the account of the *Coquille*'s pilgrimage to Botany Bay, the writer predicted that 'one day a more lasting monument will be raised to this shipwreck of an expedition devoted to useful discoveries and to the progress of civilisation'.[18] Within a few short years, this prophecy was realised. While in Sydney in 1825, as commander of yet another visiting French expedition, Hyacinthe de Bougainville, the son of the more famous imperial navigator Louis de Bougainville, went to Botany Bay's north head to assess its suitability as a site for a monument to the Lapérouse expedition. Although it was somewhat isolated, Bougainville was convinced that the headland was indeed the ideal setting for such a memorial.[19]

The French historian, Antoine Prost, suggests that a monument's significance is partly derived from the meaning of the place in which it stands.[20] As already suggested, the significance of the northern headland of Botany Bay for a monument to Lapérouse derived not only from its having been the site of the expedition's temporary encampment, but more especially from having been the last place from which the expedition had communicated with the 'enlightened world'. The epitaph that Bougainville arranged to be inscribed on the base of the monument gives emphasis to, and thus reiterates, this meaning:

This place/visited by Monsieur De La Perouse in the year MDC-CLXXXVIII/is the last/whence any account of him/has been received.

The inscription refers to the fact that, while at Botany Bay, Lapérouse had entrusted some of his voyage journals and letters to the British with instructions to deliver them to Paris by the next available ship, although this did not include his journal entries for the sojourn in Botany Bay. We know that he had acquired knowledge about the British because his published journal ends with the tantalising sentence: 'Later we had only too many opportunities of obtaining news of the English establishment whose deserters caused us a great deal of trouble and inconvenience as we will explain in the next chapter.'[21] With the ships wrecked, however, there was no next chapter. Botany Bay was not only the place from where Lapérouse had organised for his papers to be sent to Paris; one instalment had been taken overland from the east coast of Russia. The practice ensured that, while the expedition was ultimately lost, some of its 'discoveries' survived. While it had fallen short of providing France with much anticipated, highly valued information about the 'unknown world', the survival of some of Lapérouse's journals meant that the expedition had not been a total failure.

While hitherto the headland had generally been associated with the entire French expedition, the proposed new monument was primarily an edifice devoted to its commander, Lapérouse. This is reflected in the monument's form—a tall, doric column surmounted by a brass astrolabe, representing Lapérouse's ship, the *Astrolabe*, and emphasising his role as a navigator. Chris Healy has noted a tendency in nineteenth-century public history in which 'historical attributes, achievements or events that might have been claimed or associated with a number of historical actors are congealed over time around a singular personage'.[22] The Lapérouse monument at Botany Bay is illustrative of this, as was the subsequent naming of the site 'La Perouse'.

The replacement of the unofficial 'French Garden' with the official 'La Perouse' as the placename appears to have occurred some time after the erection of the monument.[23] The new name demonstrates the integral, mutually reinforcing, nature of the relationship between the edifice and its location. Not only did the monument derive meaning from its specific setting, but in turn it also contributed to the meanings about that place which coalesced over time. For many years, the column was one of only a couple of built structures on the windy headland. It was, therefore, a landmark in two senses—both a memorial to the past and a defining feature of the place. Without the monument, the association of this place with that voyage may have disappeared altogether.

Like all monuments, the Lapérouse column was originally a product of its creators' own historical sensibilities. For Bougainville, conscious of his own naval heritage, the monument honoured a national hero-navigator. But his scheme probably would not have been realised had his historical sensibility not been shared by local colonists. Bougainville received willing support from the New South Wales colonial government, in part because Lapérouse embodied colonial society's own origins, that same imperial age when scientific discovery of distant lands provided territory that could be made into colonies.

Once erected, the monument displaced the headland's mournfulness with a new and more triumphal historic presence, meaning and vision. The presence of the monument on the bleak, isolated and undeveloped headland helped to transform this landscape from one of loss to one of life. The stately structure spoke to the achievements of Lapérouse and the imperial age to which he belonged. It can be read as a vision of Lapérouse himself cast in stone, no longer prostrate on the bottom of the ocean but standing tall in a wild landscape, a landscape that poses no threat. In contrast to the image of the defeated garden overgrown with weeds, and the humble, barely visible priest's grave, the impressive column dedicated primarily to the hero-navigator suggests achievement and triumph.

This grand historical vision is far more exalted, more celebratory than the presumably prosaic details of the encounter of the expedition at the site in 1788. If the second-hand accounts of the First Fleet are anything to go by, from the point of view of the French voyagers and the British colonists, although presumably not the local indigenous people, nothing exceptional happened while the French were at Botany Bay. And, had the Lapérouse expedition returned safely to France, there might not have been a past to preserve or a history to tell about it there at all. In the complete narrative of the voyage, the northern headland of Botany Bay would have been just another unremarkable stopover among many on an epic voyage.

But, despite the motivations of the monument's makers, this was never exclusively a historic site. Rather, it was a popular one, in both senses of that word. For the steady stream of colonial visitors to the Lapérouse column in the nineteenth century, its appeal, and the enduring enigma of its location, derived not from a desire to acknowledge Lapérouse's heroic deeds but because lost voyagers like him typically provoke a certain intrigue and pathos. Shipwrecks, hero-navigators who lost their lives in pursuit of new lands, pirates, cannibals and beachcombers all captured the popular colonial imagination. It was the stock of stories and rumours which circulated, many far-fetched—that Lapérouse and his crew had survived and gone 'native' or that they had been eaten by 'natives'—that made this such a popular landmark in the wider Sydney landscape. As evidence of its popular appeal, a large number of illustrations of the monument were produced in the nineteenth century by well-known artists and amateurs alike.[24]

Did the steady stream of visitors to the monument ever encounter Aborigines on their excursions? I have found only one visual image of the monument from that period which depicts an Aboriginal presence at the site. A painting made in 1854 by Frederick Terry shows both Lapérouse's monument and Receveur's grave, and depicts a group of Aboriginal people and their dogs in the foreground. The image had been commissioned to accompany the tree stump engraved by the crew of the *Coquille* in 1824, which was to be taken from Botany Bay to be displayed first in Sydney at the 1854 Exhibition of Arts and Industry and then the following year in Paris at the Universal Exhibition. The image is by no means incontrovertible evidence that Aboriginal people were living near the French monuments on Botany Bay's north head at this time. They may have been invention, or more figurative rather than real.[25] If the former, they were perhaps included to make a statement about Aboriginal people's anticipated passing in the wake of the imperial age that Lapérouse embodied. On the other hand,

Frederick Terry's *Vue du tombeau du père Receveur*, 1854. The painting was sent to the Universal Exhibition in Paris in 1855 along with the tree stump engraved by sailors from the *Coquille* in 1824. The tree stump and a copy of the painting were returned to Botany Bay in 1988 for display at the Lapérouse Museum which opened that year. Terry's painting is unusual for showing Aboriginal people and for depicting all three memorials at the site: the priest's grave, the engraved tree stump and the monument to Lapérouse.
(Musée national de la Marine, Paris)

perhaps the painting does document an Aboriginal presence in this place at that time: certainly a decade or so after it had been created such a presence was more palpable and more permanent at the site (as discussed in Chapter 2).

French intentions?

Although the Lapérouse expedition had a quite visible memorial presence at Botany Bay compared, for example, with Captain Cook, in Australian historiography more generally it was relatively absent and, if mentioned at all, was typically done so only in passing. For the writers of Australian history, it was difficult to know what to do with the French presence in Botany Bay in 1788, particularly when they were seeking to narrate a solid national history based on the supposedly rightful, and unshakeable, British possession of the territory. In Australian historiography, at least prior to the late twentieth century, the main question implicitly posed by the French presence in Botany Bay in 1788 was whether or not it constituted a threat to the British possession of New Holland. At least until recently, most twentieth-century Australian histories dealing with the matter have generally concluded that it did not, and to give substance to their conclusion represented the French presence at the moment of British colonisation in benign terms. The apparently banal nature of visits exchanged between the French and British camps over the six weeks when they both occupied the littoral fringe of New Holland's east coast is typically proffered as evidence that the French did not have any thought of territorial disputation. The visits between the camps are characterised, in most Australian historical texts, as courteous, even cordial. Moreover, the French are routinely commended for the hospitality they extended when the British paid them visits. This emphasis on cordiality mutes any suggestion of potential territorial threat. I am not saying that the visits between the French and the British camps were not indeed friendly; rather, I point out that this fact has been used as evidence to quash any suspicion that more was at stake. That this was thought necessary is perhaps more telling about the role that Australian history, at least prior to the 1970s, played in producing a confident narrative for the nation about the certainty and calibre of British colonisation.

In a similar mode, any traces of territorial dispute that the French might have provoked have been muffled historiographically by representing Lapérouse as a navigator in company with Captain Cook, rather than a coloniser in company with Governor Phillip. This is typically achieved by reference to an account about one of the visits between the French and the British in 1788, one in which Lapérouse was reported as saying: 'Enfin, Monsieur Cook à tant fait qu'il ne m'a rien laissé a faire que d'admirer ses œuvres. (In short,

Mr Cook has done so much that he has left me nothing to do but to admire his works.)'[26]

This complimentary, and comforting, statement has been repeated by some Australian historians seeking to defuse the canard that the French posed a serious territorial threat to British colonisation. In some cases, Lapérouse's admiration of Captain Cook is deployed as evidence that the expedition did not enter the waters of Botany Bay to challenge the British. By this means, the more thorny matter of strained diplomatic relations is side-stepped.

However, no matter what historians say to diffuse the popular belief that the French posed a threat to British possession, there is always something a little troubling about the French presence at the nation's foundational moment. And its enduring memorial presence at Botany Bay—a birthplace of the nation—is at times perceived as, if not completely disturbing, then at least a little undesirable. The Lapérouse monument, standing majestically over Botany Bay and clearly visible from Captain Cook's Landing Place reserve, can sometimes seem out of place, like a gatecrasher at a private party.

An alternative history

As Botany Bay was more explicitly fashioned in the twentieth century as a birthplace of the nation, efforts were made to incorporate, often clumsily, the curious foreign memory site on the north shore, with its French nomenclature, Lapérouse's column and Père Receveur's grave. The rapprochement was often uneasy. In this period, and perhaps in order to deflect attention away from its own particular historical associations, Botany Bay's north head was more often than not referred to as the 'gateway to the birth of the nation' or as 'historic La Perouse facing the birthplace of Australia'.[27]

This proudly French memorial site on Botany Bay's north head did not fit easily into a landscape marking Australia's British origins, mainly because the French expedition did not fit seamlessly into a recognisable national Australian story. While the Lapérouse story had at times been more or less seamlessly grafted on to an imperial narrative about voyagers and their discoveries, this was more difficult when the matter of national foundations became the main focus for public history-making at Botany Bay. The Lapérouse expedition was too obviously foreign, and its presence at the founding of the colony in 1788 too problematical, to be fully embraced as part of the story that was being told at Botany Bay about the nation's past.

For this reason, La Perouse on Botany Bay's north head is one of those rare, but important, sites where one can play a game that David Malouf has called the 'game of alternative beginnings, or imagining an Australia that might have been French'.[28] The French presence at Botany Bay in 1788 offers an occasion for contemplating an alternative origin story, and thus another present and another future. The game retains its potency despite the mantra of historians that the French did not pose a threat to the British in 1788 or beyond. That is because the act of imagining alternative beginnings has little to do with history *per se*. It derives its power from the trajectory of possibilities—of other pasts, other presents and other futures. In this respect, the small portion of Botany Bay claimed for French memory, rather than reifying national Australian origins through, for example, reference to the same imperial past, can expose the implausibility of them. As a heterotopia, to use Foucault's description, the quest for true origins becomes unattainable.

However, while the French presence at Botany Bay in 1788 provides opportunities for contemplating substitute national beginnings, local Aboriginal people have had to deal with the French often being ascribed the local honour of having founded the place where they and their ancestors have lived for many generations. In local histories of Botany Bay's northern headland, Lapérouse and his expedition occupy a pivotal position. They have become 'pioneers' of a sort. A local history guide published in 1989 states:

> While Phillip founded the British Colony of NSW on the southern shore of Port Jackson, Laperouse [*sic*] and his party erected a stockaded camp near the present Frenchmans Bay. They stayed for about 6 weeks, being the first European residents of the area which became the Municipality of Randwick.[29]

As first 'residents', they did not stay long. This is one of those reversals that Ann Curthoys identifies when she writes that: 'Aboriginal people who stay on their own land as far as they can, to protect it, become in white Australian mythology, the nomads . . . while the true wanderers . . . are named the settlers.'[30] As the more permanent and continuous residents of the place, by the late twentieth century local Aboriginal people at La Perouse were calling for the site to be renamed Guriwal (also spelt Gooriwaal or Goorawahl), the name believed to be the original one for the area. 'La Perouse is the longest continuing [Aboriginal] community since first contact with whites,' claimed Beryl Beller (nee Timbery), 'and it should go by its original name, Guriwal, not a French name.'[31]

A little piece of France

During the first half of the twentieth century when Botany Bay was more explicitly inscribed as a national historical landscape (described in Chapter 3), the Frenchness of the north headland became more, not less, pronounced—a reversal of what might have been expected, given the historical sensitivities involved. But this continually growing cache of Frenchness was fed by a new impulse which was neither a desire to commemorate the imperial past nor a wish to honour a French navigator who had been tragically shipwrecked. This time the impetus was a new relationship between the modern national states of France and Australia, forged in more recent times and in completely new contexts. While this development was strongly supported by French nationals themselves, either visiting or living in Sydney, it was by no means exclusively a product of French tenacity to preserve French historical memory. This time the initiative came from within.

On Bastille Day 1917, the New South Wales government announced, on two separate occasions, that it was ceding the sites of the French memorials on Botany Bay's north head to France.[32] The scheme had been devised by the premier, W.A. Holman, and was construed as a symbolic gesture to express the alliance between France and Australia being forged at the time on the battlefields of

Europe. To express its sympathy with France, the New South Wales government offered it a piece of its own soil. Long imagined, symbolically at least, as a 'little piece of France', it was now actually to become that. The proposed land grant was, however, never made. After legal opinion advised that it would be ruled by the laws of France, and thus could be used by criminals as a safe haven, the Bill enacting transfer of title was withdrawn. However, despite disclaimers intermittently published in Sydney newspapers, the belief that La Perouse does indeed belong to France—is *terre de la France*—continues unabated.

That no land was ceded mattered not. In the context of the Great War, the French monuments at Botany Bay, and the historical moment when Lapérouse and Phillip encountered each other on the 'edges of empire', became a medium for expressing and celebrating the new alliance that now existed between France and Australia.[33] And so, when in 1918 Henry Selkirk, a fellow of the Royal Australian Historical Society, gave a lecture and lantern slide presentation about the French monuments at La Perouse, he opened by juxtaposing the scene at Botany Bay in January 1788 with that on the recent battlefields in France. He urged his audience to:

> Picture that opening chapter when Governor Phillip extended the hospitality of the infant Colony to those gallant Frenchmen in their hour of need, just 130 years ago; now turn to the present, the infant has attained to man's estate, the penal settlement expanded into a great Commonwealth; the new-world Commonwealth and the old-world Nation linked in a bond of blood brotherhood, fighting shoulder to shoulder on the fair fields of France in the cause of civilisation, of truth, and of righteousness against the powers of evil.[34]

Drawing parallels between events at Botany Bay at the end of the eighteenth century and the battlefields of France at the beginning of the twentieth requires a level of historical acrobatics which is both admirable and disturbing. Selkirk's evocative opening indicates precisely how relations between France and Australia were imagined in this period and, moreover, how the events at Botany Bay in 1788 were deployed as a source for them.

The French Mission to Australia in 1918 at the Lapérouse monument. Henry Selkirk used this image in his lantern-slide lecture in the same year to the Royal Australian Historical Society on the French monuments. This was the year after the New South Wales government had hatched a plan to cede the site to France. (Mitchell Library, State Library of New South Wales)

At least by World War II, and perhaps earlier, the 'little piece of France' on Botany Bay had became the site for annual Bastille Day ceremonies.[35] It is a tradition that has endured to the present. The event is usually attended by French government officials in Sydney, members of New South Wales state and local governments along with members of the Sydney French–Australian community, including many war veterans. For the occasion, the Lapérouse monument is regaled with French flags and wreaths are piled around its base. Children from the local La Perouse Public School, including many Aboriginal children, used to perform the French national anthem, the *Marseillaise*.

The lingering imperial meaning of the site has sometimes been evoked in press coverage of Bastille Day events through images of local Aboriginal children from La Perouse alongside French dignitaries. In one particularly stark image from 1959, Captain Loric Keraly of the tanker *Astrolabe* is shown walking past Aboriginal children lying semi-naked on the ground.[36] Another from 1975 shows the French Consul-General M. Armand Gandon, dressed in full naval regalia, 'making friends with a group of aboriginal children at the La Perouse Monument Reserve'.[37] In recent times, these types of messages have been far less common. Indeed, in the period of decolonisation in the Pacific, Bastille Day at Botany Bay has at times provided an occasion for protest against France's presence in the region. This period saw the end of the participation of the local La Perouse Primary School in Bastille Day when, in 1983, the school elected to boycott the celebration as a protest against French nuclear testing in the Pacific. The school has not been involved since.

The Lapérouse Museum

Partly as a result of the tradition of celebrating France's national day there, the French monument site on Botany Bay has been embraced by some sections of the expatriate French community in Sydney, who identify strongly with it and with the historical and symbolic associations it now holds. This attachment played a part in the most recent phase of memorial activity around Lapérouse and his expedition during the 1988 bicentennial year—the bicentennial anniversary not only of the arrival of Phillip, but also of the arrival, departure and disappearance of Lapérouse and his men. For the local expatriate French community in Sydney, this historical anniversary was worth celebrating in style. A museum was proposed.

The driving force behind this bicentennial commemoration was a group known as the Lapérouse Association for the Australian Bicentenary, formed in 1984 by a group of Australian and French residents.[38] The newly formed association set about developing a proposal for a museum that would honour the memory of Lapérouse and celebrate the history of French voyages of scientific discovery in Australia and the Pacific. The proposal attracted considerable financial assistance from private companies such as the Banque Nationale de Paris and from the French government, as well as from the New South Wales state government through its bicentennial grants program. An old late nineteenth-century building, conveniently situated between the Lapérouse column and Pere Receveur's grave, originally used as a cable station and later as a women's refuge, was made available through local and state government intervention for the proposed museum.

Local Aboriginal people had also been developing plans to exhibit and celebrate their history as part of the bicentennial commemorative year, through establishing their own cultural centre and museum on the headland, but they were having rather more difficulty than the French group in raising the necessary finance or securing government support. For them, the Lapérouse Museum project was dispiriting and insulting. Once again, Aboriginal pasts were to be overshadowed by an excessive emphasis on the fleeting presence of the French at Botany Bay. Local Aborigines found themselves forced to contest public history-making in their own backyard on two fronts. Many were already involved in organising the broader national Aboriginal protests against the Australian bicentenary, in which many local, state and national commemorative projects were focused on Botany Bay (discussed in detail in Chapter 7). With the Lapérouse museum project proceeding, they were also faced with the prospect of trying to stem as best they could the tide of French national sentiment. The dual commemoration—French and Australian—was itself a re-enactment of sorts, recalling the experience of those early weeks of 1788 when local indigenous people had suffered an assault from two sides: from a colonising force and an imperial one. Their efforts to stop the museum failed, although a compromise was reached at the eleventh hour when the local Aboriginal community was given a couple of rooms in the cable station building to establish a small museum and retail outlet for locally made Aboriginal arts and crafts.

The Lapérouse Museum opened on 23 February 1988, 200 years after the Lapérouse expedition had visited Botany Bay. In a mode reminiscent of the commemoration of Lapérouse on the headland throughout the nineteenth century, this memorial sought to communicate and celebrate a story which was global in scope, while remaining absolutely dependent upon the anniversary of a very local event for its impetus, momentum and justification. The museum uses the expedition's fleeting historical association with the place as a starting point for telling other, more global histories, primarily about imperial French navigation, cartography and exploration in the Pacific and other parts of the world, and about a French national figure, Lapérouse, cast once again as imperial hero-navigator. The exhibition's narrative is presented in a series of rooms, organised thematically but moving backwards and forwards chronologically. It begins locally in Botany Bay before moving outwards across time and space. The first room, entitled 'Encounter', establishes the connection of the Lapérouse expedition with the museum's site, which serves to validate the continued commemoration of Lapérouse here and in 1988. The encounter is between the French and the British, and not between the French and local indigenous people as might be expected. From here the narrative moves back in time to consider the place of the Lapérouse expedition in a temporally longer and geographically wider history of imperial voyaging before moving forward again to the story about his ships' wreck, and the later discovery of them at the bottom of the ocean.

A heroic narrative about French scientific endeavour in the imperial age is the interpretive frame for all the objects and images on display in the museum, many of them highly valuable and on loan from distinguished museums in Europe. This contributes to a somewhat clumsy, and one hopes unwitting, interpretation of an early nineteenth-century ethnographic sketch of an Aboriginal man named Timbéré. The sketch was produced in 1819 by a French artist, Jacques Arago, a member of Freycinet's expedition.[39]

A copy of the sketch was hung in one of the opening rooms of the Lapérouse Museum, along with others of indigenous people from Tasmania and from the south coast of New South Wales. Its function was to show the type of ethnographic drawings that had been produced in the course of French navigational expeditions exploring the Australian coastline in the late eighteenth and early nineteenth centuries, including some on the lookout for evidence about what had happened to the Lapérouse expedition. The sketch, therefore, was displayed as evidence supporting the main story

This etching of *Timbéré, a native of new south Wales, taken when at port Jackson*, by Jacques Arago was published in the artist's 1823 journal of that voyage, *Narrative of a Voyage Around the World: In the* Uranie *and* Physcienne *Corvettes commanded by Captain Freycinet . . . 1817, 1818, 1819 and 1820*. This published version is on display at the Lapérouse Museum at La Perouse. The original sketch on which it is based is held by the Mitchell Library, Sydney. (Mitchell Library, State Library of New South Wales)

told in the museum, that is, the critical role that France played in imperial science, navigation and discovery.

But this sketch of Timbéré has another meaning, one not evident in the item itself. The sketch is treasured by the Timbery family, a prominent local Aboriginal family at La Perouse. They claim Timbéré as an ancestor. The sketch belongs to a series of archival fragments that this family draws on to demonstrate an enduring association with the region that extends from the north shore of Botany Bay south to the Five Islands area near Wollongong and west to Liverpool and Campbelltown. For example, a government blanket return in 1834 shows a man named Timbéré, aged about 50, living at Wollongong. A breastplate excavated at La Perouse in 1929, but undated (see page 90), is inscribed 'Joe Timbrey, Chief of the Five Islands'. Photographs and texts, mainly produced by missionaries, about Queen Emma Timbery who was married to George Timbery (also sometimes recorded as Timberley), indicates her matriarchal role in the La Perouse Aboriginal settlement in the 1880s and 1890s.

As one in this series of historical fragments, the Timbéré sketch is part of a narrative, not about French anthropology in the antipodes, but about the possibility of Aboriginal continuity in time and place in the colonial period. And that Timbéré does link present to past is highly plausible, even if one only makes reference to physical resemblances between the man in the sketch and more recent Timbery men. Were the Timberys able to prove direct connection—some clear genealogical link—between the Timbéré in the sketch and those later Timbery men and women who make an appearance from time to time in the archival record, the present generation's oft-repeated claim of unbroken lineage from the time of the first encounter to the present would be difficult to dispute. But in the Lapérouse Museum this other more intimate, more local, but indeed more far-reaching narrative surrounding the sketch is completely absent. At one level, this absence serves to reinforce yet further the way in which the Lapérouse Museum is only connected to the locality in which it stands in tenuous ways. At another level, and more seriously, it contributes to and produces a process whereby local Aboriginal people's pasts are obscured under the weight of other histories.

The French curatorial gaffe added fuel to a fire that was already raging around the Lapérouse Museum, one that had begun to burn even before it was officially opened. From the time the museum was first mooted, it was a potent site for often tense negotiations between local Aboriginal people and the museum's sponsors and supporters about the meaning of the imperial past in and for the local present. In the mid-1990s, community consultations about the future of the museum, initiated and facilitated by the New South Wales Premier's Department (which was the government agency by then responsible for it) provided an opportunity to air grievances yet again. These meetings typically exposed the contest between Botany Bay's national and global imperial meanings and its local indigenous ones. Aboriginal people were angry about how the Lapérouse story persisted as the predominant one told on the headland, and indeed how it continued to take up such an inordinate amount of space, literally and figuratively. The long shadow cast by Lapérouse's memory was considered incommensurate with his actual contribution to the place. To evoke this perceived discrepancy between historical event and historical memory, local Aboriginal people commonly reduce Lapérouse's deeds at Botany Bay in 1788 to little more than a bit of gardening, or the planting of some carrots.[40]

FROM SHANTYTOWNS TO SUBURBS

Botany Bay's residential landscape

Governor Arthur Phillip was a latecomer to Botany Bay's memorial landscape. As founder of the colony, rather than imperial discoverer, it was only proper that Sydney Cove had been his premier *lieu de memoire*. However, in 1950, the Royal Australian Historical Society proposed that a memorial plaque should be erected at both of Phillip's historic landing places: Botany Bay as well as Sydney Cove. The discussions in the Society's Historical Memorials Committee meetings about the inscriptions for the respective plaques reflect how history was being made from the act of Phillip stepping on shore. His landing at Sydney Cove was commemorated with little difficulty as a decisive act of possession. The inscription for that memorial plaque reads in part:

> Governor Arthur Phillip and party landed on the shore of this cove on January 26, 1788. The Union Jack was displayed/a Royal Salute fired/and the Royal Proclamation was recited/the cove was named after Viscount Sydney.

In contrast, the actual purpose and effect of Phillip's landing at Botany Bay was ambiguous. There was little that was monumental about it. No possession ceremony had been performed, no name applied, no settlement established. Indeed, this landing had ultimately led to rejection: Botany Bay, Phillip decided, was not the place to establish the community of convicts after all.

This historical uncertainty led to quite protracted discussions about what should be included on the inscription, as well as what form a monument should take. Should a monument mark the site of Phillip's landfall on the Botany Bay shore, or his ship's mooring place in the bay instead? Given that monuments in water are not practical, as any shipwreck historian will attest, it was proposed that a monument on land could point to where Phillip's ship and the others in his fleet had dropped anchor in the bay. Such a monument would also overcome the problem of lack of clarity in the records about precisely where Phillip had first stepped ashore. Ultimately, after exhaustive research had been commissioned by the Society to determine as confidently as possible where Phillip had indeed landed,[1] it was agreed that a monument be built at his landing place. This was Yarra Bay on Botany Bay's north shore. The inscription would announce that he had 'arrived'.

For most of the first half of the twentieth century, the land around where Phillip had landed at Yarra Bay had been home to extensive and relatively long-term 'shantytowns'. These shanty-towns had originated in the late 1920s; two decades later, they were still there. Throughout their existence, the shantytowns had been quarters for a somewhat diverse population. From the outset, they had been occupied by white, Aboriginal and 'mixed race' families. In the 1940s, many new arrivals to the shantytowns were refugees from European countries, rather than Australian-born. But, immediately prior to the erection in 1956 of Phillip's monument, the last residents of the local shantytowns had been evicted and their shacks demolished. This meant that Phillip, the founder of a nation which in the mid-twentieth century valued whiteness highly, landed in monumental form in the middle of the detritus, and still-raw memories, of what had for some time been a makeshift, messy, mixed, multicultural, even miscegenational neighbourhood.

Phillip's memorial presence in the landscape was welcomed by at least some among the new wave of locals who were settling on the north head of Botany Bay in the same period. The erection of the monument to Captain Phillip coincided with the area's suburbanisation and, as the locality was progressively transformed from shantytown to suburb, Phillip and the national history he had come to represent were mobilised by new locals for new purposes.

'We were poor but happy'

The foreshores of Botany Bay, particularly around the north head-land and the south shore, were ideal locations for shantytowns. They possessed many natural features conducive to cheap, temporary residence: the sea could be used for bathing; the scrubby coastal heath afforded good shelter for huts; streams and springs provided access to a fresh water supply; and there were fish in the bay. Moreover, there was land available to set up camp, most of it recreation reserves or vacant Crown land. When the Depression hit in the late 1920s and early 1930s, sprawling unauthorised camps grew among the coastal heath along Botany Bay's foreshore. These camps blurred the boundaries between the recreational and residential uses of Sydney's southern littoral fringe: the largest shantytowns were situated on recreational reserves, such as at former pleasure grounds at Yarra Bay on the north shore and the camping area at Captain Cook's Landing Place reserve at Kurnell on the south shore. And some of the new residents in the area, evicted from their homes in the inner city, had simply moved into their 'weekenders'—little huts that they had built illegally in the scrubland for weekend fishing trips.[2]

The main Depression-era camps on Botany Bay's north head were Happy Valley, Hill 60 and Frog Hollow. These names were by no means original; the ubiquitous Happy Valley could be found throughout Australia in the same period. Although not unique, the names nonetheless reflected some specific topographical character-istics of each site: Happy Valley hugged the slopes leading down to Congwong Bay; Hill 60 could be found at the base of the hill leading up to Botany Cemetery, and Frog Hollow was in the flats around the foreshores of Yarra Bay and Frenchmans Bay. The names are, however, misnomers in two senses. On the one hand, they suggest clear demarcation between camps, whereas the entire north headland was often perceived as one continuous shantytown. On the other, they mask the highly calibrated structure within the tent town. Small enclaves, rather than the camp as a whole, were the most common level of identification for residents. An enclave tended to be based on family affiliations and, to some extent, race and/or place of origin. For instance, at Happy Valley there were quite a large number of Aboriginal families, most of whom had originally come from Salt Pan Creek on the Georges River and the South Coast. They congregated in its northern corner, on the edge closest to Bunnerong Road. By all accounts, their relationship to Happy Valley proper was fluid, both a part of and separate from it.

A somewhat unusual, but by no means unique, feature of the Botany Bay shantytowns, especially those on the north shore rather than those along its southern one, is that Aboriginal people lived in them. They had taken up residence in the unemployment camps for various reasons. Some had been working alongside whites in industries such as timber milling, which were adversely affected by the economic recession. They saw themselves as unemployed, and so moved into the camps alongside other unemployed people. Others were seeking to escape the confines of life on a government-controlled Aboriginal reserve. Given that this was a period when Aboriginal reserves in New South Wales were 'increasingly the site of the exercise of Protection Board power' and 'more and more like living in a prison, under intense scrutiny and rigid controls', moving to an unauthorised unemployment camp was, for many Aboriginal people, a viable and often far more desirable option than living on one of the reserves.[3] Others had no choice but to live in the unemployment camps, such as Aboriginal women married to white men who were disqualified from living on the Aboriginal reserves. Gladys Ardler, who as a child lived with her non-Aboriginal father and Aboriginal mother in the Happy Valley camp, recalled that 'my father wasn't allowed there [on the Aboriginal reserve] but my mother used to go down and see her father and her brothers and sisters. They lived there and we just went down for visits.'[4] Many Aboriginal people who moved into the unemployment camps on Botany Bay's north head had relatives living at the local Aboriginal settlement on the foreshores of Frenchmans Bay. That there was already a large Aboriginal population in the area explains in part why the unemployment camps on Botany Bay's north head attracted Aboriginal people more than others in the vicinity and in other parts of the state.

The cultural diversity of the unemployed camps at Botany Bay has tended to be subsumed by popular representations of the Depression, both at the time and since, that emphasise shared experience. Depression-era camps have been typically depicted as homogenous, unified and cohesive communities. This was certainly true of Happy Valley. Happy Valley's reputation as a cohesive community was sealed when the Governor of New South Wales, Sir Phillip Game, and his wife, visited it in June 1931. In media coverage, the camp was portrayed as one that deserved its name: 'there the persons are bound together by a common misfortune, and determined to make the best of things with a smile and a laugh.'[5] This theme, distilled in the oft-repeated line 'we were poor but happy', lies at the heart of the Great Depression mythology.[6]

Yet, the large archive of the Botany Bay unemployment camps contains considerable evidence of conflict among campers.[7] And, although it is not as well documented, competition for local resources, both among campers and between campers and permanent residents, existed and was probably inevitable. The Depression brought rapid and unprecedented growth in the population on Botany Bay's north head and a radical change in land use. According to the reports produced by the Lands Department, by late 1931, the Happy Valley camp at Congwong Bay consisted of 110 camps housing 350 adults and children. Between February and November 1931 the number of people camped on public land around Yarra Bay rose from 42 to slightly over 500 adults and children.

The north headland had swiftly been transformed from a place sparsely settled by a mainly Aboriginal population, who made extensive use of the natural resources in the bush and the sea, to one crowded with campers, who drew upon many of the same natural resources to supplement their own meagre existence. With everyone trying to provide for themselves with whatever was available, local resources were spread more thinly. Yet, despite evidence of conflict within the unemployed camps on the one hand, and competition for resources on the other, it is a narrative of happiness, of cooperation and of resilience ('we were poor but happy') that dominates local remembrance, both Aboriginal and non-Aboriginal, of the Depression. This narrative seemed to have developed quite soon after the Depression ended, or at least eased. For instance, on the basis of her ethnographic fieldwork in the area in the mid-1940s, a decade or so after the Depression-era, anthropologist Pamela Nixon, wrote:

> Practically every person to whom one talks of the Depression days, especially those who lived in 'The Valley', insists that the name 'Happy Valley' was actually justified in fact. That in despite of the Depression, and the fact that all 'The Valley's' inhabitants were unemployed, the whole atmosphere was one of happiness and good feeling towards one another.[8]

This impression has not subsided with time. In oral history interviews I recorded in the 1990s with ex-residents of Happy Valley, and with the children of ex-residents, similar sentiments were expressed. For instance, Lucy Porter, a non-Aboriginal woman who had lived as a young child with her family in Happy Valley, told me that her mother 'said in retrospect that it was the happiest time of her life'.[9] Aboriginal people who lived in the camp, or who lived in the local area when the Depression camps existed, likewise emphasise the theme of community spirit, often focusing their narratives around activities and events that best encapsulate cooperation between residents, regardless of race. For example, the effort by Aboriginal and non-Aboriginal men alike to 'eke out a living' by fishing or by caddying and 'pilling' for golf balls on nearby golf courses, which prior to the Depression had been the preserve of local Aboriginal men, features in many Aboriginal people's accounts of those times.[10]

But, while I have suggested that common tropes like 'all being in the same boat' mask differences, in both senses of that word, at the same time it is worth noting that the 'hard times' were indeed an historical experience shared by Aboriginal and non-Aboriginal people, not only at Botany Bay, but in other parts of the country. And, at the very least, the Depression provided an occasion when the lives of some Aborigines and some non-Aborigines became joined, either because they lived in close quarters with each other or sought to subsist in similar ways. This sometimes led to the formation of intimate relationships between black and white. Yet, while courageously sharing hardship might have been publicly applauded, sharing beds was not.

The flipside to the story of the Botany Bay unemployment camps as close-knit, cohesive communities was an angst-ridden one about them transgressing racial boundaries. The Botany Bay camps provoked and intensified a general anxiety, prevalent in this interwar period, about miscegenation in Australian society. Attention was repeatedly drawn to the allegedly increasing number of mixed-race unions formed in the shantytowns. Expressing his own anxiety about interracial unions and a concomitant growth in the local 'half caste' population, and giving voice to the concerns of others, the mayor of Randwick was quoted in 1938 as saying that 'the number of legitimate and illegitimate children has risen sharply. The half-caste population has almost doubled since the campers began to move into La Perouse.'[11] Confirming this, a local Aboriginal man named Allen Foster who had lived in the area at the time, including spending some time in the camps, later recalled that 'there was that many mixed people over here during the Depression you know'.[12]

An attendant anxiety was that the Depression was contributing to the collapse of spatial boundaries on the headland that hitherto demarcated an Aboriginal living space from non-Aboriginal ones. Given that quite large numbers of Aboriginal people had taken up residence in the shantytowns during the 1930s, including some who had earlier been living within the confines of the local Aboriginal reserve, the previous separation of Aboriginal and non-Aboriginal domiciles was muddied. That the boundaries had been unsettled was for some local white residents a source of distress. 'Before the advent of these camps', the president of the Property Owners and Ratepayers Association of La Perouse and District wrote in 1937, 'no aboriginal was allowed to camp anywhere in La Perouse outside the reservation controlled by the Aborigines Protection Board. Today they would appear to have come from all over the State and taken up blocks of valuable crown land to build humpies on.'[13] This concern with keeping blacks and whites apart was also evident on a much smaller scale: the principal of the local school, which now serviced all the children in the camps as well as those living at the local Aboriginal reserve, made a special request to the Education Department for single, rather than the standard-issue double, desks. The request was made in order to avoid the situation whereby white children might be required to sit next to black children.[14]

With the impact of the Depression, particularly the emergence of the shantytowns, it seemed Botany Bay was no longer simply the place where blacks and whites had first encountered each other, or where blacks were later kept out of sight and separate from whites. It had become, instead, a place that witnessed how the lives of some blacks and whites were entangled, sometimes intimately. In a landscape that symbolically celebrated the British origins, the local shantytowns told a different story about how the nation's British stock was no longer as 'pure' as it once was, or as many desired it to be. The shantytowns unsettled the nation's cherished ideal of whiteness. This was Botany Bay as 'hybrid' landscape.

'A meeting place of many races'

The Depression began to ease around 1934, but the shantytowns on Botany Bay's north head remained well after that time. Some people resident in the camps were simply not prepared to move from them. Many of the Aboriginal and 'mixed-race' families who now called this place home had nowhere else to go, or were simply loathe to take up residence on a government-controlled Aboriginal reserve. Some people did move out of the camps, either to houses they had been able to acquire in the local area through the Unemployed Homes Trust Scheme, which had been established in the mid-1930s as an incentive for people to move out of the camps, or to where they had lived prior to the Depression. But, as some of the Depression-era residents left during the late 1930s, others gradually moved in to take their place.

During the war and in the postwar period, the newcomers to the shantytowns on Botany Bay's north head were increasingly likely to be non-British migrants, mainly from Poland, Russia, the

Ukraine and Malta. 'At the end of the 1940s the people from the wars in other countries came and put their places up' in Frog Hollow near Yarra Bay, recalled Gloria Ardler (nee Hoskins).[15] A 1953 census of the residents living at the old Yarra Bay Pleasure Grounds confirms this, listing Bronislaws, Stanislaws and Vassallos, among others. Compare this with a similar survey conducted during the Depression fifteen years earlier, which was made up almost entirely of Anglo-Celtic names like Martin, McCaffery and Smith. And, while most residents listed in the 1937 census were recorded as being unemployed and living on government food rations and relief work, the residents of the Yarra Bay camps in the 1940s and early 1950s were employed, many as unskilled labourers. Their places of employment included the local tannery, cemetery and market gardens and the nearby paper mills, Coast Hospital and ICI (Imperial Chemicals Industry) plant. Others were skilled tradesmen, including carpenters, fitters, monument masons, boat-builders and a blacksmith. It was not unemployment that contributed to the continuation of the camps in the postwar period. Rather, it was because of an acute housing shortage in Sydney that the camps endured. New residents might have been employed, but they were effectively homeless.

In physical terms, the postwar shantytowns strongly resembled the Depression-era camps. Individual humpies were made of tin, wood and hessian, and the whole area was crowded with a hotch-potch of cramped dwellings. However, while the Depression-era camps had typically been represented as aberrant and temporary, the result of a blip in the world economic market, descriptions of the postwar shantytowns emphasised the increasing permanency of dwellings. In 1953, the metropolitan land inspector reported that, while 'there were no structures on Crown Land at "Happy Valley" other centres at La Perouse and Yarra Bay including "Hill 60", "Goat Hill" and the area adjoining Aboriginal reserve, have remained unchanged and contain many permanent residents'.[16] According to some reports, these permanent residents had substantially improved their humpies over the years. One newspaper account alleged that a resident had spent £600 on his shack, and went on to say that 'there is a small but thriving real estate market

there and some new Australians, mostly Maltese with large families, have paid up to £400 for homes.'[17] In addition to shacks being
bought and sold, this alleged real estate market included rent being
charged on some places. Claims that a thriving real estate market
existed in the camps, whether they are true or not, clearly contributed to a perception that the shantytowns were no longer a
temporary presence, but were becoming permanent. The migrants
were settling down.

A new wave of Aboriginal residents also arrived during the war
and in the immediate postwar period, particularly from country
areas. Many were drawn to the city for better employment and educational opportunities and to escape the control that the Aborigines
Welfare Board continued to exercise over their lives. The war and
postwar employment boom in Sydney provided substantial new
economic opportunities for many Aborigines. The war years were
'good', according to Gladys Ardler, 'because there was plenty of work

This shantytown was situated behind Frenchmans Beach and was
commonly known as Frogs Hollow. The photograph was probably
taken in the late 1940s and so depicts the period after the
Depression when the postwar shantytowns threatened to become
permanent fixtures on the landscape and were occupied mainly by
Aboriginal families and postwar migrants. (Fairfax)

and that around. Everybody was working . . . My husband was in a good job. There was plenty of work around . . . There was no one on the dole . . . Everyone had plenty of money.'[18] The industrial development of nearby areas contributed to a local employment boom. For instance, in 1948, the BORAL oil refinery was established at nearby Matraville. Pam Koeneman, a local Aboriginal woman, recalled that 'a number of people were involved in working at BORAL's oil refinery and my dad was one of them and Mr Ella and Mr Stewart . . . Paper mill was another area [for Aboriginal employment]'.[19] Local Aboriginal men worked at nearby factories too, such as Davis Gelatine, and Felt and Textiles. Aboriginal women worked as maids and cooks at the Coast Hospital as well as in local factories.[20] This high rate of employment is reflected in the Aborigines Welfare Board manager's report for 1948, which reported that the population on the La Perouse Aborigines reserve was 106, with 98 per cent of adult residents in regular employment.[21]

During the postwar period, Botany Bay's north head regularly presented a paradoxical image, of being both backward and progressive at the same time. It was sometimes represented as a cosmopolitan place, a place shared by many cultures living and working alongside each other. A 'meeting place of many races' was how one journalist described the La Perouse Public School in the early 1950s.[22] Warming to this theme, the writer described a Ukrainian student singing a lullaby in the 'original aboriginal dialect', and an Aboriginal girl dressing up her doll as a 'Polish peasant'. Indeed, La Perouse Public School was often held up as an example of a school that had overcome 'the colour bar'.[23] The school was hailed as a model of progressive education, a place where pupils were taught that the 'colour of one's skin means nothing'.[24] Beyond the school gates, the general locality was also represented as an urban frontier where the 'colour bar was collapsing'.[25] The local Aboriginal population was often depicted as benefiting from the modernising influences of the city and the community promoted as an example of assimilation-in-action. Such representations unsettled and complicated its pre-existing, and to some extent enduring, reputation as an abject place. Rather than a place left behind, it was depicted as a place of the future: as modern, civilised and progressive and the antithesis of rural Australia, where widespread racism reportedly endured.

But its not too distant past shadowed, and at times interrupted, this more sanitised, harmonious and assimilated image. Rather than being a site of modernity and progress, the area could be presented, through the vista of the shantytowns that still dotted the headland, as a turgid backwater, a place where some people experienced far worse living conditions than the general population. For instance, alongside images promoting supposedly assimilated, even affluent, Aborigines, were others showing Aboriginal people living close to the city in appalling conditions, and still falling victim to racial discrimination. Some local Aboriginal people publicly claimed that they were forced to live in shantytowns because they could not find anywhere else to live. They identified their 'colour' as the major obstacle to finding accommodation elsewhere, contradicting the rosier image of an assimilated Australia and of assimilated Aborigines.[26]

This almost split imagery inscribed Botany Bay's north head as simultaneously a modern and a pre-modern place. These contradictory representations clearly depicted a place and a problem in flux. The narrative told about local Aboriginal people was about them in transition from past to future, a common story of the period. Here was a place that was witness to this apparently inevitable process—a place caught somewhere between its past and its future. Its late nineteenth-century and early twentieth-century local past had been black; its mid-twentieth-century present was mixed and messy, but haltingly modern; its imminent future was imagined as assimilated and as white.

Tidying the 'cradle of the nation'

From the late 1940s onwards, the north head of Botany Bay became attractive to new suburban settlers because housing blocks there were relatively cheap, and because industrial growth in neighbouring suburbs meant jobs were available close by. Over the decade, large numbers of new residents moved in. According to one estimate, by the late 1950s the local white population of La Perouse totalled well over 2000 people, 90 per cent of whom had arrived since 1950.[27]

The postwar suburbanisation of the north head of Botany Bay was typically represented as a much-desired break with a recent and local past, and as a rapprochement with an earlier and now national past. It was sometimes characterised as a shift from an old order, or what was more precisely perceived as a period of disorder, to a new order. It involved a process of restoration. The area apparently needed to be tidied or cleaned up because it had fallen into disarray. Moreover, its allegedly messy state was not in keeping with the site's national historical significance. One particularly evocative image of the process was the description of 'tidying [of] the "cradle of the nation"', suggesting metaphorically that those involved were devoted mothers and housewives who were putting things in order, which fitted nicely with the 1950s suburban vision through which the local area was being remade.[28] They were tidying up the mess made by those who had occupied the area before them. Those earlier residents were commonly accused of having been neglectful custodians of this historically significant landscape.

The shantytowns that remained on the headland at the beginning of the 1950s especially epitomised the alleged level of disorder and disarray to which this pocket of Botany Bay had supposedly sunk. Not surprisingly, they were among the first material traces belonging to a so-called shameful recent local past that were removed from the landscape as part of the process of suburbanisation. Between 1952 and 1955, the local municipal council carried out a concerted campaign to rid the area of the shantytowns, and to reclaim the land they occupied for residential and recreational development. As part of its removal operation, the council instituted eviction proceedings against the shantytowns' remaining residents, non-Aboriginal and Aboriginal alike.[29] Some remaining residents contested the council's eviction orders or ignored them, simply refusing to leave. There were some who had been living in their shacks for more than a decade, and therefore considered them their permanent place of residence. Some reports at the time, and subsequently, claimed that in the face of this intransigence the council had by 1955 resorted to demolishing shacks that were still occupied.

This photograph taken in June 1954 shows Crown land at Yarra Bay after it was cleared to make way for new housing. (Government Printing Office collection, State Library of New South Wales)

Ultimately, however, the residents' resistance to enforced removal was to no avail. By the late 1950s, the shantytowns were completely gone. Many of their residents relocated to government housing estates on Sydney's western fringe because they could not afford to buy a housing block and build a new home for themselves in the area. Before long, solid suburban houses, lined up neatly along soon-to-be-curbed streets, replaced the higgledy-piggledy shantytowns. Fibro or fibro-cement houses became the new local vernacular architecture. In addition, there were some slightly more upmarket houses situated on a hill overlooking Botany Bay, which one observer described as an 'all-brick area'.[30]

After Randwick Municipal Council had finally succeeded in closing down the shantytowns, any remaining physical trace of them on the landscape was removed. The shantytowns were completely razed, and the sites where they had once stood were subsequently excavated to provide fill for new developments in Botany Bay, such as a new runway at the Sydney (Kingsford Smith)

Airport. These past places were recycled to make new ones. By this means, their original locations were altered beyond recognition. The hill of Hill 60 was reduced to a gaping hole, the hollows of Frog Hollow flattened, and the steepness of Happy Valley eroded. 'Hill 60,' George Cann Jnr recalled, 'was one of the Depression camps. The hill was a lot higher then because the sand miners come in here about 30 odd years ago [i.e. 1960s] and took a lot of the sand and unfortunately they left it as it is. But it used to be a beautiful big hill.'[31] With all material signs that the shantytowns had once existed expunged their previous presence remained mainly in the memories of older residents. For some, places such as Frog Hollow and Hill 60 continued (and continue still) to be used as reference points in storytelling about the local past. Knowledge about and memories of these now absent places distinguish old residents from new. These remembered absent presences, 'bear the marks of a continuous agency'.[32]

It was in this area, only recently cleared of shantytowns, that the monument marking the historical moment of Phillip's first landing at Botany Bay was erected in 1956. While the monument was located at the place where Phillip had supposedly come ashore, the main inscription on it made history from his arrival in the bay, not his landing on the shore:

To Found the Colony of New South Wales
Captain Arthur Phillip, R.N.
Arrived
In Botany Bay in the ship 'SUPPLY'
Which was moored off the site
On January 18th, 1788

This might have been the only inscription on the monument had it not been for some involved who pressed for further information to be included about the landing, and particularly about Phillip's encounter with local indigenous men. While on the north shore, Phillip had exchanged trinkets, words and signs with the locals, who directed him and his men to water. Giving the locals some trinkets had produced better results than Captain Cook's earlier attempt, perhaps precisely because they had had some previous experience in this type of exchange. Phillip's official journal notes:

> at the very first landing of Governor Phillip on the shore of Botany Bay, an interview with the natives took place. They were all armed, but on seeing the Governor approach with signs of friendship, alone and unarmed, they readily returned his confidence by laying down their weapons . . . The presents offered by their new visitors were all readily accepted, nor did any kind of disagreement arise while the ships remained in Botany Bay.[33]

Phillip's mid twentieth-century memorialists reached a compromise: these details would be included on a smaller, supplementary plaque attached to the monument with the inscription:

> In this vicinity, about 3pm on 18th January 1788, Governor Phillip first set foot on Australian soil. He was seeking fresh water. On his approach, a group of natives, who had watched him land, withdrew into the bush. Later that afternoon, some of them directed him to a stream nearby (Bunnerong Creek?).[34]

Placed on a separate, smaller plaque below the main inscription, it can be read as a footnote to the real story that the monument told. That real story was, yet again, about colonial and national foundations. Here was one more monument to the late eighteenth century in a landscape that already excessively memorialised that particular past.

On 18 January 1956 at three o'clock, exactly 168 years after the event that it marked, a group of people gathered at the new monument to participate in an unveiling ceremony. The ceremony included predictable elements: the performance of a historical re-enactment of Phillip arriving on shore in a long boat and speeches by dignitaries that served as history lessons, for instance. But it seems that local Aboriginal people ensured that their contemporary presence in the place was also acknowledged. One newspaper report noted that there were 'about 800 sightseers, many of them from the La Perouse reserve'. Among them was an old Aboriginal man,

This photograph accompanied an article published in January 1956 about the unveiling of Captain Phillip's landing place memorial at Yarra Bay. The article was titled 'In the Beginning'. (News Limited)

Robert Timbery, who was holding a large boomerang. He explained to some official that he had 'made this boomerang myself for the Governor. Souvenir for him. Show we're still friendly.'[35] Reportedly on this basis, Timbery was invited to sit on the dais along with the official guests and, after the formal program was over, to present the boomerang to the governor.

The improvised exchange between Timbery and the governor has been depicted as symbolically re-enacting the relations between Phillip and local Aborigines that had occurred during the actual encounter at the site in January 1788. It nicely filled a gap in proceedings, given that this particular scene had not been included in the official re-enactment due to be staged that day. That it was, at least in spirit, an authentic representation of the original encounter was underscored by repeated reference to two powerful links connecting the present-day participants with the past. The recipient of the boomerang, the governor of New South Wales, was described as the thirty-third in direct line from Governor Phillip to hold that office. Robert Timbery, the maker and presenter of the boomerang, described himself as the 'oldest direct descendant at Yarra Bay of the tribe which was there when Captain Phillip arrived'.[36] This claimed continuous descent from those 'natives' who had encountered Phillip in 1788 is yet another example of a long-standing local tradition, dating from at least the late nineteenth century, which I have traced in other chapters in relation to Captain Cook.

More than simply indicating that an encounter between black and white had occurred at Yarra Bay in 1788, Timbery's presentation of the boomerang was mobilised by those present and by the journalists who covered the event to emphasise the apparent 'friendliness' of that encounter. Timbery himself had suggested the narrative of 'friendliness', which once more suggests that local Aboriginal people had an acute appreciation of Australian historiography and historical mythology, given that Phillip was typically cast as the 'friendly coloniser'. The friendly theme was picked up by the metropolitan press. In coverage of the ceremony the following day, a photograph appeared in the *Daily Telegraph* showing two local Aboriginal children waving enthusiastically at the boat carrying the person playing Phillip coming ashore. The caption read: 'As their ancestors did on January 18, 1788, these two aborigines stood on the shore of Botany Bay yesterday waving to a longboat coming ashore.'[37] It wasn't quite historically accurate, but the message is clear. It is more than likely that the photograph was staged, with the two boys encouraged to wave at the boat. They, like Robert Timbery, agreed to perform a spontaneous re-enactment of sorts of the encounter between Phillip and the 'natives' described on the monument.

The emphasis on the original encounter and its momentary friendliness, inscribed on the monument and reinforced in the unveiling ceremony and press coverage, overshadows the subsequent effects on Aborigines of Phillip's founding of the colony. Yet, there was another Aboriginal participant in the unveiling ceremony, who seems to have used his short speech to draw attention to the enduring legacies of the past on the present. Herbert Groves, who was then the Aboriginal representative on the New South

Wales Aborigines Welfare Board and had been a long-time Aboriginal activist, had been officially invited to participate in the unveiling ceremony. What he said to the audience on the day is not known, although it is likely that an article he published in *Dawn* magazine a month or so later is based on his speech. 'The commemoration of this historic occasion that we so proudly celebrate marks the beginning of progress, law and order in Australia (white man's progress!), by a great Pioneer,' he begins. But in the very next sentence he notes: 'The Aborigines could have been forgiven had they regarded it as a day of mourning instead of a day of rejoicing.'[38] By reference to a day of mourning, Groves was harking back to the sesquicentenary of Phillip's arrival held in 1938, twenty or so years earlier. On that occasion a group of New South Wales Aboriginal people, some of them from the La Perouse Aboriginal settlement, had declared 26 January, the day Phillip had performed his possession ceremony at Sydney Cove, a day of mourning. By evoking this particular past, Groves drew attention to how the present-day disadvantage that Aboriginal people experienced was a product of the past, inaugurated when Phillip landed. Moreover, he implied that Aboriginal people had continuously mourned the past that the colonisers celebrated.

This somewhat unusual commemorative performance, staged on the shores of Yarra Bay in 1956, at a time when the enforced removal of the shantytowns and the displacement of their residents was still a fresh local memory, acknowledged local Aboriginal people, albeit somewhat clumsily and in part through their own insistence, as occupying a central place in the locality's history. However, while their place in history was momentarily recognised, some of the new suburbanites moving into the area believed that local Aboriginal people had little or no part to play in the much-anticipated modern local future.

Reservations about the reserve

After the closure of the shantytowns during the first half of the 1950s, local Aboriginal people were concentrated in two main areas on the northern headland of Botany Bay. They predominantly occupied the remnants of pre-war housing stock, which were mainly houses that had been built under the Unemployed Homes Trust Scheme, established in the mid-1930s as the Depression eased in order to encourage families to move out of the unemployment camps. These were concentrated in the streets that bordered the Aboriginal reserve. Some Aboriginal families had managed to secure these houses through the Homes Trust in the 1930s. Others acquired a house after it had been vacated by its original occupants during World War II. The other main concentration of Aboriginal people in the local area was in the Aboriginal reserve. Originally located on the foreshores of Frenchmans Beach, the Aboriginal reserve was now located a short way up the hill behind the beach, close to the housing blocks that newcomers were acquiring. It had been relocated in 1930 and in the process, the Aboriginal settlement was completely remodelled with new houses. In the late 1940s, the size of the Aboriginal reserve had been slightly increased to incorporate an area on its perimeter where some Aboriginal families had established homes during the shantytown era. This development enabled these mainly young Aboriginal families to remain resident in the area.

During the suburban redevelopment of this part of Botany Bay in the 1950s, the local government authority carried out a series of town planning surveys in which it consistently designated the concentrations of Aboriginal residence on the headland as local slum areas of a sort. When the entire headland had been dominated by shanties rather than newly built suburban houses, these areas had been at worst indistinguishable from, and at best better than, those that surrounded them. However, with the shantytowns gone and many new houses now dotting the headland, these old pockets of housing stuck out like sore thumbs. Yet the problem was not simply that the houses were old; rather, it was that their occupants were Aboriginal. The continuing existence of the Aboriginal reserve especially was an affront to some local suburban settlers specifically, and to a mid-twentieth century Australian sensibility more generally. In these assimilationist times, Aborigines as a distinct and separate group within Australian society were something that belonged to the past, not to the modern present and future. Their highly visible spatial separateness in this new suburban area was considered out of place and out of date.

In this period, the suburb was imagined as a space for whites (or whiteness) more so than for Aborigines (or for Aboriginality). Within Australian suburbia, representations of Aboriginality functioned as signs of the cultural other, reminders of a previous presence that was now largely absent. The most popular images of Aboriginality that might appear in 1950s suburban homes tended to reinforce conventional notions of 'primitivism', including the geographical location of Aborigines mainly in rural and desert landscapes, rather than urban ones. Images which adorned ceramic-ware or teatowels, of 'native' women sitting on the ground with a child, or a 'traditional' man standing on one leg with shield and spear looking into the distance, are classic examples. Likewise, the assignation of a traditional Aboriginal word as a name for a twentieth-century suburb or suburban street was by no means the acknowledgment of a continuing indigenous presence in the landscape, but instead an act of re-bestowal. Its function was to highlight, and indeed reinforce, the actual absence of Aborigines from these places. But despite this, Aborigines were present within the newly suburbanised 1950s Botany Bay landscape, and their presence was palpable.

The most vociferous opposition to the continued existence of the ostensibly segregated Aboriginal reserve came from some of the new suburbanites who reportedly 'had sunk money into La Perouse, and . . . want[ed] it, if possible, to become a white district', according to one newspaper report in the late 1950s.[39] Some of the new locals, according to the anthropologist James Harle Bell, blamed Aborigines 'for the poor reputation of the suburb (La Perouse is known throughout the metropolitan area as "the place where the blacks live"), and for low real estate values'.[40] Ironically, it was the area's poor reputation that had contributed to the affordability of housing blocks there and that made it possible for some of the new suburban settlers now complaining about the Aborigines to move into the area in the first place.

Those outspoken in their opposition to the continued presence of a separate Aboriginal settlement within their suburb were often characterised as racist. For instance, Pamela Nixon, the anthropologist who had carried out her ethnographic study of the area in the late 1940s, a decade or so before Bell, claimed that the whites, taking up residence there in the immediate postwar period, who she labelled 'middle class', were openly 'anti-coloured'.[41] Likewise, newspaper coverage of the 1950s campaign by local whites to remove local blacks was typically presented as a racial struggle—one investigative report, for instance, was titled, somewhat sensationally, 'Racial antagonism: A hatred in early flower'.[42] But those accused of being racist were not necessarily expressing views any different from those prevalent at the time. What the local effort to close down the Aboriginal reserve ultimately aimed to achieve was the removal of any visible signs that spatial segregation on the basis of race had a place in modern Australian society, and especially in suburbia.

Yet removing the Aboriginal reserve from the local landscape was not quite as straightforward as razing the shantytowns had been. The Aboriginal reserve was not public land, and its residents were not illegally occupying it. The reserve, like all such reserves in New South Wales at the time, was under the control of the New South Wales Aborigines Welfare Board. As such, the board had the final say in the matter. And it was responding to the call to remove the Aboriginal settlement from the local landscape with a 'yes . . . but not yet'. The board, pursuing a program of assimilation, was in principle opposed to the continuing presence of separate Aboriginal settlements, including—and indeed especially—this one. But for the time being the reserve would remain, at least until such time, according to the board, as its 'aboriginal residents are in a position to establish themselves in homes in the general community'.[43] Assimilation was therefore a goal shared by some local white neighbours of the Aboriginal reserve and the government authority responsible for it. The only difference was that some new suburban settlers wanted it now, while the board's view was that its inevitable realisation was in the future. And so, for the time being at least, the newcomers would share the space of their new home with a segregated Aboriginal settlement.

Renaming Aborigines Avenue

Some of the new settlers who had arrived since 1950 deployed Botany Bay's national historical associations to make their own mark on the local landscape; at the same time, they sought to erase other local pasts, and indeed presences, they preferred to forget. This process can be characterised by a shift from local memory to national memory in place-making, and is most obvious in a new nomenclature applied to the local landscape. Many new names applied to the local landscape in this period drew on the comparatively distant colonial and nationally significant past to replace more recent and localised associations. For instance, in 1959, after representations from the local progress association to Randwick Municipal Council, Yarra Bay was rejected as the name for the suburb that was growing in the vicinity, and Phillip Bay, after Captain Phillip, was proposed in its place.[44] Long-time local resident George Cann Jnr tells the story:

> [This area] was known originally as Yarra Bay in my time [but] some of the other people coming out this way [to settle in the 1950s] didn't like the name of Yarra Bay because it was bringing back the Depression years—there'd be no value in their land, so unbeknown to a lot of us, who'd lived here for a lot of years, they just went through and had it changed to Phillip Bay. The people who had lived here all their lives had no idea it had been changed until it was changed. I certainly didn't hear of it being changed. Nobody come and asked me to sign a petition.[45]

The new monument to Phillip was no doubt the inspiration for this name. The name change from Yarra Bay to Phillip Bay replaced a reference to a relatively recent local past with a much earlier, more nationally significant one. In this sense, the name change was both an act of memorialisation and one of erasure.

It is worth stressing that the name Yarra Bay was deemed unsuitable for the new suburb because of its associations with the shantytowns of the Depression (and beyond) and not because Yarra was an Aboriginal word. The use of traditional Aboriginal words for

placenames in the area did not seem to cause offence and was sometimes even championed, as some names chosen for new suburban
streets in the area, such as Elaroo and Goorawahl, indicate.[46]
However, in the late 1950s there was one Aboriginal name on the
local map that some newcomers particularly did not like. A road
running through the middle of the newly refashioned local landscape was called Aborigines Avenue, a name left over from the past.
Aborigines Avenue was straightforwardly descriptive. It was the
road that ran along the border of the Aboriginal reserve. In the
period before the 1930s, when the Aboriginal settlement was still at
its original site next to the beach, the avenue had led directly into
it. The name for the road had probably been organic, emerging naturally from its everyday uses. But it had subsequently become
formalised through its inclusion on maps. Aborigines Avenue was
the only name the road was known by. In the 1950s, the street
name's ostensible function had not changed: it still provided directions to the place where Aboriginal people lived. Follow it and you'd
find Aborigines.

But the context in which it now existed had changed markedly.
By the late 1950s, and within what was now part of Sydney suburbia, the name had become anathema to some and an anachronism
to others. This name was too immediately and directly associated
with an actual Aboriginal presence, rather than the more acceptable
memory of a previous one which no longer existed in the place. And
so the local progress association had Aborigines Avenue renamed to
Endeavour Avenue, after Captain Cook's vessel.[47]

The change from Aborigines Avenue to Endeavour Avenue was
one more example of a shift from local memory to national memory
that accompanied the suburbanisation of the northern headland of
Botany Bay. But scratching out Aborigines Avenue on the local map
and writing in Endeavour Avenue was a hollow victory. It came at
the tail end of the campaign, fought over a number of years, to
remove the actual presence of Aborigines from the locality. Had
that campaign succeeded, the name change would have celebrated
the victory. Yet in 1959, the year the avenue's name was changed,
the new settlers' own endeavour had failed. The Aborigines were
staying where they were.

The road formerly known as Aborigines Avenue, like the old shantytowns, lives on in some local Aboriginal and non-Aboriginal people's memory, particularly those now aged 60 years or more who have lived in the area most of their lives. It is a remembered landscape feature that typically resurfaces in discussions about threats—both past and present and specific and general—to the Aboriginal settlement on Botany Bay and to its long-time residents. As such, Aborigines-now-Endeavour Avenue is a type of local shorthand, standing in for a larger, messier story about when suburban settlers arrived on the local scene and brought their own visions for the suburb, the nation and the past.

From history to heritage

The former site of the Happy Valley camp is now part of the Botany Bay National Park, and it is in the process of becoming part of the historic heritage of the local area. A walking trail alerts visitors to its previous presence. Its historical significance is explained largely in reference to the Depression generally, rather than to the types of local idiosyncrasies and specificities discussed above. The unemployment camps that continued to exist after Happy Valley had closed down soon after the end of the Depression, however, have not yet been incorporated into the local heritage landscape or into local histories. Their broader historical significance is still too uncertain. While Happy Valley can be valorised by reference to a popular historical narrative about 'ordinary' Australians struggling against the odds, evoking qualities that are seen to be essentially Australian, as yet no similar story exists to give shape to the meaning of the postwar camps. They are still largely viewed as merely a temporary solution to a short-term housing problem; that they were occupied by postwar migrants adds to their uncertain historical significance, local and otherwise. Hill 60 and the other shantytowns from the 1940s and first half of the 1950s still engender an ambiguous and somewhat aberrant recent past, one that is not yet easily assimilated into a local or national story. This is symptomatic of a more difficult and more pressing issue in Australian history, recently described by Ann Curthoys.[48] Calling for a deeper historical understanding of the diversity within Australian settler society, Curthoys has argued that more is required than simply revealing hitherto little-known non-British migrant pasts and incorporating them into Australian histories, local and national. What is needed is an understanding of the nature of the relationship that non-British migrants have to the histories of British colonisation, as well as to the historical experiences of indigenous Australians. One starting point for this type of historical analysis is that short, but important, period in the middle of the twentieth century when the postwar shantytowns, local Aboriginal reserve and fledgling suburban settlement all co-existed on the foreshores of Botany Bay—under the shadows of captains Cook and Phillip and their historical legacy.

THE PAST AS FUTURE

Industrial development and environmental politics

The 1960s and 1970s was a period of unprecedented development as Botany Bay was turned into Sydney's second port, servicing large container ships; as heavy industry grew along its foreshores; and as the Sydney (Kingsford Smith) Airport was expanded. Amid this, concern intensified for Botany Bay's natural environment. Almost all attempts either to stop the encroachment of industry altogether or protect remnant ecosystems made reference to the botanical work carried out by Cook's expedition, and especially invoked Sir Joseph Banks as renowned naturalist. For instance, in the mid-1960s when some remnant Crown land behind Congwong Bay on the north head was earmarked for development, the National Trust of Australia and a local group known as the La Perouse Peninsula Fauna and Flora Protection Society stepped in, lobbying for the land in question to be 'preserved for all time as a national reserve'. The National Trust argued that the area was significant and required preservation because it had been 'traversed by Captain Cook and Sir Joseph Banks in 1770 and [was] where part of the famous botanical collection was made'.[1] In an era when Botany Bay's natural native environment became something to defend, Banks was especially useful in his dual role as national forefather and as transnational botanist. He enabled local natural heritage campaigns to be framed in both historical and ecological terms, and be given national and international—not simply local—significance.

But the preservationists were not the only ones to use this past for their present purposes. Cook and Banks also became figureheads for those pushing development—for those with a 'progressionist' rather than a 'preservationist' impulse. During this period, the significance of Botany Bay was typically represented as lying in the future in addition to, or sometimes instead of, lying in the past, as had hitherto been the case. Botany Bay was now not only where the nation had purportedly begun, but was also where the nation's modern potential would be realised. Its future, typically cast as inevitable and much anticipated, was understood as fundamentally dependent upon its late eighteenth-century past, which Banks and Cook embodied. In this respect, the imagined relationship between Botany Bay's past and future was somewhat circular. The late eighteenth-century past was interpreted through a logic of precedence: it was significant for what it had apparently enabled to happen in the twentieth century and for what it would continue to make possible in the imagined future. In turn, the present and imagined future were perceived as the product of history—a history that was understood to be inherently progressive. The present and future apparently unfolding at Botany Bay in the 1960s and 1970s were, then, simply the proper, indeed predictable, fulfilment of the late eighteenth-century past, or so the story went.

At the heart of this story, which tied the past and the future so tightly together, was modern science. Botany Bay's future was imagined as a scientific and technological one. And this is why Cook and Banks were so useful: they were forefather figures in the scientific revolution being played out there almost 200 years after their own scientific enterprise in the same place. As such, Botany Bay was framed as the ideal landscape for a modernising impulse driven by science and technology, precisely because its own origins had been 'scientific'.

Yet there was an unavoidable dilemma at the heart of this story about where Botany Bay was heading. In a Frankenstein-type scenario, it soon became obvious that the new science giving Botany Bay a future was despoiling, indeed destroying, relics from its highly valued past. The 'scientific laboratory' where Cook and Banks made their 'discoveries', especially where Banks had made his botanical collection, was under threat as development proceeded. In this situation, rather than a natural memorial preserving a particular past, Botany Bay was now recast as a witness to the present-day legacies of that past—a textbook example of what happens when imperial Europeans and their descendants enter Eden. Thus, from the mid-twentieth century onwards, Botany Bay became an accidental memorial to 'what happened next' rather than to 'the moment before'. The tragedy was that its fall from grace, from pristine nature that had turned the late eighteenth-century scientific world on its head to environmental disaster zone, was so rapid.

In the midst of campaigns to preserve natural remnants of the pre-colonial past from the destruction caused by industrial development, local Aboriginal people were engaged in a hard-fought struggle to hold on to their own little piece of Botany Bay. Their reserve was once more under threat precisely because it was deemed a relic from a past that had no place in the modern future. But local Aboriginal people desperately wanted to preserve their reserve, not because it was a relic from a past that was supposedly over, but rather because it was custodian of and witness to a past that for them was continuous with the present and without which they believed they had no future.

Industrialisation

Prior to the 1950s, the encroachment of industry around Botany Bay had been piecemeal. The story of its industrialisation typically begins in 1930, the year that petroleum was first shipped through Botany Bay to a terminal on the Alexandra Canal on its western shore. The next milestone in the saga was the first oil refinery, which was established in 1948 on the north head at Matraville and was owned by BORAL (Bitumen Oil Refineries Australia Limited). It was followed in 1955 by another oil refinery established on the opposite side of the bay, on the Kurnell peninsula, 'just south of Captain Cook's landing site', owned by the North American company Caltex, but trading as Australian Oil Refinery.[2] This refinery, which required extensive sand dredging to make this comparatively shallow dock navigable by oil tankers, contributed a long jetty jutting out into the bay. Development at Sydney (Kingsford Smith) Airport began in 1948, and continued throughout the following two decades. Its first encroachment into the bay was in the early 1960s, when its main runway was extended out into the water, complementing the Kurnell Oil Refinery's own finger-like protrusion opposite. The runway was made from sand that had been dredged from the bay's floor and from along its foreshores, including some from the sites of the old shantytowns on Botany Bay's north head described in Chapter 5. The process by which Botany Bay's physical landscape was refashioned was analogous to a radical body makeover: a bit of skin taken from one part was used to fashion new appendages that were grafted on to the body.

During the closing years of the 1950s and the opening years of the 1960s, mechanisms were gradually put in place to enable Botany Bay to be developed as Sydney's second port. In 1961, the Maritime Services Board of New South Wales assumed responsibility for Botany Bay, an act that was widely interpreted as evidence that the government had decided that a cargo handing facility was required. From this moment on, the trajectory of port development seemed unstoppable. Prior to this, Botany Bay's industrial development had been somewhat ad hoc—an oil refinery here, an oil refinery there. However, with the entry of the New South Wales state government as the main proponent of maritime development at Botany Bay, the narrative of industrialisation becomes a more confident tale about improvement, progress and development. The rhetoric that accompanied the development positioned Botany Bay at the forefront of a new frontier—the frontier of modern science and technology that would enable the development of state-of-the-art transport and communications systems fundamental to any progressive, competitive and prosperous society, which is how Australia increasingly saw itself in the postwar period.

Throughout Botany Bay's port development, the public relations machine worked overtime. By the time the Maritime Services Board produced the short promotional film *Botany Bay: Two Centuries After*

Cook in 1989, the script was already well rehearsed. The signs that this bay would become a major maritime port in a global shipping industry had been there from the very start, or so the story went. By entering the Botany Bay heads in 1770, Cook's ship, the *Endeavour*, had unwittingly forged a route for the untold ships that would follow in its wake. In publicity of this type, Botany Bay is repeatedly depicted as Australia's first port rather than Sydney's second one. Implicit in the description 'first port' are two meanings: a temporal one and a qualitative one. Because it was put on the map as a result of the late eighteenth-century global maritime enterprise, Botany Bay is imagined as Australia's first, or original, port. Because it was being turned into the largest, most modern and most technologically advanced port in Australia in the second half of the twentieth century, it was the nation's superior port, the first among all ports. The paradox in this doubled first-ness is that so much had to happen to make the bay that Cook had brought into the realm of global shipping through his own maritime adventures suitable for his twentieth-century followers. As one commentator wryly observed: 'If Port Jackson has a well-earned reputation as the best harbour and the worst port in the world, it may be suggested by the cynic that NSW planners are attempting to make in Botany Bay one of the best ports out of one of the worst harbours.'[3]

The Maritime Services Board was well aware that Botany Bay had serious natural limitations as a port, particularly for large cargo ships, but its proximity to Sydney made it the state government's prime choice for desperately needed new port facilities. In 1962, the Maritime Services Board commissioned a British firm, Sir Alexander Gibb & Partners, to provide the technical advice necessary to make a decision. It was not about whether the port development at Botany Bay should proceed—that decision had already been taken in principle. Rather, the advice sought was about which part of Botany Bay would be most suitable, and what was required to make it port-worthy. Over the next four years, Botany Bay was described, mapped, measured, tested, simulated and studied in minute and excruciatingly technical detail.

The consultants' report, delivered to the Maritime Services Board in 1966 and known ominously as the Stage 1 Report, confirmed what was already known, albeit in almost impenetrable language: Botany Bay was not an ideal site for the type of port facilities desired, but with some intervention it could be transformed. This report can be read as the 'classical scientific narrative of enlightenment and discovery' which John Morton and Nicholas Smith argue 'is both pure (revealing nature as "she" really is) and applied (transforming "her" for human benefit)'.[4] Like the original surveyors of Botany Bay's nature two centuries earlier, whose reports had been consulted in assessing the potential of the site for colonial settlement, the British scientists commissioned by the New South Wales government revealed the bay as wanting, in many respects, but suitable nonetheless. All it would take was some modification of its natural limitations: the 1966 Stage 1 Report outlined what those adjustments would entail, and a mountain of subsequent reports would describe those transformations in yet more excruciating detail.

The part of Botany Bay favoured by the British scientists for the port development was its north shore, not because this was naturally superior but because it could be modified more easily. It was more malleable. On previous occasions, Botany Bay's natural disadvantages had saved it from development, but that was only when there were better alternatives close by. Phillip was able to reject Botany Bay in 1788 because Port Jackson, around the corner, was apparently not being used. Two hundred or so years later, the other options available had withered considerably, and Botany Bay, or so the argument ran, was really the only bay sufficiently close to Sydney to serve as a complementary port to Sydney Harbour. This time around, its natural limitations did not rule it out; they were merely obstacles to be overcome. This line of thought was nicely captured when the Maritime Services Board noted that the government's authorisation for the port development to proceed had followed seven years of 'detailed study to determine the best ways of overcoming the major problems which had prevented major development in the area in the past'.[5] Nature was no longer Botany Bay's destiny.

The upshot of those seven years of study was the finding that Botany Bay was too shallow for the container ships that the proposed port would service. The answer was to create sufficiently deep channels by dredging its seabed to allow the passage of very big ships. But this remodelling of its bottom would affect natural tides, currents, waves and winds. This, however, could be moderated by constructing long groynes, which would help to readjust wind and wave movement. Before long, Botany Bay would boast yet more finger-like constructions poking out into the water. The end result was that the length of the Botany Bay shoreline was increased by 20 per cent. A short film produced in association with the Maritime Services Board during the port development, released in 1974 and entitled *Birth of a Port*, graphically depicts how Botany Bay's deficiencies were overcome. It shows the sand dredging boats that worked continually for two years removing 20 million cubic yards of sand from the bay. It shows cranes lowering pre-cast concrete units to form a protective armoury around the wharves. It shows front-end loaders pushing rocks into the water to form a jetty. This film is a testament to, and a celebration of, the science, technology, machinery and human resources that made the birth of the port possible. Only momentarily was the machinery of development overcome by nature when a violent storm undid some of the work that had already been achieved. But the storm merely reinforced the message that the entire port project was 'man striving against the forces of nature'.[6]

Like other promotional material, *Birth of a Port* also deployed the historical past to tell its story. Predictably, the opening scene shows the *Endeavour* in Botany Bay and the narrator tells the viewer: 'This was the beginning.' Yet it is not a seamless historical narrative. In this version, in the beginning, Captain Cook got it wrong. Botany Bay was, according to the script, 'an anchorage that Cook described *somewhat optimistically* as a capacious, safe and convenient harbour' (emphasis added). But 'those who followed', we are told, 'didn't agree'. Botany Bay remained unchanged for almost 200 years, while Port Jackson became one of the world's busiest ports. However, with the selection of Botany Bay as a Sydney's second shipping terminal, Captain Cook's skewed vision was at last to be put right: 'Two centuries later [the redevelopment of Botany Bay] will vindicate Captain Cook's opinion of a capacious, safe and convenient harbour.' And so Cook might have begun the story, but it was those who followed him who provided the ending.

Botany Bay's industrial landscape: Port Botany. (*Dock Botany Bay* from the photographic series 'Bound', 1992. Ian Provest)

Botany Bay's natural landscape: Towra Point. (*Mangroves Botany Bay* from the photographic series 'Bound', 1992. Ian Provest)

Defending the environment

If the Stage 1 Report produced by British scientists and the many other technical reports that followed can be read as a classical scientific narrative of enlightenment and discovery, the statements, petitions, pamphlets and posters produced by the anti-port development lobby can be read as romantic narratives. A romantic vision elevates nature, seeing in it the possibility of a return to origins and the chance of redemption. In this vision, nature becomes especially valued as people become, or perceive themselves as becoming, increasingly alienated from nature, for instance, as urbanisation occurs. In this context, city dwellers assume a closeness to, or fondness for, the natural environment, and in Australia the most highly valued nature is that belonging to the pre-1788 past. The urban environmentalists bring with them an ethic of conservation that is also conservative: a desire to return to an idealised past is often a response to accelerated processes of change. Late twentieth-century Botany Bay was the perfect environment for the emergence of a newfound ecological sensibility. It was a landscape that had recently been urbanised but not overly so, situated on the edge of a large metropolis, prized for pre-colonial nature and for the late eighteenth-century historic botanical work that had described it, but which was now on the brink of major industrial development that threatened the local environment.

When the decision to develop Botany Bay as Sydney's second port was publicly announced in 1969, it prompted an immediate groundswell of opposition, particularly from local residents who in turn found ready support from an emergent environmentalist movement. To fight the development, various community-based groups were formed, including the Botany Bay Planning and Protection Council and an umbrella group known as the Botany Bay Coordinating and Action Committee. The Action Committee, formed in 1976, called for a 'moratorium on the developments' so that an inquiry could be made into the impacts of the port development. Resident and environmental groups were concerned that, while study after study had been conducted into how Botany Bay could be turned into a port, no comprehensive analysis of the ment was made in the lead-up to a state government election.

effects, both environmental and social, had been carried out. There was a call for a Royal Commission into the port development, a call that was strongly resisted by the then New South Wales Liberal government. In his policy statement issued in April 1975, the responsible minister, L.A. Punch, restated the government's commitment to the construction of the port, which by that time was well underway. The statement countered the demand for a total environmental impact assessment by claiming that environmental studies had been carried out at every stage of development, and reiterating that the 'government is determined that the natural areas at Towra Point will be preserved'.[7] Towra Point was a remnant fragile ecosystem, consisting mainly of wetlands, located on the southern shore near Kurnell, that had for some time been a focus for nature conservation.

Punch's policy statement about the Botany Bay Port development was made in the lead-up to a state government election. As part of its electioneering, the Labor opposition supported a moratorium on the development until a comprehensive environmental impact assessment had been made. Labor gained power in May 1976, and the Botany Bay Port and Environment Inquiry (also known as the Simblist Inquiry after its commissioner) was established two months later in July. It reported in November that year.[8]

The inquiry provided an opportunity for those mainly local residents who were against the development to put forward their case. They typically drew upon its past to make a case for its future. For instance, Mrs Hannan from the La Perouse Society said in her spoken submission:

> I guess everyone knows that Botany Bay is the birthplace of Australia. It's possibly the most important historic area in Australia and there again with development of the port we feel that it will suffer. Instead of being a place where the future generations can come and be proud of their heritage it will be destroyed.

Mrs Moore from the Randwick Historical Society told the commissioner that:

It is stack-full [*sic*] of history, the whole Bay . . . we have to keep something that resembles the original historic site. I don't know that we could put up a screen or something to hide all the works, but you can't have it both ways with all these tourists coming out and still have it looking good with the coal loader and supertankers around.

Botany Bay could either have a past or a future, but not both. That also seemed to be the message from E. White from Kurnell, who wrote to the commissioner that:

Last but not least this area of Kurnell for me and all Australians should still be looked upon as the Birth Place of Australia, and therefore same [*sic*] way of beautifying the Kurnell Peninsula, and I have never seen beauty come aut [*sic*] of any industrial take over. Cluta Industry from Swizerland [*sic*] can not dictation [*sic*] to The Australian people and to take away from the Australian the birth place of Australia.[9]

Despite the mountains of evidence, the ultimate outcome of the inquiry was expected. The terms of reference that had been set made it almost impossible for its commissioner to recommend that the port development should cease. In January 1977, two months after the report was released, the New South Wales Labor government gave the green light for the port development to proceed.

Not surprisingly, many interpreted the inquiry as a cynical political ploy. Environmental groups denounced it and, as a result, Botany Bay became the focus for one of the first campaigns fought by Australia's first non-government environmental agency, the Total Environment Centre. The Centre produced its own report, entitled *City in Peril*, which reviewed the Simblist Report and gave its own assessment of the potential damage that the port facility would wreak at Botany Bay. It concluded that 'the effect of the developments . . . will be extremely unfavourable for the people of Sydney and for the environment'.[10]

Although the pro-development lobby was using a classical narrative of progress and transformation of nature for the social good, and the anti-developers were using a romantic narrative of redemption of an alienated society through preservation of nature, each was struggling with the same antagonistic dualism between nature and culture. Either modern society was going to control and tame nature for social and economic benefit, or to care for and nourish it in ways that were also ultimately aimed at the benefit of humans. Within this melee of claim and counterclaim was another position, advanced by a group of academics in Canberra contributing to a project dubbed the Botany Bay Project. The project likewise grappled with the nature/culture antagonism, but also sought to achieve and reconcile the dual impulses for control over the future and restoration of the past.

The Botany Bay Project

Almost as soon as the New South Wales state government decided in 1971 to develop Botany Bay as Sydney's second port, a collaborative academic research project was instigated.[11] Spearheaded by economic historian Noel Butlin, the Botany Bay Project brought together the Australian Academy of Science, the Australian Academy of the Humanities and the Academy of the Social Sciences in Australia, and it initially received quite substantial federal and state government funding. It was conceived as an interdisciplinary project, bringing together scientists, humanists and social scientists to examine questions about environmental policy, planning and control, and to contribute to the development of environmental planning procedures in Australia during a period when 'the environment', particularly environmental degradation, was becoming a significant public issue.

Botany Bay was chosen as a case study. According to one of the project's reports, *Environmental Policy in Australia*, published in 1973:

> this area [Botany Bay] was chosen as one raising major existing and future environmental problems which are generally comparable to those in urban areas elsewhere—a developed but also developing industrial, commercial, residential and recreational area housing a large and growing population.[12]

That it was Botany Bay, birthplace of the nation, added to its obvious appeal as an exemplary locale through which to examine how environmental degradation affects 'the immediate and long-run welfare of the mass of Australians'.[13] Its inherent, imagined nation-ness came to the fore. Botany Bay would function nicely as a local case with nationwide application precisely because it was a locality of national significance. It would capture the imagination not only of the researchers and the public, but also the politicians upon whom the project depended for funding.

'As the cradle of white Australian society,' the project's reports stated, 'Botany Bay summarises much of the impact of Europeans on the Australian continent.'[14] But this statement confuses Botany Bay's *symbolic* historical meaning with an *actual* past. While it is the case that Botany Bay had experienced some environmental damage post-1788, and was certainly on the precipice of experiencing considerably more once the major port development was complete and functioning, that damage had not necessarily followed the same historical contours as experienced elsewhere, and was by no means representative of far more ubiquitous and serious environmental devastation that had occurred in other parts of the continent as a result of colonisation. Indeed, Botany Bay had long been spared from some of the worst environmental damage that is now increasingly evident across the country, such as salination caused by extensive land clearance. Once more, it seemed, Botany Bay was conveniently, but oddly, being used to tell stories about pasts that had occurred somewhere else. But, because it was so deeply symbolically associated with the coming of Europeans to the continent, it provided an evocative site through which to document the types of damage that colonial settlers typically wreaked in new lands.

The Botany Bay Project set out to achieve its overall aim of contributing to the development of environmental policy and practice in late twentieth-century Australia by assessing both 'the damage already done' and 'the likely impact of future development' at Botany Bay. But, more than simply assessing the past and the future, the project went further: to contribute to the development of means by which to restore and redevelop past damage and by which to assert 'control' over the future.[15]

The role of the historians involved in the project is worth considering. Hugh Stretton, in a review of the Botany Bay Project,
argues that they often found themselves in a difficult position
because the judgments that they were inclined to make about the
social effects of rapid urban change could not be based purely on the
accumulation of detailed knowledge.[16] Stretton points to a conundrum at the core of the Botany Bay Project: while it produced
mainly technical and scientific reports that clearly spelt out the
effects of urbanisation and industrialisation on various measurable
things, such as air, noise and water pollution, even the aesthetic
qualities of the landscape, there was 'no purely objective way to
bring together the results . . . in order to understand the whole
physical system of a city, or to relate its management to the interests and conflicts and ideas of justice which concern the mass of the
citizens'.[17] The hard science collected and collated had revealed
environmental degradation—nothing surprising there—but it was
still unclear how that knowledge could be assessed in social terms.
What was one to do with historically produced contemporary disadvantage? Stretton argues that, for those types of assessments to be
made, questions about equality and justice had to be addressed, but
the Botany Bay Project largely failed to do this. It resulted, like so
many Botany Bay projects before it, in the accumulation of yet
more descriptions of this place, but little appreciation of what could
be done about the social effects of the colonial past that had been
inaugurated here.
    As they strove to make sense of the technical and scientific
information about the scale of environmental damage at Botany
Bay in social terms, the historians not surprisingly were asking questions about causes, and they were doing so in a broader context in
which certainties about the achievements of colonisation were
being seriously questioned. In this respect, the Botany Bay Project
can be read as evidence for, and as a product of, an emerging
historical sensibility in which narratives about colonisation as an
unmitigated good were losing ground. One highly visible reminder
that progress had come at a price was the degradation of the natural
environment. The other, of course, was the terrible state and status
of Aborigines in this apparently progressive, modern society. That a

landscape as symbolically central to the nation's history as Botany Bay had also become a site through which historians were telling stories about the impact of colonisation on the environment is symptomatic of the way in which nature had become a parchment for a new Australian history. Noel Butlin subsequently went on to write *Our Original Aggression*, published in 1983, about the disastrous impact of the arrival of Europeans on Aboriginal populations of south-eastern Australia between 1788 and 1850.[18] His analysis of the social costs of colonisation was perhaps already forming in his mind, as it was in the minds of some other Australian historians, when he was working on the Botany Bay Project in the 1970s.

Redeeming the past through nature

A narrative of redemption, casting Botany Bay as a place where one might transcend rather than celebrate the colonial past, was most evident in the rhetoric used by environmentalists. This was not necessarily difficult to do because symbols of birth had long been used to describe Botany Bay. Those symbols simply needed to be reconfigured for the foundation of a new era. For instance, the National Trust of Australia, alert to these possibilities, made a public plea in 1970—the bicentennial of Captain Cook's arrival in Botany Bay (discussed in more detail in Chapter 7)—to 'Let Kurnell [Captain Cook's Landing Place] be the birthplace of a *new* Australian attitude to land and land use, of loving and caring for the land itself, and respecting its special qualities and needs' (emphasis added).[19] Botany Bay could become, the National Trust and other environmental groups regularly argued, the site for a new beginning where an ethics of care for the environment was privileged over its destruction. What such an ethics of care would entail was to be demonstrated through various environmental conservation projects aimed at restoring damaged ecosystems to their former glory. Indeed, as it became increasingly clear during the 1970s that, despite the various research projects and government inquiries, the port and other developments would proceed at Botany Bay as planned, attention was directed away from trying to halt them and channelled into an effort to preserve, protect and rehabilitate pockets of original, but now fragile and vulnerable, nature. There were only a few pockets of remnant landscape remaining, including Towra Point near Kurnell on the south shore and parts of Cape Banks on the north shore.

During this period, Towra Point became one of the most highly valued remnants of Botany Bay's natural (for this, read pre-colonial) environment, a refuge where the modern post-colonial future would be kept at bay. The recognition of its significance was initially international. The first practical government support for protecting and preserving Towra Point emerged at a Commonwealth government level, when in 1975, an area of 282 hectares of land was acquired by the Commonwealth to satisfy the Japanese and Australian Migratory Birds Agreement (JAMBA), signed in Tokyo in February 1974. But while the Commonwealth acquired the land so that the habitat of rare migratory birds could be protected, it was not until 1982 that it officially became a nature reserve. By this time, quite extensive parts of Botany Bay's south and north heads had been turned into a national park. Two years after being declared a nature reserve, the Towra Point wetlands were included on the Ramsar world listing of wetlands of international importance. But, despite its internationally recognised credentials as a significant ecosystem—a nesting place for threatened birds and a wetlands providing a window onto deep time—the value of Towra Point was not purely and objectively ecological. Nature never is. Its meanings were saturated with sentimentality and nostalgia for long-lost time. It represented an original past that might possibly be returned to.

This little pocket of Botany Bay had the advantage not just of being close to the point where Cook had landed, but of apparently still looking exactly as it had when he had been there. The same could not be said for his official landing place: it was by then a completely refashioned landscape. Towra Point provided a small space within a much larger landscape where one could imagine being returned to an 'original' pre-colonial landscape, but to achieve that vision, one's sight had to be trained, blocking out the airport to the west, the oil refinery to the south and the port development to the north. Paul Carter's description in the opening pages of *The Road to Botany Bay* captures something of the possibilities for seeing the past on the present landscape, and something of the challenges too. 'A more sensuous trace of aircraft and oil refineries,' he writes, 'stains the prospect but, with a selective eye, the outlines of what Cook saw, the rim of the shore on which Banks' natives remained absorbed in their own preoccupations, these material facts remain discernible.'[20] In his description of Botany Bay, Nicholas Thomas also sees traces of the past in today's heavily industrialised landscape. 'Botany Bay,' he writes:

> is still beautiful, despite the oil refineries massed around this 'South shore', the airport runways that stab into its waters from the northwest, and diverse other excrescences of suburban and industrial Sydney. There are places behind the dune where all this can be imagined away, where the shallow waters are stained yellow-brown from bracken and wattle blown or washed into the water, where sandbars have become crab ghettoes, where flathead and mullet are motionless in the hot still water at the top of the tide.[21]

These are the wetlands of Towra Point. Towra Point's preservation has served its purpose: here time stands still.

In these descriptions, and others like them, nature becomes the means by which to enter the historical past—to be one with Cook and Banks as they traverse this landscape. Thomas, in his beautifully written description of his experience of visiting the Botany Bay wetlands in the closing years of the twentieth century, transcends even historical time, and through this pocket of nature enters the 'Dreamtime'. He continues his evocation of the landscape by cataloguing the rock paintings that remain faintly on the sandstone ledges along the water's edge:

> At dawn and dusk, as the low sun picks out the pocks and lines in this stone, you discover—and can still discover—old rock engravings, etched tracks and weird figures as well as naturalistic wallabies. This stone is not just natural, these are not just animals, but mythic beings, dreamtime ancestors of this land.[22]

Thomas' suggestion that one can 'still discover' these pre-colonial etchings allows contemporary Australians to imagine contributing to the discovery project that Cook and Banks inaugurated in this place. Moreover, the evocation of an Aboriginal presence in the Botany Bay landscape through reference to their material traces can be read as a continuation of the mode of the dialogue that Cook and Banks had with the 'natives' in 1770—one that was with their material culture rather than face to face. Banks and Cook learnt about the locals through reading the signs of their presence on the landscape, and from the objects left by them in their huts and on the ground, which Banks and Cook collected.

Thomas sees in the landscape three different temporalities: his own present; the past belonging to Banks and Cook; and the 'Dreaming', that transcendental time belonging to indigenous Australians. For a brief moment in the muddy flats behind the sand dunes at Kurnell, one can imagine that very moment when European (historical) time met indigenous transcendental (prehistorical) time. That moment remains suspended . . . until the roar of a plane jolts one back to the present and the 'excrescences of suburban and industrial Sydney' blur one's vision again.

'Pocks and lines'

During the development of Botany Bay in the 1960s and 1970s, concern was expressed not only about the future of botanical relics from pre-colonial time, but also about other pre-colonial traces, particularly Aboriginal rock carvings, those 'pocks and lines' on the sandstone ledges along the shore. For instance, a Mr I. Sim, considered an authority on Sydney rock art, wrote repeatedly to local authorities to point out that old rock carvings were being threatened by the building of new roads and to ask that something be done to protect them.[23] His petitions fell on deaf ears and so, underneath one road known paradoxically as the Scenic Drive, are many rock carvings now permanently hidden from view. Many others were lost through the reclamation of foreshore for the port on the north shore and for the expansion of industry on the south.

Like other parts of the Sydney coastline, the sandstone ledges around Botany Bay were a crowded canvas. They overflowed with sometimes overlapping images of fish, whales, kangaroos, men, spears, Dreaming figures and so on. Some had been faithfully recorded by amateur archaeologists, a process that seems to have begun in the late nineteenth century and to have been carried out intermittently since. Among the first recorders were the surveyors, R.H. Mathews and W.D. Campbell. For instance, Mathews records going to the Aboriginal settlement at La Perouse in the early 1890s 'in order to research the habits of the natives'. During the visit, 'they showed me drawings of three large fish carved into smooth slabs of *Hawkesbury* sandstone (which surrounds the bay), adding that it was the work of their ancestors before the arrival of the white man'.[24] Campbell, too, talked with the locals when he went to Botany Bay to look for rock carvings a few years after Mathews. Coming across a large carving on the north head, the one already recorded by Mathews in an article published in 1895, Campbell recorded in his journal that 'when questioning the blacks at the native encampment nearby [I] was informed by an old black woman that this was a "Bora" whale'.[25] But not all who came across these carvings in this period, when they were still quite visible, believed that the local Aborigines possessed knowledge about them.

E.W. O'Sullivan, one-time Minister for Lands in the New South Wales government, wrote a short piece about the La Perouse headland in 1906, which he entitled 'Where Three Histories Meet'. There are no prizes for guessing the three histories with which he was concerned. After dealing with Cook, Phillip and Lapérouse, O'Sullivan mentions a 'large whale carving', the same one described by Mathews (although he in fact believed it to be a shark) and Campbell only a decade or so earlier. O'Sullivan placed the carving outside both the realm of local Aborigines and of history. 'On the rocks, a little to the right of the [French] monument,' he writes, 'there is an aboriginal carving representing a whale, with eye, fins, and tail complete. It is nearly 50ft long, and at one time the lines were several inches deeper than they are now. As a specimen of barbaric art it is most interesting.'[26] Having situated the carving squarely in the realm of the primitive by characterising it as

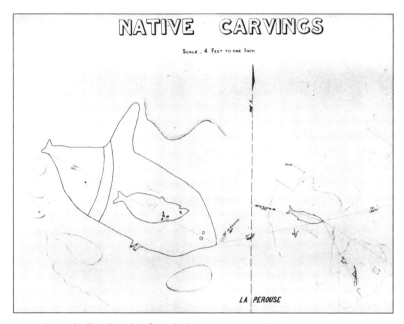

W.D. Campbell's sketch of a whale carving on the La Perouse headland, c.1893–6. Campbell's sketch indicates the position of the carving in relation to the monument to Lapérouse. As discussed in Chapter 7, in the 1990s the carving became a focus for local Aboriginal people's efforts to create their own monumental presence in the Botany Bay landscape. (Mitchell Library, State Library of New South Wales)

barbaric, O'Sullivan goes on three paragraphs later to describe the Aboriginal people living in the settlement nearby. He describes them as being 'of various hues [who] seem to eke out an existence there'.[27] In his narrative, no relationship is drawn between the Aborigines then living at La Perouse and the carving of the whale. They are removed both spatially and temporally from each other. This is somewhat different from the impression that one gets from both Mathews' and Campbell's descriptions, which suggest a quite close connection between the carving and the local Aboriginal people.

During the twentieth century, Aboriginal people living within the confines of the Aboriginal reserve were no longer producing this type of art, and no longer spending their days punching holes on to the sandstone ledges leading to the water. They had, however, been imprinting the landscape with their presence and with meaning in other ways. This became obvious during their hard-fought campaign to hold on to their piece of Botany Bay, a campaign waged during the second half of the 1960s.

'Our heritage bestowed upon us'

During roughly the same period that some efforts to preserve pockets of Botany Bay's natural environment were getting underway, local Aboriginal people were involved in a struggle to preserve the reserve that they occupied on the north head. In the mid-1960s, they were once again facing the prospect of forced removal from the place they called home. While they were no doubt concerned about the preservation of traces in the landscape belonging to the precolonial past, throughout this particular struggle they were mainly seeking to protect the stuff of their post-contact (post-1770) historical presence in the place. Because of this, the ideological basis of their struggle was quite different from those of the environmental and natural heritage preservation campaigns of the same period. In their campaign, local Aboriginal people were not defending something called 'primitivism', or arguing about the significance of a type of essential nativeness, or making claims about the universal value of traces surviving from deep time. Their claims were starkly historical, not prehistorical, and they were not yet founded predominantly on a cultural definition of Aboriginality that we would recognise today. Local Aboriginal people involved in the campaign were primarily concerned about preserving a still-remembered past rather than, or at least in addition to, a distant one. It was in some ways a curious situation: concurrently at Botany Bay, non-Aboriginal people were seeking to preserve material traces from prehistoric or pre-colonial time and Aboriginal people were seeking to preserve material traces from historic or colonial time. The memorial tables had turned.

In the mid-1960s, the New South Wales parliament had established a parliamentary inquiry into the welfare of Aborigines. The inquiry provided an opportunity for a renewal of pressure to disband the Aboriginal settlement on Botany Bay—the only Aboriginal settlement in a metropolitan area. In its submission to a parliamentary inquiry, the New South Wales Aborigines Welfare Board, which had only five or so years earlier resisted local pressure to shut down the settlement by saying 'not yet' (as discussed in Chapter 5) was now saying that the time was ripe for the settlement's remaining residents to take their place in the wider community. Mr Kingsmill, then chairman of the board explained:

> At the present time the board is faced with the problem of heavy expenditure on houses on the La Perouse Aborigines Reserve, where residents are employed in local industry and quite capable of seeking housing in the community in the same manner as other persons in the district. In fact the board has reached the conclusion that . . . the reserve has outlived its usefulness and the majority of residents should be expected within a reasonable period to find accommodation elsewhere.[28]

The notion that the reserve had 'outlived its usefulness' reflected the conventional bureaucratic definition of Aboriginal settlements as transitional places, where Aboriginal residents were trained for assimilation into the general community.[29] Considered in this way, this particular reserve no longer had a function because its residents were considered already assimilated. In spoken evidence to the parliamentary inquiry, Kingsmill elaborated on the board's position: 'I think that reserves in the metropolitan area are incongruous, and I do not think they do anything to promote the object of assimilation.'[30] In this sense, the perceived redundancy of the La Perouse Aboriginal reserve was understood in both temporal and spatial ways—it had 'outlived its usefulness' and was 'incongruous with the metropolitan area'. Bureaucratically, at least, the reserve was considered an anachronism, a leftover from the past that no longer had a place in the modern landscape that Botany Bay had by then become. At the same time, particularly as the Welfare Board was under pressure to explain the perceived slowness with which Aborigines were assimilating, this particular reserve was a highly visible and unwanted reminder of the board's failure to achieve its policy aims.

Local Aboriginal people and their supporters took every opportunity possible to challenge the public statements and intentions of the board. In evidence to the inquiry, some Aboriginal people questioned the assumption that the board's aim of assimilation required that Aboriginal people live apart from each other. Indeed, some of those who spoke to the press or gave evidence to the inquiry did not repudiate suggestions that they were assimilated, when assimilatedness was simply measured in terms of external signs such as participation in employment. For example, one local Aboriginal woman told a newspaper reporter: 'We've grown up here with these white people around us . . . We're integrated and we're happy about it.'[31] What they did not accept, however, was that certain forms of participation in white society cancelled their right to live on the Aboriginal reserve, where they had lived their whole lives and where their parents and grandparents had lived before them. Cliff Cooke, one of the Aboriginal witnesses to the inquiry, told the committee that, while he personally had no objection to living off the reserve, others would because 'they have had their roots in the place for so many years now'.[32] Rather than represent their relationship to the reserve as an inalienable one founded on fixed notions of traditional culture, residents of the reserve articulated their attachment to the place historically.[33] Hubert Timbery, another Aboriginal man, told reporters that he was 'going to stick to [the reserve]',[34] on the basis of a belief that it had been a grant in perpetuity from Queen Victoria. What this claim emphasised was that Aboriginal people understood that length of occupation of a reserve continuously over generations was a strong basis for their right to retain it. Yet, from the bureaucratic point of view, this same history of occupation constituted the inevitable demise of the reserve, at least in its present configuration. The longer it existed, the less sure its future was because bureaucratically it was understood as a place where Aboriginal people were being prepared for their inevitable assimilation into white society.

It is worth noting that, a generation earlier, local Aboriginal people had used quite similar arguments to resist their removal from Botany Bay. In the late 1920s, the local municipal council authority had made a concerted effort to force Aboriginal people out in order for the area to be developed for recreation and leisure. The council seemed unwilling to acknowledge that it was Aboriginal people themselves who were part of the attraction for visitors (as discussed in Chapter 3). In their campaign opposing the council's plan, Aboriginal people typically articulated their right to remain in historical terms. According to one newspaper report at the time, when they were 'asked if they would go . . . they [the Aborigines] strenuously objected', on the grounds that 'many of them were born on the reserve, and naturally regarded it as their home'.[35] The local Aboriginal people organised a petition against their removal in which they worded their claim to remain at Botany Bay in terms of the land on which they lived being 'our heritage bestowed upon us'.[36] What did they mean by this?

In the early twentieth century, heritage was a relatively common concept. In that period, it retained its predominantly familial meanings whereby it referred to things held in common from one generation to the next. It encapsulated the notion of inheritance. But it was also quite commonly applied to larger collectivities, such as local communities or the nation. Those communities were understood as sharing a common heritage, such as links to the same past as well as traditions and values, which bound them together. By describing the Aboriginal reserve as 'our heritage bestowed upon us', its residents were emphasising that it had been passed down to them and it was held in common by them. Those Aboriginal families, like others living on Aboriginal reserves throughout New South Wales that had been created in the late nineteenth century, believed that the land had been granted to them directly by Queen Victoria, the reigning monarch, just as Hubert Timbery did 40 or so years later. As a gift from the Queen, they understood that the reserve would remain in their possession as long as it was occupied by the descendants of the original grantees. It was their heritage because they had inherited it; it was what they held in common; and it was what they strongly identified with. Further, they understood that they had been given exclusive rights to this little piece of land because they had been alienated from the rest of their country. Their dispossession was the common past they shared. Finally, they expected to be in a

position to pass the reserve on as an inheritance to those later born
into the place so that their common heritage would continue.

'I like the view'

In March 1966, some members of the parliamentary committee of
inquiry went out to the Aboriginal reserve at La Perouse to talk with
residents.[37] Iris Williams remembers that the chairman of the committee visited her and her husband in their home. He asked her
husband, Tom, why he did not want to move off the reserve. They
were standing on the front porch of Tom and Iris's house, which
overlooked Botany Bay, when Tom answered: 'Because I like the
view.'[38] It was a nuanced response, exposing the powerful ways of
seeing that were at the centre of the dispute. The view to which
Tom Williams referred was the immediately visible one and another
less obvious one. Looking from the Aboriginal reserve across
Botany Bay, the view is indeed delightful, and was more so then
because it had not yet been marred by the considerable port development that began in the 1970s. But the view to which Tom
referred was also an historical one—a vista that the present-day
landscape provided on the past.

   The land in question had become desirable, which, it must be
said, was not the fate shared by all Aboriginal reserves throughout
New South Wales. This bolstered a generally held view that it was
not just the government but also, and perhaps more importantly,
developers who were behind the campaign to move Aboriginal
people away from their settlement on the foreshore of Botany Bay.
For instance, in response to Kingsmill's statements, Charles Perkins,
then chair of the Foundation for Aboriginal Affairs, told the media
that 'the reserve should be retained for the people and not speculated
on for real estate'.[39] The considerable trade union involvement in the
local campaign to save the reserve was motivated by, and helped to
frame, the struggle in these predominantly capitalist terms. This was
also the case with other Aboriginal land campaigns at the time, in
New South Wales and elsewhere. Stan Sharkey, a trade union activist
from the nearby suburb of Matraville, and workmate of some of the

Aboriginal men from the reserve, was actively involved in the campaign to retain the reserve. When I spoke to him about it, he insisted that it was essentially a working-class fight against private capital. In his view, 'the land was going to be developed by LJ Hooker as prime residential area'. 'The excuse that the Askin government used,' he explained, 'was that it was a shantytown, there were tin sheds and many of them had sand floors. So they were using that as an excuse to carry out their greedy and racist policy. And [it was] very close to happening.'[40] As Sharkey understood it, the government's assimilation policy was secondary to aggressive capitalism as a force intervening in local Aboriginal people's lives. Indeed, Sharkey went further and described the struggle as a precursor to the well-known green bans applied by left-wing unions on inner-city developments around the harbourside suburbs of Woolloomooloo and the Rocks in the 1970s.[41]

But this was not the main platform upon which local Aboriginal people were protesting their removal. The key plank in their desire to remain at La Perouse, and the basis upon which they argued their case to retain their reserve, was their historical attachment to the place. In this respect, the landscape, as seen through the eyes of Tom Williams and other Aboriginal residents, was a storehouse of memories, an intimate, local historical text.[42] This landscape told their stories. The view they liked from their houses took in, among other things, the site of the old Aboriginal reserve on Frenchmans Beach, a place where ancestors had been born and where they had been buried.

While many material traces of this history of occupation no longer physically existed on the landscape, and were held only in memory, some tangible markers remained. Among others, King Billy's shack was still standing. King Billy was also known as William John Wentworth.[43] Some local Aboriginal people believe he received the surname Wentworth from his employers, the well-known colonial family, the Wentworths of Vaucluse. He is believed to have moved out to the La Perouse settlement in the late nineteenth century. His little house was made partly from materials used in the original government supply houses on the Aborigines reserve in the 1880s, thus providing a tangible link between the old reserve and the new one. King Billy died in 1906. The shack was eventually demolished in 1974, but its presence has since been memorialised by stories published about it.[44] In the absence of the old shack, a nearby tree has taken on significance as the marker of its location on the original reserve on the foreshores of Frenchmans Bay. 'There isn't anything to remind us of our old people because we don't have monuments and statues,' wrote Iris Williams in a community history called *La Perouse: The Place, the People and the Sea*. 'There are three Moreton Bay fig trees on the old reserve and one stands alone just a few yards from the tin shack where King Billy died. His shack was painted red and it was the last house built of government tin to be demolished. . . . We all know that the old people lived under the tree and the children played around it and it was never damaged in any way.'[45]

This photograph shows King Billy's red tin hut in the foreground, under a Moreton Bay fig tree, c. late 1960s. The little hut was demolished in 1974 but the fig tree still remains and today functions as a memorial to the 'old people'. (Randwick and District Historical Society)

The Endeavour Project

By the end of the 1960s, the Aboriginal residents of the La Perouse reserve had won the right to remain, although this had not been achieved completely through the strength of their own arguments. The broader social and political currents had shifted in their favour. Rather than the late 1960s signalling the end of the little Aboriginal reserve on the foreshores of Botany Bay (or, indeed, of others throughout New South Wales), it was the demise of the Aborigines Welfare Board that characterised this era in Aboriginal politics. But, while the residents got to stay on their reserve, they did not get the title to it that they had hoped for. Their settlement eventually became the responsibility of the New South Wales Housing Commission, for development as a medium-density housing project.[46] This state of affairs gave rise to some new anxieties among local non-Aboriginal residents, many of whom were spooked by the spectre of urban ghettoes, and so came up with their own visions for how the continuing local Aboriginal presence might be accommodated.

The Endeavour Project was one such scheme.[47] It received widespread support from an unusual consortium of government agencies, including the New South Wales National Parks and Wildlife Service and the New South Wales Department of Housing. The project, initiated by Dr Gaven Andrews, a resident of the suburb of La Perouse, a psychiatrist and a lecturer at the University of New South Wales, was influenced by social science discourse which held that social reformation could be achieved by modifying the environment in which people live. In this case, the aim was to reform, educate and socialise the Aboriginal people living at La Perouse through substantially transforming their physical environment. Some involved in the Endeavour Project believed that local Aboriginal people were caught between two worlds, alienated from their cultural past and not yet fully acculturated into the modern present. There was a heightened concern that, as Botany Bay became increasingly modernised, industrialised and urbanised, local Aboriginal people would be left behind, unable to keep pace with 'progress'. The Endeavour Project was conceived to address this perceived problem. Key to the proposed development of a new environment to assist the transition of local Aborigines into the modern future was a return to nature. In this period, 'traditionally-oriented' Aboriginal people were commonly perceived as essentially one with nature. At Botany Bay, on Sydney's suburban fringe, Aboriginal people were, by contrast, typically characterised as dangerously alienated from it. According to the rationale that underpinned the Endeavour Project this, in part, explained their alleged anti-social behaviour, or their potential to become social deviants.

At the core of the proposed Endeavour Project was the creation of a holistic environment consisting of a village-like housing settlement which would be shared by Aboriginal and non-Aboriginal people, including an educational centre and local craft workshops in which Aboriginal people would produce traditional arts and crafts. All of this was to be situated within an extensive park, which was to be landscaped with native flora.[48] Both the natural bushland setting and the traditional craft workshops were explained in terms of providing links with a pre-modern cultural life, which would supposedly help to breakdown the alienation considered a basic (indeed defining) feature of modern, urban life.

The plan, like many others that had been proposed during the 1950s and 1960s to deal with the supposed problem of the Aboriginal settlement on Botany Bay's north head, did not get past the drawing board, despite the considerable interest it generated. In the end, Commonwealth money was used to provide completely new housing on the Aboriginal settlement, designed and built by the New South Wales Housing Commission. With the new houses replacing the old ones including King Billy's shack, the settlement ultimately looked like any other housing commission estate found on Sydney's suburban fringe. The Aboriginal settlement had gone suburban, while still remaining spatially separate. The much-prized view over Botany Bay was, however, marred by the unstoppable port development that continued throughout this period, and the whole thing fell far short of the utopian, landscaped village that those behind the Endeavour Project had envisaged and championed. Local Aboriginal residents, however, seemed pleased to have at last some new accommodation and amenities.[49]

A quiet reflection

In 1999, historian Geoffrey Moorhouse reflected on what the costs of the development of Botany Bay as Sydney's second port had been. 'The disaster is not simply the erosion of the shoreline', he wrote. 'The disaster is not even—though it is very much also— because some people happen to have lived a long time inside the northern arm of the bay at La Perouse but, being aboriginal, they were not consulted.' Over and above, or at least in addition to these two disasters, Moorhouse argued that the 'disaster is as much . . . to do with the defilement of Australia's history, with the very beginning of European settlement on this continent'. Indeed, he accuses those responsible for having 'spat on their own past'. More than simply the defilement of the past, Moorhouse also believes that the original and continued development of Botany Bay constitutes a lost opportunity for Australians to deal with the past in the present. 'Cook's Landing [Place reserve] . . . could have been a place for quiet reflection about many things in Australia's past,' he writes, 'not least on the relationship between the two peoples who have a particular attachment to Botany Bay.'[50] But, despite the jumbo jets, tankers and oil stacks, Botany Bay *is* a site, and increasingly so, for reflection on the relationship between black and white. The only thing that is missing from Moorhouse's vision for Botany Bay as a place to meditate on the historical dimension of the relationship between Aborigines and non-Aborigines is the quiet.

REMEMBERING DISPOSSESSION AND SURVIVAL

Botany Bay stories revisited

On 18 January 1988, the First Fleet sailed into Botany Bay for a second time. It had been 200 years between visits. This re-enactment, although not an official event, was nonetheless a greatly anticipated, well-publicised and popular one among the many held during Australia's bicentennial year. Crowds lined Botany Bay's foreshores to see history being remade. Most were in a welcoming mood, but others were not. Quite a large group of Aboriginal people and their supporters had gathered to protest the return of the First Fleet. This was not the first time that an historical re-enactment of this type had attracted both onlookers and opposers. In 1970, the 200th anniversary celebrations of Captain Cook's arrival in Botany Bay, had also attracted large crowds who wanted to witness the re-enactment, and a small group of Aboriginal people who wanted to express their opposition.

The Aboriginal protest staged at Botany Bay in 1988 was itself a re-enactment of sorts. It specifically drew upon the 1970 protest, which in turn had drawn on the 1938 day of mourning held in Sydney on the occasion of the sesquicentenary of the arrival of the First Fleet. It can thus be interpreted as part of a tradition whereby Aboriginal people, in their struggle for recognition and rights, challenged the historical narratives that non-Aboriginal people told about the colonial past. These protests, held on the occasion of national anniversaries, were forceful statements about what had been forgotten or denied in national histories. During the 1970 and 1988 protests, Botany Bay, as a national historical landscape, was mobilised by Aboriginal activists in new ways and in the process acquired new significance. It became a place through which to remember the dispossession of Aboriginal people across the country and through which to remind all Australians about the underside of the national history conventionally celebrated there.

Although Aboriginal people who lived at Botany Bay throughout the twentieth century had long been engaging with, and at times unsettling, national commemorative performances and historical narratives in an almost everyday way, from the time of the 1970 protest their local history-making became enmeshed in an emerging national Aboriginal politics and was increasingly influenced by the national Aboriginal consciousness, including the historical consciousness, of the time. But, while it is true that Botany Bay and its Aboriginal residents became embroiled in the new national Aboriginal politics, local ways of doing and using history also continued. This is because, even though local Botany Bay Aborigines were participants, often key participants, in the national protests held in their own backyard, they were also the ones who, after the staged national protests were over, remained resident in a locale with a surfeit of signs pointing to the national past, but in which their own specific, intimate, familial and quotidian history had hardly any visibility at all. Their response, as it had consistently been, was to tell their own stories, both to one another and to others willing to listen, about what this place meant to them, and to imprint as best they could their presence—past and present—on it.

By the close of the twentieth century and the beginning of the twenty-first, Botany Bay was not only being mobilised to expose, as the popular saying put it, that 'white Australia has a black history'. It was also a site through which to return to the moment when blacks and whites first encountered each other. This act of return to the foundational meeting was performed to confront that moment in order to escape its burden, or to creatively examine how it might have been done differently, or to experiment with how a different story might be told about it. Rather than being exclusively a place to celebrate that historical moment, Botany Bay increasingly became somewhere where non-Aboriginal and Aboriginal people alike sought to unsettle its symbolic power and to reconfigure its role in shaping the nature of their relationship to each other.

A mourning ceremony

When a re-enactment of the *Endeavour* arriving in Botany Bay, and Captain Cook landing on its shore, was staged on 29 April 1970, there were large crowds of onlookers there to greet him, among them Queen Elizabeth II and other members of the British royal family. The arrival and landing was performed with a degree of verisimilitude: Aboriginal people performed the role of uninterested witnesses, paddling about in canoes paying scant attention to the strange ship and its occupants. A lengthy display of spearing a stingray was part of their act, evidence that there was some laxity in interpreting the script. In 1770, this was an activity Cook's own crew had engaged in rather than the locals. With the stingray killed, the Aboriginal actors took their place on the beach as Cook and his men approached in their longboat. The voyagers threw beads and trinkets on to the beach as they approached; the infamous shot was fired; the natives retreated; and the all-important landing was enacted.

While the re-enactment was being performed, directly opposite on the northern headland a small group of Aboriginal activists and their supporters staged what they dubbed a mourning ceremony. It had been organised by the Federal Council for the Advancement of Aborigines and Torres Strait Islanders and the National Tribal Council, and its aims were to draw attention to Aboriginal people's dispossession from their land and to appeal for national land rights. In a symbolic gesture highlighting the death and the loss caused to Aboriginal people across Australia by colonisation—which, for Aboriginal people, was directly tied to the arrival of Captain Cook in Botany Bay in 1770—wreaths were thrown into the bay. Aboriginal poet, Kath Walker (Oodgeroo Noonuccal), read an oration she had written.[1] It underscored how British colonisation had resulted in dispossession, the end of sacred ceremonies and an unhappy people with an unhappy past. She described Aboriginal people as 'the strangers now'. The protestors wore red headbands, symbolising blood spilt, and carried signs with the names of 'lost tribes'. The symbols, actions and words used in the mourning ceremony provided a potent contrast with those of birth and beginnings that characterised the re-enactment at Kurnell, and with the bicentennial celebrations held throughout 1970. The northern headland of Botany Bay was an ideal stage for the mourning ceremony. Staged directly opposite Captain Cook's Landing Place reserve at Kurnell on the south shore, the mourning ceremony enabled protestors and commentators alike to make immediate and highly visible juxtapositions between metaphoric death and birth that were at the centre of the respective events.

Moreover, and perhaps more importantly, the mourning ceremony drew some of its symbolic power from the history and the meaning of the land on which it was staged: that tiny slice of Botany Bay's northern headland long occupied by an Aboriginal settlement. In 1970, this handkerchief of reserve land remained occupied by a relatively large Aboriginal settlement but was still vested in government hands. Only months earlier, it had been under the direct control of the New South Wales Aborigines Welfare Board, which had been formally disbanded in 1969. A process of transition was underway, typically characterised as a shift from paternalism to self-management. A central element in this broader push for Aboriginal self-determination was the demand for rights to, and ownership of, land that had been taken from Aborigines during the colonial period. Within this broader political context, this piece of Botany Bay, with its post-1770 history of an Aboriginal presence over generations, was now mobilised in the campaign for an Australia-wide Aboriginal struggle for rights to land. One Aboriginal leader described the Aboriginal reserve on Botany Bay's north head as 'a tiny part, an outpost of "our Israel", the tribal Promised Lands for whose return the Aboriginal militants most urgently yearn'.[2] Statements like this positioned the small Aboriginal reserve within a much broader, national context as one pocket of land among many over which Aboriginal people sought rights. In this context, Botany

Bay's dual, and somewhat contradictory, meaning came to the fore: it was at one and the same time a place possessed by Aborigines, through their actual presence in it and through their public historical claims to it, as well as being the symbolic origin point for the historical dispossession of all Aborigines.

As part of the mourning ceremony, claims of continual occupation of that place, which local Aboriginal people at Botany Bay had been asserting for some time, were made public. The claims by local Aboriginal people of direct descent from those who had lived in the area at the time of Captain Cook were prominent in the media coverage of the protest. Newspaper reports made reference to a local Aboriginal woman, Trudy Longbottom, who, having declined an invitation to meet Queen Elizabeth II at Kurnell, participated in the mourning ceremony instead. She was described in reports as 'a direct descendant of the Illawarra tribe, which lived around Botany Bay more than two centuries ago'.[3] The Aboriginal reserve on Botany Bay's north head was likewise used to represent historical continuity, but of a slightly different kind. By this time, the settlement on the reserve was a conglomeration of run-down houses and shacks. This was the result, many residents claimed, of purposeful government neglect while the Welfare Board had, throughout the 1960s, sought its complete closure (discussed in Chapter 6). In this physical state, the Aboriginal reserve provided tangible and graphic evidence of the continuing consequences of colonisation for Aboriginal people, including the most recent era of government paternalism when it was under the control of the board. Perched on Botany Bay's shore, the Aboriginal settlement was used effectively as a backdrop for the mourning ceremony, communicating through graphic images more effectively than words the plight of Aboriginal people both here and, by extension, across Australia. It functioned as a type of historical tableau, depicting the flipside of the historical moment that was being celebrated in grand style across the bay. By means of these two slightly different uses of the Aboriginal reserve and its residents— one to narrate continuity of descent, the other continuity of disadvantage—a powerful symbolic connection was drawn between present and past. This practice of emphasising continuity over discontinuity, while also paradoxically acknowledging the radical temporal break and the brokenness produced by colonisation, had long been a *modus operandi* in local Aboriginal forms of history and historical remembrance.

Although the local Aboriginal reserve and some of its residents took part in it, the mourning ceremony was primarily national in its aims and scope. And, as a national Aboriginal protest, it had an ambiguous, and to some extent uneasy, relationship with the local Aboriginal settlement and their historical claims upon which it drew. While some use was made of local historical traditions, such as the claims about continuous occupation of the place from before Captain Cook until the present, in the process of the protest the pre-existing functions and meanings of these local traditions within a local context became somewhat obscured. Mobilised for national purposes, they were cast and interpreted in national terms, overshadowing the specific origins and uses of the local historical traditions, which had been produced and told by Aboriginal people intermittently over the previous century. At the same time, the long history of local people struggling successfully to hold on to that tiny piece of Botany Bay, was eclipsed by the new, bolder national land rights movement. In this movement, rights to land were increasingly conceptualised on the basis of Aboriginality, or cultural difference, rather than on attachments to land that had been forged historically, experienced intimately and explained locally not nationally.

'The children are not taken away'

After the 1970 mourning ceremony was over, local Aboriginal people returned to the task of trying to secure tenure to the land they occupied so that they would not need to live under the threat of expulsion from it, which had characterised their experience for most of the twentieth century (as discussed in previous chapters). While the local Aboriginal reserve momentarily provided the stage for a symbolic national Aboriginal protest in 1970, and was used to highlight the call for national land rights, the campaign to secure better living conditions on it and for security of tenure over it continued throughout the 1970s and into the 1980s. By 1972, the reserve settlement had been redeveloped, with new housing built by the New South Wales Housing Commission and made possible by Commonwealth funding. The redeveloped settlement made the continued presence of Aboriginal people in this local/national landscape more secure, even though in visual terms it now looked little different from the suburban housing that surrounded it. Yet the matter of ownership of the land remained unresolved. Initially, and for a short period of time, responsibility for the Aboriginal settlement was vested in the New South Wales Directorate of Social Welfare, before being handed over to the newly established New South Wales Aboriginal Lands Trust in 1973. From this period on, the campaign to gain security of tenure over the reserve was embroiled within a process of legislative reform concerning Aboriginal land rights in New South Wales generally. When the New South Wales *Aboriginal Land Rights Act* 1983 was eventually passed, provision was made for the establishment of local Aboriginal land councils. The deeds to the land upon which the local settlement was built were handed to the La Perouse Local Aboriginal Land Council in 1984, fourteen years after the 1970 Captain Cook bicentenary and four years before the 1988 First Fleet one. The transference of the deeds to the land from the state to a local Aboriginal organisation was essentially a ceremonial acknowledgment of what local Aboriginal people had always considered to be the case. Upon receiving the deeds, Tom Williams, who had become the chairperson of the land council, stated: 'We always considered it our own.'[4] Media coverage of the ceremony at which the deeds to the 2.6-hectare area of land were handed over made reference to the land being near to the place of 'first contact', adding some further historical symbolism to the event. One local newspaper report noted:

> It was an historic day for our [*sic*] Aboriginal community and it was apt that the recognition of Aboriginal land rights should take place only a few steps from the place where officers of the First Fleet landed in Australia and the dispossession of the Aborigines began.[5]

The arrangement whereby the reserve was controlled by a local Aboriginal organisation marked a new era for the local people. Explaining the meaning of this development, Iris Williams wrote:

[The Aboriginal Lands Trust] was abolished in March 1983 when new legislation came in and set up Local Lands Councils so now we are responsible to ourselves only. We pay rent and are much happier and freer, free to have our white friends in our home. The children are not taken away.[6]

The phrases 'free to have our white friends in our home' and 'the children are not taken away' are vernacular for the long history of the reserve as a site of government control. The change in ownership represented the removal of dehumanising and demoralising restrictions on residents. At the same time, the creation of a local Aboriginal organisation to manage local Aboriginal affairs provided a new context for the production of new forms of local Aboriginal history-making, and especially new modes for making them public.

The year after the deeds to the reserve were handed over, and in anticipation of the upcoming 1988 bicentenary, a group of local Aboriginal people organised a project, supported by TAFE (the New South Wales Department of Technical and Further Education), to write their own history of this place. Calling themselves the Individual Heritage Group, they met over the following two years to record their memories and stories and to research the lives of their ancestors. The result was the publication of a book entitled *La Perouse: The Place, the People and the Sea*, and a photographic display which told, through word and image, the histories of individual families and the settlement as a whole. The desire to record and make public their own local and family histories had emerged in part from dissatisfaction with a centenary history of the Randwick Municipal Council, within the boundaries of which their reserve settlement is located, and from an expectation, based on previous experience, of the types of localised celebratory histories that would be produced as part of the impending national historical anniversary in 1988.

There was a strong perception among those involved in the Individual Heritage Group, as there was among Aboriginal people generally at the time, that national and local celebrations of foundational histories had the tendency to elide, if not erase, the specific meanings of the past for Aboriginal people. The Individual Heritage Group can be understood, then, as an explicit intervention into forms of public history, both local and national, occurring at the time. It was a public history project which told a new local history of a national landscape, and which contested both local and national histories that were blind to, or purposefully excluded, the pasts of Aboriginal people. And it exposed the structures of forgetting upon which those histories were typically based.

La Perouse: The Place, the People and the Sea gives an account of the historical presence of Aboriginal people at Botany Bay. Read as a whole, the collection constructs links between contemporary Aboriginal residents and the historical traces of a previous Aboriginal presence in the same area. At the same time, the collection excavates a landscape rich in historical significance—an historical landscape that is beyond the colonial monumental one that dominates Botany Bay and which tends to assume or consume the entire historical significance of the place. The memorial landscape mapped by these local Aboriginal historians is also beyond the boundaries of the Aboriginal reserve, the site almost exclusively associated with a local Aboriginal historical presence. The histories and memories they recorded ascribe significance to many of the same places that commonly feature in non-Aboriginal accounts of the landscape's historical heritage. The jukebox at the café, the tram terminus, the Colonnade dancehall, the local public school were all part of the map of the vernacular landscape constructed by local Aboriginal people as they went about their day-to-day lives. By narrating other, less visible pasts, and inscribing known places with hitherto unknown meanings, an alternative, somewhat subversive, local history was made public. While in local historiography Aboriginal people are largely absent, or at least their presence is contained with the bounds of the local reserve, by their own account the places associated mainly with non-Aboriginal people and their activities are shown to have mattered to, and held significance for, them too.

From Invasion Day to Survival Day

By the time 1988 arrived, much had changed in black–white relations in Australia. Some advances had been made in the pursuit of Aboriginal land rights across the nation, although the legislation introduced in the period generally fell short of Aboriginal people's hopes. Perhaps more importantly, white Australia's consciousness about the historical experiences of Aboriginal people had altered and was on the verge of changing even more. This reconstituted national historical consciousness had been in part the product of the 'breaking of the great Australian silence' about the nature of relations between blacks and whites in the colonial period, including the often violent nature of those relations.[7] The breaking of the great Australian silence is an achievement usually claimed by academic historians, which ascribes to their profession the dual honour of responsibility for building the wall of silence and for tearing it down. This process was accompanied by a considerable amount of Aboriginal people's own historical production and their loud rejection of the old history that had hitherto denied their historical experiences. The 1988 bicentennial celebrations provided another opportunity for Aboriginal people collectively to make statements about what was wrong with the conventional interpretation of the national past.

The crowd that protested against the 1988 re-enactment of the re-arrival of the First Fleet in Botany Bay was considerably larger than had been the case for the mourning ceremony staged on the occasion of the *Endeavour*'s re-arrival in 1970. As their predecessors had, the protestors gathered on the open stretch of land between the Aboriginal settlement and Frenchmans Beach. This time, a huge Aboriginal flag was pegged to the ground, which told those on board the ships that this was Aboriginal land. And in 1988 the land upon which the protestors stood was now legally held in Aboriginal hands under the provisions of the New South Wales *Aboriginal Land Rights Act* 1983. But the flag's message was not merely literal. The point the protestors sought to make was that this land had been occupied when the fleet arrived the first time, and it had not been surrendered in the interim. And, as owners—legal and moral—the local Aboriginal leaders had some say over who could set foot on it. A first fleeter descendent who had travelled from England on board one of the ships had wanted to re-enact not only the voyage but also the first landing. He was told not to come ashore.

The protest was photographed: a now iconic image of an Aboriginal woman standing on the rise above the beach wearing a t-shirt with the slogan 'White Australia has a Black History' captured the mood and the moment.[8] Since 1988, it has become, along with some other visual images of protests against the bicentenary, shorthand for the demands for historical recognition that Aboriginal people were making. The image, once simply a visual record of an event, can now be read as representing a new Australian historical project, one that might be broadly characterised as anti- or post-colonial.

The protest against the unofficial re-enactment of the First Fleet (known as the Tall Ships) in Botany Bay was simply a curtain raiser for the main event. The major national celebrations were to be held on Australia Day, renamed Invasion Day by Aboriginal people, and focused on Sydney Harbour. This was the day and the place for the large anti-bicentennial protests organised by Aboriginal people and their supporters. The key event was billed as a March for Freedom, Justice and Hope from Redfern to Hyde Park, where a rally and concert were held. The Invasion Day protest was by far the largest national gathering of Aboriginal people ever,

White Australia has a Black History, La Perouse, 1988.
(Copyright Juno Gemes)

attracting thousands from across Australia. It was an Aboriginal protest against national foundation myths, and an indication that Aboriginality was now itself a national phenomenon.

Sections of this national Aboriginal community made their temporary home at Botany Bay during the course of the protests. In the week leading up to Invasion Day, the land vested in the La Perouse Local Aboriginal Land Council, including the large Yarra Bay House which was the council's offices, became a temporary national Aboriginal village; here busloads of Aborigines from across Australia set up camp, transforming the place into a hub for the protests. And Botany Bay was the place to which many of the protestors returned after their day of protest in the city. They returned to dance, to sing and to perform ceremonies. While the national celebrations around Sydney Harbour continued on into the night, culminating with a fireworks display, an alternative and more modest celebration was held on the foreshores of Botany Bay. In the sand hills behind Kurnell, Aborigines and their invited guests held an all-night vigil, dancing and singing to reclaim the land, to restore the past and to create new beginnings. The event heralded a turn towards the celebration of survival, which was to become an increasingly central motif in Aboriginal identity politics post-1988. The symbolism of Botany Bay as a landscape for celebrating survival is clear. Botany Bay, as a place associated with national beginnings, provided an ideal setting for acknowledging the endurance of Aboriginal existence within the imagined space of the nation. At the same time, by holding this ceremony at Botany Bay rather than near Sydney Harbour, Aborigines suggested that, while they had a place in the national community, they also existed outside it, or at least on its edges.

The all-night vigil at Kurnell, like some of the visual images of the 1988 protests, has been deployed in subsequent critiques as a powerful metaphor to convey just how much Australian historical sensibility had changed and was changing. For some Australian historians, Kurnell, Australia Day, 1988 constitutes a turning point in their own historical narrative—a disjuncture marking the end of one chapter and the beginning of the next. For instance, Heather Goodall frames the epilogue to her comprehensive history of Aboriginal people's struggles for land in New South Wales from 1770 onwards around 'Kurnell, 1988'. It serves her purposes nicely. On the one hand, she represents the event as evidence of her thesis: 'that relations between land and people remain at the centre of Aboriginal politics and symbolism', and thus represents a continuation with the past. On the other hand, the night at Kurnell represented the beginning of a new era in the history of land in Aboriginal politics, particularly because the Aborigines leading it 'said their work was about restoration and new beginnings'.[9] Similarly, for Chris Healy, the Invasion Day 1988 protests, culminating in the sand hills at Kurnell that night, were about opening up the possibilities for other, more explicitly post- or anti-colonial, approaches to writing Australian history. The vigil encapsulated the processes of translation between black and white interpretations of the same past, which were necessary for this imagined, and longed for, new history. This is how he describes 'Kurnell 1988': 'The flag of Captain Cook was hauled down. The Other's flag is raised slowly, an inch at a time. At the top of the flagpole a breath of wind opens the cloth, bright in the very first rays of a new sun.'[10] It is yet another utopian image of new beginnings, one ultimately forged on renewed understandings of the past.

In the wake of 1988, Botany Bay was claimed by Aboriginal people as a landscape to celebrate historical continuity, or survival. The turning point was in the early 1990s, when the first Invasion Day concert was proposed to be staged at La Perouse on Botany Bay's north head. By the time the concert was staged, a decision had been made to call it Survival Day, a semantic shift that encapsulated the emphasis on continuity over discontinuity. At the same time, the name change put emphasis on Aboriginal people and took it away from the colonisers. In this formulation, Aboriginal people become the main actors in history, creatively and heroically maintaining their own culture—surviving in the face of colonisation.

The Survival Day concerts brought together Aboriginal performers—dancers, singers, bands, storytellers, musicians—from across Australia to express their cultural identity as Aboriginal people and to celebrate the survival of Aboriginal cultural life. At the same time, events like this were part and parcel of a broader process, already in train for some time, by which a national Aboriginal community and a pan-Aboriginal identity were forged in late

Aboriginal Survival Day concert, La Perouse, 26 January 1993.
(Copyright Ben Apfelbaum. Mitchell Library, State Library of
New South Wales)

twentieth-century Australia. It has long been observed that telling
stories about the past has been a resource for Aboriginal identity (or
Aboriginality), something which had been previously evident in
small-scale settings such as in local communities and in families,
but which was becoming more obvious on a national scale. The
sense that Aboriginal people across Australia were now part of an
imagined national Aboriginal community which transcended geography was both produced and made palpable on these alternative
Australia Day celebrations. Even if people could not attend the
concerts in person, they were known and shared events, able to be
participated in virtually because they received considerable media
coverage, including television. For those who did attend, the sensa-
tion of belonging to 'the Aboriginal community' was literally
experienced through being in the presence of other Aborigines. 'I
came here because I needed to be around black people,' one Aboriginal participant told a journalist. 'Coming here gives you a sense
of belonging.'[11] On a more symbolic level, the trope of community,

or of belonging to a national family, was reiterated through the statements that the performers made to the press, and through the typical media representation of the concert, in which the apparent fact of survival as a distinct cultural group within the Australian population was what bound together the members of this imagined indigenous community.

New historical traditions were being forged through these occasions. The Survival Day concert was conceived in part as a memorial to the protests, unprecedented in scope, that had been staged in 1988, when Aborigines had first come together in such large numbers to voice their collective grievances and demands. The concerts were therefore another Aboriginal re-enactment of sorts, and thus were sometimes grafted on to that longer tradition, which included the various mourning ceremonies held since 1938, whereby Aboriginal people challenged national forms of history that denied their own historical experiences. Harold Stewart, the chairman of the La Perouse Aboriginal Land Council when the first Survival Day concert was staged in 1992, was reported as saying that 'people come together to mark what was the biggest Aboriginal gathering in Australia's history', referring to the 1988 protests.[12] The idea for the concerts had emerged directly out of the 1988 protests, and at one level had been an attempt to capture some of the strength that Aboriginal people had experienced when they were gathered together in one place with Aboriginal people from all parts of Australia to express a collective grievance.[13] Two people who had been a motivating force behind the inaugural Survival Day concert in 1992, Rosalie Graham and Peter MacKenzie, were both originally from La Perouse on Botany Bay, having grown up there in the 1940s and 1950s. When publicly explaining what had motivated them to stage the concert, they consistently referred to the gathering of Aboriginal people from different corners of Australia at Yarra Bay House at La Perouse in January 1988 as their inspiration.

This part of Botany Bay was an ideal stage for the concerts for other significant reasons. In the developmental stage, Rosalie Graham had pushed La Perouse as the location because, as she told Leah Purcell in a documentary: 'We wanted an awareness to come out to the wider community that La Perouse has always been a community here—there's still a community and it was before the onslaught of invasion.'[14] Continuity of an Aboriginal presence in the place—that there were Aboriginal people there before whites arrived and there were Aboriginal people there 200 years later—was what mattered. Whatever the historical realities in the interim between first arrival and the contemporary moment, the fact of an Aboriginal presence in a place that had been the site for national foundational events was powerful. 'La Perouse was chosen,' one newspaper report claimed in 1992, 'because it was the site of the first landings by British and French explorers. La Perouse is also significant because it is the only area in metropolitan Sydney where an Aboriginal community has survived more than 200 years of European settlement.'[15] Like the various other protests before it, the Survival Day concerts both derived their symbolic meaning and power from their stage at Botany Bay, and breathed new life into and added new meaning to that already layered locality. The Survival Day concerts held on the fore-shores of Botany Bay on Australia Day insisted that there was no history of Australia without the history of Aboriginal people.

Reclaiming the landscape

Before, during and immediately after the large national Aboriginal protests in January 1988, local Botany Bay Aboriginal people were faced with the prospect of a plethora of new memorial gestures and structures to mark 1788 *and all that*. One of the more ambitious, and indeed bizarre, was a scheme for the establishment of a 24-hectare heritage park and a year-long heritage festival at the site of Captain Phillip's first landing at Botany Bay in 1788. Its centre-piece was to be a geodesic dome in which live, simulated displays of traditional Aboriginal life would be performed. The proposed dome and surrounding area were to be designed to include a space for corroborees, decorated with rock engravings and paintings, shell middens and streams. Along with the dome, there was a proposal to construct a First Fleet centre that would tell the story of the fleet's long journey from Portsmouth to Botany Bay and include a re-enactment of the meeting between Captain Phillip and the local indigenous population.[16] The envisioned re-enactment of the meeting between Phillip and indigenous people was designed to emphasise its supposed friendliness and to promote the theme of the bicentennial year: 'Living Together'. The aim of the entire project was to reconstruct as authentically as possible the moment of contact in 1788, and thus a major component of the scheme was the rehabilitation of the area to make it the way it was when Phillip first set eyes on it.

After efforts to secure funding failed, the project was scaled down and proposals were made simply to landscape the park area around Phillip's landing place monument (discussed in Chapter 5). The garden design which eventually won the contract retained some interpretive elements of the original scheme—the reported friendliness of the meeting between Captain Phillip and local Aboriginal people in 1788, for instance. This was symbolised by trees planted in a circular design to represent, according to the winning landscape architects, 'a neutral meeting place'.[17] The entire design was explicitly shaped by a sanitised and depoliticised version of this significant colonial encounter, a version popular during the bicentenary. 'Not a monument celebrating or apologising for colonisation,' insisted the landscape architects in the submission that won the contract, 'but rather a space commemorating the meeting of two cultures which led to the birth of our country.'[18] This is gardener as interpreter of the past in the present. 'Just as the bulldozer desecrated the ground,' writes Paul Carter, 'so the landscape architect resacralises it.'[19]

The notion of this original encounter as a meeting of two cultures implies an equivalence between the two cultures that clearly did not exist. At the same time, the excessive concentration on the moment of meeting elides the subsequent history to which that initial encounter gave rise, confining the entire history of contact to one solitary event. The memorial acknowledged an Aboriginal presence, but ossified it in a fixed moment in time—the moment of contact. This demonstrates a very narrow historical vision, one that fails to take into account the historical experiences of Aboriginal people after that meeting, either at Botany Bay or elsewhere. Material evidence for some aspects of that post-1788 history was there in the landscape for all to see, simply by casting one's gaze in the direction of the local Aboriginal settlement, just a stone's throw from the newly refashioned parkland.

In the mid-1990s, local Aboriginal people engaged in their own form of memorial gardening, seeking to refashion the landscape through pre-colonial eyes. Around Yarra Bay House, the headquarters of the La Perouse Local Aboriginal Land Council, a group of Community Development Employment Project workers, involved in a training program as landscape gardeners, reclaimed a piece of land upon which to build a bush tucker track.[20] The track was in part designed as a re-creation of the landscape as it would have been pre-1788. It was replanted with native foliage, and structures associated with pre-contact Aboriginal life, such as gunyahs, were built. The track was dotted with wooden poles carved and painted with traditional designs, some giving indigenous names for features on the landscape. On the surface, the bush tucker track suggests a return to the pre-colonial past. But a tour of the track with the men and women who built it suggested that the project was less an effort to return to some distant past and more an attempt to restore to the present that which had been deemed to be lost. A tour of the track provided both an explanation of its genesis and construction, and the meanings, personal and otherwise, of various objects dotted along the path. The descriptions of the objects given by their makers cast them as contemporary expressions of an existing and evolving relationship to the place that drew upon symbols of Aboriginality based on pre-contact life as the language for telling new stories. As the guide told his or her own biography and story of association to the contemporary landscape of Botany Bay, the objects, while appearing as imitations of traditional objects, were brought to life as personal and intensely intimate texts.

Whale carving as monument

This development whereby traditional motifs were increasingly mobilised in local forms of Aboriginal history-making was also evident in projects aimed at protecting and conserving rock art around the bay that emerged during this post-1988 period. A project to re-groove the whale carving on the headland (discussed in Chapter 6) is one such example. By this period, the carving was literally disappearing: its erosion from exposure to the natural elements was hastened by increased air pollution due especially to the airport, Port Botany and the Kurnell oil refinery. Despite its fading, or perhaps because of it, the whale carving became increasingly significant to local Aboriginal people, and since the mid-1990s sustained efforts have been made to restore it to prevent its complete disappearance from the landscape. The process of seeking its restoration was initiated by members of the Individual Heritage Group, which had re-established itself as the Burraga Aboriginal History and Writing Group, along with some other concerned local Aboriginal people, including the sites officer employed by the Local Aboriginal Land Council. They worked in collaboration with staff of the Botany Bay National Park, which has management responsibility for the carving, and received assistance from the Australian Institute of Aboriginal and Torres Strait Islander Studies in Canberra. The project involved not only experimenting with technical ways in which the carving might be re-grooved some time in the future, but also recording its meanings and the stories that had become attached to it.

While earlier recordings by Mathews and Campbell detailed the exact location and accurately measured the dimensions of the carving, as well as provided the additional information that it was a 'bora' site, the emphasis in the recent recordings about the carving made by local Aboriginal people has been on explaining its contemporary significance to them. Indeed, the project to preserve this material trace from pre-contact times provided an occasion for telling some new stories about it, particularly ones that emphasised how it links people to place.

At Botany Bay, as elsewhere, tribal boundaries are unclear and the subject for contestation between groups. Many local Aborigines living on the north head claim that they belong to the Dharawal people, the tribal group that extends southward from Botany Bay along the coast at least to Jervis Bay, although perhaps further. There is some uncertainty about the pre-colonial northern limits of

Dharawal territory—whether it includes the north shore of Botany Bay or only extends as far as the southern one. Despite this, many Aboriginal people who lived on Botany Bay's north head in the late nineteenth century and during the twentieth century, and those living there now, identify as Dharawal. In recent years, some have deployed the whale carving to demonstrate that the land they live on is Dharawal land.

A large whale features in a 'Dreaming' story collected by R.H. Mathews in the late nineteenth century which explains the origin of the Dharawal people.[21] The story describes how the whale and his descendants swam up and down the coast at certain times of the year. This story is now associated with the whale on the headland. By attaching the recorded story to it, the now-faint whale carving on Botany Bay's north head is transformed into an *aide de memoire* for the original whale and its descendants. Through this type of re-signification, the whale carving bridges historical time to Dreaming time. This is not to rule out the possibility that the carving is connected to this story, or others like it. It might well be. Rather, it is to highlight that it has acquired new significance, deployed to support claims about tribal allegiances, in a period in which they matter a great deal, especially in the native title context of the 1990s. The linking of Dreaming story to the whale carving—connecting tradition to trace—occurred in a period in which local Aboriginal people were not only seeking to prove their own continuous connection to place, but also resisting the incursion of Aboriginal people from neighbouring groups who claimed, as part of their own native title applications, that the northern headland of Botany Bay belonged to a different tribal group. Native title requires Aboriginal people to transcend the historical period, for fear they get washed away by it, and return to a moment in which tribal boundaries were supposedly fixed. In this moment belonging to the late twentieth century, the whale carving and a whale story, both recorded in the late nineteenth century, were floated for a new narrative about how local Aboriginal people were connected to Botany Bay.

But this is to miss the carving's place in internal local politics, not at all imbricated in native title issues or the associated threat posed by neighbouring Aboriginal groups. As the headland continued to bend under the weight of memorials to the late eighteenth-century past, this enduring, although hardly visible, carving became an historical monument of sorts. This particular carving has received more attention than most because it is so proximate to the monuments to imperial and colonial pasts that dominate Botany Bay's north and south heads. The carving is adjacent to the French monuments and is on a trajectory leading directly to Captain Cook's Landing Place reserve at Kurnell. The whale-as-local-tribal-forefather counters the excessive memorialisation of other forefather figures on the headland.[22] For it to come to prominence as part of the headland's monument precinct, re-grooving is required, but this is not possible under current heritage legislation. In pursuit of this ultimate goal, the outline of the whale carving has been re-surveyed and a computerised model of it has been produced. This will be invaluable if, in the future, permission is granted by the relevant government authority to re-groove the carving in order to bring it back to visibility. For the time being, however, it continues to disappear slowly.

Botany Bay as reconciliation landscape

At the beginning of the twenty-first century, Botany Bay has become a landscape through which to return imaginatively to the original moment when Captain Cook arrived, in order to perform it differently or to confront its legacy. This began in earnest in the lead-up to the 2000 Sydney Olympic Games, when Botany Bay became the stage for the opening of the Olympic Arts Festival. The Olympic Arts Festival was launched by a three-part performance called *Tubowgule* (pronounced tie-bah-gool), choreographed by the Bangarra Dance Theatre. *Tubowgule* means 'meeting of the waters' in the language spoken by indigenous people living around the new British colony at Port Jackson, the language and the people now commonly referred to as Eora. The performance comprised a series of 'welcoming ceremonies'—one at dawn, one at noon and one at dusk—staged at three different venues in Sydney. A beach just inside the north head of Botany Bay was the location for the dawn ceremony. Huddled in the pre-dawn darkness on a cold August morning on a beach looking out to the Botany Bay heads, the audience, many of them international journalists, witnessed a highly stylised performance. There was no clear narrative, but lots of symbols. A circle in red, black and yellow marked out the performance space on the sand. The Aboriginal opera singer Deborah Cheetham sang hauntingly in the early morning light, while local Aboriginal children danced. Some wore grey blankets, reminiscent of the government-issued ones given to Aboriginal people in the colonial period. The finale was the launching of a burning sculptural raft made from eucalyptus. Could this have been an effigy of Cook's ship? From comments overheard among those who witnessed the performance, many (and I would include myself among them) were not sure what it had all meant, but there was certainly a strong sense that it was Aboriginal people who were in control of the storyline this time. The opening scene was being played by those who were on the beach.

In a subsequent effort to give greater visibility to the meaning of Botany Bay for those on the beach, a proposal was made to rename Botany Bay National Park as Kamay Botany Bay National Park. The gesture, according to those behind it, was to show that 'when Cook turned up there were already people here'.[23] Similarly, the New South Wales National Parks and Wildlife Service is now actively including local Aboriginal people in annual commemorations of Captain Cook's arrival in Botany Bay. As part of these commemorations, wreaths are cast on the water, drawing yet again on past Aboriginal memorial events emphasising mourning while at the same time evoking the continuing theme that the meaning of Cook's arrival has another side. But this is less a protest than a symbolic acknowledgment of a pre-existing presence and an act of remembrance for the loss that has occurred between then and now. The act of casting wreaths marks both death *and* survival. Similarly, local National Aboriginal and Islander Day of Commemoration (NAIDOC) celebrations are regularly held at Captain Cook's Landing Place reserve, also organised in collaboration with the staff of the Botany Bay National Park. Rather than an explicit protest against colonial histories, these ceremonies are now incorporated

Tubowgule, ceremonial performance at Congwong Beach, Sydney,
18 August 2000. (Loui Seselja. National Library of Australia)

into, and form part of, the process whereby Botany Bay is being
inscribed as a type of origin point for what is characterised as a
shared history. This is Botany Bay as reconciliation landscape.

And so when, in April 2001, a replica *Endeavour* sailed into
Botany Bay, the commemorations surrounding its arrival could
deviate considerably from previous Cook re-enactments. Rather
than a re-enactment with verisimilitude, perhaps accompanied by
Aboriginal protest, the man playing the part of Captain Cook did
something that had not been in the original script: he asked permission to come ashore. Attuned to the post-colonial sensitivities now
surrounding the original encounter, the twenty-first century Captain
Cook sought to perform the landing in a way that was acceptable to
those on the shore. As he stepped ashore, he asked for permission

from the locals to land. A local Aboriginal woman, Beryl Beller, was there to receive his request. She asked whether he had come in peace, and when he said he had, she welcomed him ashore.

The landing was followed by a weekend of activities, dubbed the Festival of the Sails, organised by the local municipal council. It finished on a Sunday afternoon with a 'meeting of the two cultures' ceremony staged at Captain Cook's Landing Place reserve. Beryl Beller opened the ceremony with a welcome to country speech. In a mode consistent with other forms of local Aboriginal history-making at Botany Bay over the previous hundred or so years, she used her speech to draw continuities between a local present and the national past commemorated. She identified herself as a descendant of those who had been on shore when Captain Cook arrived the first time, and went further by saying that she was feeling what they had felt. Before welcoming the audience to country, she asserted ownership of the land by describing it as 'our land'. By this means she reinstated her right to welcome.

The various commemorative performances staged that week did not amount to re-enactments of a past event. Rather, they constituted a reworking of that event and its meanings. Momentarily, a state of affairs that both sides (perhaps) desired was instated. On the white side, it was possible to imagine that they had done the right thing: asked permission to come ashore and in turn been welcomed; on the black, it was possible that, despite the arrival of whites after Cook, their sovereignty had been retained. But neither proposition was true. For this reason the festival constituted a mode of reconciliation that was less a reckoning with the past as it happened and more an effort to transcend the burden of that past by performing and imagining it in more palatable, and indeed benign, terms. The headline of an article about the welcome that Beryl Beller extended to Chris Blake, the captain of the replica *Endeavour*, perhaps summed it up best: 'Once more with feeling'. This suggests that the original encounter perhaps could have been done properly the first time, if only those involved were as enlightened as the present generation.

In this same period, some non-Aboriginal artists, writers and film-makers had already begun to play around with Botany Bay's foundational meanings, using it as a place to raise questions about the psychological pull that origins can have on individuals and nations alike. Margot Nash's film *Vacant Possession* released in 1994 is in this genre. It uses Botany Bay for a-return-to-origins story, but constantly overlays the protagonist's story with elements in the national past. The locked cupboard of the protagonist Tessa's psyche is simultaneously the 'locked cupboard of Australian history'.[24] The doubled meaning in the film's title signals its interest in the troubled and ambiguous foundational moment in the nation's past when the British claimed the country as their own. It asks the viewer: Is possession a hollow reality? Was it illegitimate? Was the land empty or vacant when originally possessed?

In the film, Tessa, a professional gambler, returns, after her mother's death, to her family home at Kurnell on the south side of Botany Bay, and there meets again an Aboriginal family who she had grown up with. The mystery at the centre of the film is her relationship as a teenager with an Aboriginal boy, a relationship that functions as a metaphor for the way in which the Australian past is a shared past. The film opens with a dream sequence, replete with familiar psychoanalytical concepts—death, a house, snakes, a womb. Tessa is dreaming that she is on a boat on Botany Bay. To the sound of lapping water, she explains:

> This dream returned to me again and again. I knew it was about home because it started here on a boat heading for Botany Bay—birthplace of a nation—my birthplace, my home. The heads lay in front of me like an entrance to a womb and the great land whispered behind it. All I could think of was that my mother was dying and I wouldn't reach her in time.[25]

This opening sets the tone and the theme of the film, communicating to its audience how the return (real and imaginary) to origins lies at the heart of the story that follows. This scene, and the film itself, can be interpreted as a quest, or a desire, to recover and uncover one's origins in the hope of grasping some sort of truth. In *Vacant Possession*, Tessa is both self and nation, and Botany Bay functions as a personal and a symbolic birthplace: it is the place where self and nation are simultaneously born and thus inseparable from each other. But it is also a place that one rejects, but in truth never totally escapes from. As an adult, Tessa returns to this birth-place, seeking some answers and looking for resolution. The film gestures towards the popular notion that reconciliation with the past, a coming to terms with one's origins, is critical in a process of acquiring self-knowledge—a concept now applied equally to indi-viduals and to nations.

At one level, *Vacant Possession* can be read as a deployment of the original encounter story as the stuff for imagining a new type of relationship between black and white, although arguably it remains a particularly 'white' story as the protagonist works through her own 'dark' past predominantly in order to complete her own process of self-realisation. In this way, it belongs very much to a late twentieth-century rhetoric about national maturity as being funda-mentally dependent on owning up to shameful past secrets in order to be liberated from their burden. In a memorable line towards the end of the film, Tessa says that 'there were so many questions left unanswered; so many stories still to tell. But that night I looked to the future, and to the past, for the first time without fear.'

'A meeting of cultures'

The development of Botany Bay as a site for reconciliation seems set to continue given that the New South Wales state government has endorsed and committed funds to a project to turn Captain Cook's Landing Place reserve into a site celebrating the 'meeting of cultures'. In his foreword to the Botany Bay National Park Plan of Management, endorsed on 27 May 2002, the Minister for the Environment explains that 'the role of Botany Bay National Park as a "meeting place" is a central theme for the park. The park offers a unique opportunity to explore the history of meetings between indigenous and other cultures in Australia.'[26] The definition of meeting place given in the plan of management incorporates both the past and present:

> The term 'meeting place' reflects the history of Botany Bay National Park as a key location in which peoples of different cultural backgrounds first

encountered each other. However, it also denotes an ongoing role for the park as a meeting place. The historic role of the park as the site of first meetings makes it uniquely appropriate as a place in which to discuss the broader and ongoing nature of cultural meetings in Australia, particularly in relation to the reconciliation process currently underway.[27]

This attempt to use the concept of first encounters—which in the plan of management includes both those between indigenous people and Cook in 1770 and indigenous people and Lapérouse in 1788—as a basis for reconciliation glosses over both the specific nature and broader historical context of those encounters as well as the histories of relations between colonisers and colonised after those encounters. What gets lost in this reworking of Botany Bay's historical significance as a reconciliation site is the tide of history that followed in the wake of Cook and Lapérouse. More disturbingly, the plan of management states that 'a precondition of this shift in emphasis is that the presentation and interpretation of the park reflects the meeting of cultures rather than the domination of one culture over another.'[28] But that was not the situation then; and it is not the situation now.

This is not the first time that Botany Bay has been imagined as an historic and historical meeting place. The same metaphor was used by E.W. O'Sullivan in 1906 when he suggested that Botany Bay was a place 'Where Three Histories Meet':

> Standing on the shore of the reserve which surrounds the first cable station at La Perouse, Botany Bay, the visitor looks upon the most historic scene in the southern world. Before him, on the southern shore, about a mile away, lies the landing place of Captain Cook. Within a few hundred yards of where the visitor stands is the anchorage of the First Fleet, and around him is the soil trodden by La Perouse [sic].[29]

O'Sullivan is standing in the same spot I described in the opening lines of this book. If he were to stand there today, the Scenic Drive would encircle him. His notion of Botany Bay as a meeting place is significantly different from that currently being developed by the New South Wales National Parks and Wildlife Service and endorsed by the state government. O'Sullivan is not at all concerned with the meetings that took place between the locals and the visitors on each of those occasions. It is that Botany Bay has been the site for a series of significant historical events that constitutes the stuff of his 'meeting place' metaphor.

My use of O'Sullivan's description of Botany Bay as a place where histories meet in the subtitle for this book was intended to function in a different way yet again. My concern has been less with the most prominent past events that happened at Botany Bay, and more with the stories that have been persistently told about them, along with some other Botany Bay stories. Many of those stories might have something to say about the past, but we would not necessarily call them 'true stories'. They are ostensibly about the past, but more importantly they tell much about other things—about the shifting contours of Australian historical consciousness; about how the nation and its origins are imagined at different times; about the nature and quality of relations between Aborigines and various groups in the larger settler community. Some stories—particularly ones that might be characterised as national—elide other, usually more local ones. Others draw on the stuff of national stories in order to make a local point. Whatever the case, various Botany Bay stories exist in a dialogical relationship to each other. And, because of this, it is possible to think about Botany Bay as a place where histories meet. This is meeting in the sense of connecting and converging as well as colliding and clashing. The meeting that takes place between Botany Bay histories is not always easy, nor is it necessarily straightforward. Yet it is within the interconnection between stories, however fraught or fragile, that much of their meaning can be found. This is Botany Bay as historic meeting place.

NOTES

1 Paul Carter used *The Road to Botany Bay* as the title for his ground-breaking book on spatial history. Carter's work has influenced my study of Botany Bay in terms of thinking about how place is culturally produced through language. In my study, I wanted to show how that cultural process works on the ground and so I have begun it by overlaying Carter's now well-known metaphor to an actual road to Botany Bay.

2 Others involved in the work were Gloria Ardler, Beryl Beller, Clara Mason, Lee-Anne Mason, Sharon Williams and Leslie Davison. In 1990 they formed the Burraga Aboriginal History and Writing Group.

3 My interest in Aboriginal people's history-making is inspired by and draws upon the work of historians and anthropologists Deborah Bird Rose, Jeremy Beckett, Diane Barwick, Gillian Cowlishaw, Bain Attwood and Heather Goodall, who have shown how the act of telling stories about the past is a vital resource for Aboriginal people in producing new forms of identity in the colonial context, as well as critical, more generally, to shaping relations between various settler communities and colonised people in the post-1770 period. See especially: Deborah Bird Rose, 'Remembrance', *Aboriginal History*, vol. 13, nos 1–2, 1989, pp. 135–48; Jeremy Beckett, 'Walter Newton's history of the world—or Australia', *American Ethnologist*, vol. 20, no. 4, 1993, pp. 675–95; Jeremy Beckett (ed.), *Past and Present: The Construction of Aboriginality*, Aboriginal Studies Press, Canberra, 1988, especially J. Beckett, 'The past in the present; the present in the past: Constructing a national Aboriginality', K. Maddock, 'Myth, history and a sense of oneself' and L. Coltheart, 'The moment of Aboriginal history'; Barry Morris, 'Making histories/living history', *Social Analysis*, no. 27, April 1990, pp. 83–92; Gillian Cowlishaw, *Blackfellas, Whitefellas, and the Hidden Injuries of Race*, Blackwell Publishers, Malden, 2004; Bain Attwood and Fiona Magowan (eds), *Telling Stories: Indigenous History and Memory in Australia and New Zealand*, Allen & Unwin, Sydney, 2001; Bain Attwood (ed.), *In the Age of Mabo: History, Aborigines and Australia*, Allen & Unwin, Sydney, 1996; Heather Goodall, 'The whole truth and nothing but . . .': Some interactions of western law, Aboriginal history and community memory', in

B. Attwood and J. Arnold (eds), *Power, Knowledge and Aborigines*, La Trobe University Press, Melbourne, 1992; Heather Goodall, 'Colonialism and catastrophe: Contested memories of nuclear testing and measles epidemics at Ernabella', in K. Darian-Smith and P. Hamilton (eds), *Memory and History in Twentieth-century Australia*, Oxford University Press, Melbourne, 1994, pp. 55–76; Diane Barwick, 'Writing Aboriginal history: Comments on a book and its reviewers', *Canberra Anthropology*, vol. 4, no. 2, 1981, pp. 74–86.

4 Dolores Hayden, *The Power of Place: Urban Landscapes as Public History*, MIT Press, Boston, 1995, p. 9.

5 Maurice Halbwachs, *The Collective Memory*, first published 1950, trans. F. J. Ditter, Harper and Row, New York, 1980.

6 Patrick Hutton, *History as an Art of Memory*, University of New England Press, Hanover, 1993, p. 80.

7 Pierre Nora (ed.), *Realms of Memory: The Construction of the French Past*, vols 1–3, trans. Arthur Goldhammer, Eng. Language edn, Columbia University Press, New York, 1996–1998.

Chapter 1

1 *The Endeavour Journal of Joseph Banks: 1768–1771*, ed. J.C. Beaglehole, The Trustees of the Public Library of New South Wales in association with Angus & Robertson, Sydney, 1962, p. 50.

2 Paul Carter, *The Road to Botany Bay: An Essay in Spatial History*, Faber and Faber, London, 1987; J.C. Beaglehole, 'Textual introduction', in *The Journals of Captain James Cook, Volume 1, The Voyage of the Endeavour, 1768–1771*, ed. J.C. Beaglehole, Hakluyt Society at Cambridge University Press, Cambridge, 1968, p. cciv.

3 Greg Dening, 'MS1 Cook, J. Holograph Journal', in *Remarkable Occurrences: The National Library of Australia's First 100 Years 1901–2001*, ed. P. Cochrane, National Library of Australia, Canberra, 2001, p. 14, notes that 'Cook is enjoying himself creating names for all these new sights'.

4 *The Endeavour Journal of Joseph Banks: 1768–1771*, p. 50.

5 According to Greg Dening, the journal is the 'foundation document of the National Library of Australia'. Dening, 'MS1 Cook, J. Holograph Journal', p. 1.

6   *The Journals of Captain James Cook, Volume 1, The Voyage of the Endeavour, 1768–1771*, p. 310.

7   *The Endeavour Journal of Joseph Banks: 1768–1771*, p. 54.

8   ibid., p. 63.

9   ibid., p. 53.

10 *The Journals of Captain James Cook, Volume 1, The Voyage of the Endeavour, 1768–1771*, p. 306.

11 Sylvia Hallam, 'A view from the other side of the western frontier: or "I met a man who wasn't there . . .'", *Aboriginal History*, vol. 7, no. 2, 1983, p. 134.

12 ibid., p. 134.

13 Keith Willey, *When the Sky Fell Down: The Destruction of the Tribes of the Sydney Region, 1788–1850s*, Collins, Sydney, 1979, p. 51.

14 There is evidence from other parts of the continent that cross-cultural encounters were remembered for some time. For instance, Hallam refers to a ceremony first performed in 1801 during the time that navigator Matthew Flinders was at King George Sound, which was apparently still being performed a hundred years later. See Hallam, 'A view from the other side of the western frontier', p. 145.

15 Deborah Bird Rose, 'Hard times: An Australian study', in *Quicksands: Foundational Histories in Australia and Aotearoa New Zealand*, eds K. Neumann, N. Thomas and H. Ericksen, UNSW Press, Sydney, p. 5.

16 Inge Clendinnen, *Dancing with Strangers*, Text Publishing, Melbourne, 2003, p. 5.

17 *The Endeavour Journal of Joseph Banks: 1768–1771*, p. 59.

18 Nicholas Thomas, *Discoveries: The Voyages of Captain Cook*, Allen Lane, London, 2003, p. 114.

19 *The Journals of Captain James Cook, Volume 1, The Voyage of the Endeavour, 1768–1771*, p. 310.

20 A historian, Keith Smith, is now challenging the view that no language was recorded at Botany Bay in 1770, on the basis of three word lists reportedly compiled 'by three men from Cook's HM Bark *Endeavour*'. See Deborah Jopson, 'Endeavour crew's language lists throw new light on first contact', *Sydney Morning Herald*, 5 April 2003, p. 13.

21 Beaglehole, 'Textual introduction', in *The Journals of Captain James Cook, Volume 1, The Voyage of the Endeavour, 1768–1771*, p. ccix.

22 Beaglehole, 'Textual introduction', in *The Journals of Captain James Cook,*

Volume 1, The Voyage of the Endeavour, 1768–1771, and Thomas, *Discoveries,* trace Cook's development as a writer. See also Beaglehole, *Cook The Writer,* Sixth Arnold Wood Memorial Lecture, Sydney University Press, Sydney, 1970.

23 J.B. Hirst, *Convict Society and its Enemies: A History of Early New South Wales,* Allen & Unwin, Sydney, 1983, p. 196.

24 L.L. Robson, *The Convict Settlers of Australia: An Enquiry into the Origin and Character of the Convicts Transported to New South Wales and Van Diemen's Land 1787–1852,* Melbourne University Press, Melbourne, 1965, p. 16.

25 Hirst, *Convict Society and its Enemies,* p. 189.

26 *A Description of a wonderful large wild man, or monstrous giant, brought from Botany-Bay,* Pictures Collection, Mitchell Library, SV/44.

27 Michael Taussig, *Shamanism, Colonialism and the Wild Man: A Study in Terror and Healing,* University of Chicago Press, Chicago, 1986, p. 211.

28 Robert Holden, *Bunyips: Australia's Folklore of Fear,* National Library of Australia, Canberra, 2001, p. 46.

29 Julian Thomas, 'A history of beginnings', in *Quicksands: Foundational Histories in Australia and Aotearoa New Zealand,* eds K. Neumann, N. Thomas and H. Ericksen, UNSW Press, Sydney, p. 128.

30 Alan Frost, *Botany Bay Mirages: Illusions of Australia's Convict Beginnings,* Melbourne University Press, Melbourne, 1994, p. 7.

31 See for example Manning Clark, 'The choice of Botany Bay', *Historical Studies,* vol. 9, no. 35, November 1960, pp. 221–30.

32 L.R. Macintyre, 'Botany Bay', in *Some Australians Take Stock,* ed. J.C.G. Kevin, Longmans, Green & Co, London, 1939, p. 39.

33 Thomas, 'A history of beginnings', p. 130.

34 For an example that evokes Botany Bay, see Portia Robinson, *The Women of Botany Bay: A Reinterpretation of the Role of Women in the Origins of Australian Society,* Macquarie Library, Sydney, 1988.

35 Thomas, 'A history of beginnings', p. 130.

36 When I was the Nancy Keesing Fellow at the State Library of New South Wales in 2002, Richard Neville, Original Materials Librarian at the Mitchell Library, told me about James Martin's piece on Botany Bay and described it to me as the 'first intellectual study' of the place.

37 James Martin, *The Australian Sketch Book,* James Tegg, Sydney, 1838, pp. 45–6.

38   'At La Perouse and Botany Bay', *Illustrated Sydney News*, 4 July 1891, p. 13.

39   Charles H. Bertie, 'Captain Cook and Botany Bay', *The Royal Australian Historical Society Journal and Proceedings*, vol. x, part v, 1924, pp. 233–78. Bertie was librarian of the City of Sydney from 1909 to 1939 and a Fellow of the Royal Australian Historical Society. See Thomas, 'A history of beginnings', pp. 115, 126.

40   Cited in Bertie, 'Captain Cook and Botany Bay', p. 233.

41   Bertie, 'Captain Cook and Botany Bay', p. 233.

42   Thomas, 'A history of beginnings', p. 117.

43   Chris Healy, *From the Ruins of Colonialism: History as Social Memory*, Cambridge University Press, Melbourne, 1997, p. 22; Bertie, 'Captain Cook and Botany Bay', pp. 246–7.

44   Bertie, 'Captain Cook and Botany Bay', p. 237.

45   ibid., p. 238.

46   Jeremy Beckett, 'Aboriginality in a nation-state: The Australian case', in M.C. Howard ed., *Ethnicity and Nation-Building in the Pacific*, United Nations University, Tokyo, 1989, p. 124.

47   Cited in Bertie, 'Captain Cook and Botany Bay', p. 263.

48   Retta Long, *Providential Channels*, Australian Inland Mission, Sydney, 1935, p. 13. 'Moomiga', according to Long, was the 'great, evil spirit, of whom they were all their life held in fear'.

49   *Minutes of Evidence taken before the Select Committee on the Aborigines*, 1845.

50   Cited in Maryanne Larkin, *Sutherland Shire: A History to 1939*, Sutherland History Press, Sydney, 1998, p. 5.

51   ibid., p. 5.

52   D.M. Cooper, *Randwick 1859–1909*, Randwick Municipal Council, Sydney, 1909, p. 1.

53   Joan Kerr, 'Strange objects: A special kind of identity', in *Remarkable Occurrences*, p. 102.

54   Richard Neville, *A Rage for Curiosity: Visualising Australia 1788–1830*, State Library of New South Wales Press, Sydney, p. 10.

55   Holden, *Bunyips*, p. 76.

56   James Clifford, *Routes: Travel and Translation in the Late Twentieth Century*, Harvard University Press, Cambridge, MA, 1997, pp. 188–219.

57   Peter Cochrane, 'Introduction', *Remarkable Occurrences*, p. vii.

Chapter 2

1   *The Voyage of Governor Phillip to Botany Bay*, Angus & Robertson in association with the Royal Australian Historical Society, Sydney, 1970, p. 46.

2   *The Governor's Noble Guest: Hyacinthe de Bougainville's Account of Port Jackson, 1825*, trans. and ed. Marc Serge Rivière, The Miegunyah Press, Melbourne, 1999, p. 110.

3   Francis Myers, *Botany Bay: Past and Present*, John Woods & Company, Sydney, 1885, p. 14.

4   In this period, spatial isolation was mainly justified in terms of protecting colonial metropolitan society from the supposedly contaminating influence of undesirable others. Ann Curthoys has shown this in relation to Aboriginal people and Stephen Garton has done so in relation to the insane. See Ann Curthoys, 'Race and ethnicity: A study of the response of British colonists to Aborigines, Chinese and non British Europeans in New South Wales, 1856–1881', PhD thesis, Macquarie University, 1973; Stephen Garton, *Medicine and Madness: A Social History of Insanity in New South Wales 1880–1940*, University of New South Wales Press, Sydney, 1988.

5   'Report of the Board of Health upon the late epidemic of small-pox, 1881–2', *JNSWLC*, vol. 34, part 2, 1883, p. 357.

6   *NSW Government Gazette*, 6 December 1881, p. 6299.

7   Alison Bashford, 'Epidemic and governmentality: Smallpox in Sydney 1881', *Critical Public Health*, vol. 9, no. 4, 1999, pp. 301–16.

8   'Report of the Board of Health upon the late epidemic of small-pox, 1881–2', p. 362.

9   ibid.

10   David Collins, *An Account of the English Colony in New South Wales*, Australiana Facsimile Editions no. 76, reproduced by the Libraries Board of South Australia, Adelaide, 1971, p. 65.

11   Obed West, *Old and New Sydney*, reprinted from the *Sydney Morning Herald* by Edward Hordern and Sons, Sydney, 1882, vol. 6, p. 29.

12   Shirley Fitzgerald, *Rising Damp: Sydney 1870–90*, Oxford University Press, Melbourne, 1985, esp. Ch 3, pp. 69–100.

13   'Report of the Board of Health upon the late epidemic of small-pox, 1881–2', p. 358.

14   Elizabeth Grosz, 'Bodies-cities', *Sexuality and Space*, ed. Beatriz

Columina, *Princeton Papers on Architecture*, Princeton, New Jersey, 1992, p. 242.

15   'Report of the Board of Health upon the late epidemic of small-pox, 1881–2', p. 362.

16   NSW Board of Health, 'Report on Coast Hospital, Little Bay, 1884', *JNSWLC*, vol. 40, part 1, 1885–86, p. 883.

17   Curthoys, 'Race and ethnicity', p. 176.

18   ibid., p. 220.

19   ibid., p. 231.

20   'Report of the Protector of Aborigines, to 31 December 1882, Senior-Constable Byrne to Protector of Aborigines, 17 January 1883', *JNSWLC*, vol. 34, part 2, 1883, p. 315.

21   Daniel Matthews Papers, Diary, 4 May 1881, Mitchell Library.

22   *Sydney Morning Herald*, 17 January 1883, p. 6.

23   'Report of the Protector of Aborigines, to 31 December 1882', p. 315.

24   'Report of the Protector of Aborigines, to 31 December 1882', Appendix A, from Aboriginals William Foot and others to the Protector of the Aborigines, La Perouse, 20 January 1883, p. 317.

25   Daphne Salt, *Kurnell—Birthplace of Modern Australia: A Pictorial History*, Clarion House, Sydney, 2000, p. 29.

26   In May 1881, Bundong reportedly 'fell from a roof of a bus and was killed'. See 'Report of the Protector of Aborigines, to 31 December 1882, Senior-Constable Byrne to Protector of Aborigines, 17 January 1883', *JNSWLC*, vol. 34, part 2, 1883, p. 315.

27   ibid.

28   'A visit to the blacks' camp at La Perouse', *Sydney Morning Herald*, 16 January 1883, p. 5.

29   For details about another Aboriginal reserve settlement in the broader Sydney landscape in this same period, see Jack Brooks, *Shut Out From the World: The Hawkesbury Aborigines Reserve and Mission, 1889–1946*, Deerubbin Press, Sydney, 2nd edn, rev, 1999.

30   'Report of the Protector of Aborigines, to 31 December 1882', p. 311.

31   Curthoys, 'Race and ethnicity', p. 240.

32   'Report of the Protector of Aborigines, to 31 December 1882', p. 311.

33   'Letter to the editor', *Sydney Morning Herald*, 6 January 1883, p. 5.

34   Two correspondents in 1883 refer to the beach near the 'Blacks' Camp' at La Perouse by this name. One noted that the camp was situated near

'a beach called Cooriwal (I am not sure about the spelling, but I have very good authority of the pronunciation which I have endeavoured to indicate)'. The other, George Hill, a local from Botany, wrote in a letter to the editor of the *Sydney Morning Herald* that 'I very often go to Currewol, where the blacks are camped, almost a stone's throw of La Perouse'. Both appear in the *Sydney Morning Herald*, 16 January 1883, p. 5. In the twentieth century, the word is often written as Koorewal or Gooriwaal.

35 E.J. Telfer, *Amongst Australian Aborigines: Forty Years of Missionary Work. The Story of the United Aborigines' Mission*, Printed by Fraser & Morphet, Sydney, 1939, p. 107. For other examples of relocations to La Perouse, see NSWAPB, Minutes, 2 August and 15 August 1895, 4/7109.

36 'Special Lease at La Perouse (Correspondence)', *V&PLANSW*, 1887.

37 NSWAWB, Correspondence, Letter from Mr Trescoe Rowe to the NSWAWB, 18 May 1966, SRNSW, 8/3017.

38 A Miss Baker was an active member of the La Perouse Aborigines Mission established in the early 1890s, and lived for many years in its mission house at the La Perouse Aboriginal Settlement.

39 W.E.H. Stanner exposed the structures of forgetting at the heart of twentieth-century Australian historiography in his ABC Boyer Lectures aired in 1968 and published as *After the Dreaming*.

40 These types of claims are gradually being supported by archival research. Recent historical research, particularly about Botany Bay's southern shore, reveals that there were Aboriginal people living around the southern shore during the period from the 1830s to the 1880s. This concurs with historical research about other parts of the broader Sydney landscape, which is revealing a strong Aboriginal presence in the first half of the nineteenth century.

41 Jeremy Beckett uses the term 'beat' to describe Aboriginal patterns of movement in the post-contact period in western New South Wales. See J. Beckett, 'Kinship, mobility and community in rural New South Wales', in *Being Black: Aboriginal Cultures in Settled Australia*, ed. I. Keen, Aboriginal Studies Press, Canberra, pp. 117–36.

42 Sue Zelinka, *Tender Sympathies: A Social History of Botany Cemetery and the Eastern Suburbs Crematorium*, Hale & Iremonger, Sydney, 1991.

43 Terry Kass, 'Long Bay Complex 1896–1994: A History', unpublished final report for NSW Public Works, Sydney, March 1995.

44 Jan Morris, *Sydney*, Viking, London, 1992, p. 77.

45   Max Kelly, 'Introduction', in *Sydney—City of Suburbs*, ed. M. Kelly, UNSW Press, Sydney, 1987, p. 7.

46   Kelly, *Sydney—City of Suburbs*, p. 10.

47   John Pilger, *A Secret Country*, Vintage, London, 1990, p. 23.

48   Ruth Park, *The Companion Guide to Sydney*, Collins, Sydney, 1972, p. 427. Park's guide was revised in 1999, and it included some details about the local Aboriginal community that appears to draw primarily from *La Perouse: The Place, the People and the Sea*, Aboriginal Studies Press, Canberra, 1988.

Chapter 3

1   NSWAPB, Minutes, 9 February 1893, SRNSW, 4/7108; *NSW Government Gazette*, 30 March 1895, p. 2169.

2   Ann Curthoys, 'Race and ethnicity: A study of the response of British colonists to Aborigines, Chinese and non British Europeans in New South Wales, 1856–1881', PhD thesis, Macquarie University, 1973, p. 245.

3   Maryanne Larkin, *Sutherland Shire: A History to 1939*, Sutherland History Press, Sydney, 1998, p. 10.

4   ibid., p. 13.

5   'Captain Cook's landing; Celebrations at Kurnell', *Daily Telegraph*, 29 April 1905.

6   'The Captain Cook Anniversary', *Sydney Morning Herald*, 28 April 1905.

7   Interview, Annie Starr, NSW Bicentennial Oral History Project, National Library of Australia.

8   'The vanishing Aboriginal of Australia', *The Globe Pictorial*, 4 July 1914, p. 1.

9   'Report of Protector of Aborigines for 1882' and 'Report of Board of Protection of Aborigines for 1890, 1891 and 1892'.

10   The La Perouse snake show's original proprietor was a Professor Fred Fox, a professional showman who advertised himself as 'half snake juice, half English'. Others followed him, including Garnet See who reportedly died from a snakebite on his first day.

11   Interview, George Cann (Jnr), MN 1.

12   Gloria Ardler, 'When we were children', *La Perouse: The Place, the People and the Sea*, Aboriginal Studies Press, Canberra, 1988, p. 61.

13 F.W. Allen, 'Tourist section', in *Randwick 1859–1909*, comp. D.M. Cooper, Randwick Municipal Council, Sydney, 1909, p. 37.

14 'Lord Jellicoe', *Sydney Mail*, 20 August 1919, p. 1; *Australian Aborigines' Advocate*, no. 327, 1 August 1928, p. 12.

15 Interview, Pam Koeneman, Talking Lapa Oral History Collection, NSW Office of Board of Studies, NSW.

16 Interview, Ruth Simms, Talking Lapa Oral History Collection, NSW Office of Board of Studies, NSW.

17 'Lord Jellicoe', *Sydney Mail*, p. 1.

18 *Dawn*, 1 September 1956, p. 4.

19 Report of Aborigines Protection Board for 1890.

20 Ruth B. Phillips, 'Why not tourist art? Significant silences in Native American museum representations', *After Colonialism: Imperial Histories and Postcolonial Displacements*, ed. Gyan Prakash, Princeton University Press, Princeton, New Jersey, 1995, p. 103.

21 See La Perouse Aboriginal Community Oral History Collection, Museum of Applied Arts and Sciences, and Talking Lapa Oral History Collection, NSW Board of Studies.

22 Interview, Gladys Ardler, NSW Bicentennial Oral History Project, National Library of Australia.

23 Interview, Gladys Ardler, NSW Bicentennial Oral History Project, National Library of Australia.

24 I am indebted to Ilaria Vanni for this insight. Ilaria Vanni, '"When Jimmy Cook arrived": The production of artefacts at La Perouse', unpublished paper presented at Symbolic Souvenirs, a one-day conference on cultural tourism, Centre for Cross-cultural Research, ANU, April 1998.

25 James Clifford, *The Predicament of Culture: Twentieth-century Ethnography, Literature and Art*, Harvard University Press, Cambridge, MA, 1988, p. 1. This partly explains the relative lack of early anthropological work among Aboriginal people in New South Wales compared with northern parts of Australia where Aborigines were considered to be less touched by colonial influence.

26 See W.E.H. Stanner, 'The Aborigines', *Some Australians Take Stock*, ed. J.C.G. Kevin, Longmans, Green & Co., London, 1939, p. 5.

27 Newspaper clipping, n.d., La Perouse Aboriginal Community Archive, Social History Section, MAAS.

28 *Sydney Wants to See You!* NSW Tramways, issued for the Railway Commissioners for NSW, 1928, p. 26.

29 Frederick D. McCarthy, *New South Wales Aboriginal Place Names and Euphonious Words, with their Meanings*, Australian Museum, Sydney, 1946, lists it as Koorewal meaning strong person; name of La Perouse, Botany Bay.

30 'King Burraga to Professor A.P. Elkin, President, Association for the Protection of Native Races', 16 January 1936, reproduced in B. Attwood and A. Markus, *The Struggle for Aboriginal Rights: A Documentary History*, Allen & Unwin, Sydney, 1999, p. 74.

31 Cited in Heather Goodall, *Invasion to Embassy: Land in Aboriginal Politics in New South Wales 1770–1972*, Allen & Unwin, Sydney, 1996, p. 170.

32 'Aborigines. Relics discovered. "Chief of the Five Islands"', *Sydney Morning Herald*, 14 September 1929, p. 21.

Chapter 4

1 This term was made popular by the French historical project overseen by Pierre Nora and published as *Lieux de Mémoire*. The phrase is translated in English as 'realms of memory'.

2 Jean-François de Galaup de la Perouse, *The Voyage of Jean-François de Galaup de la Perouse, 1785–1788*, trans. and ed. John Dunmore, Hakluyt Society, London, 1995, p. 539.

3 Jocelyn Linnekan, 'Ignoble savages and other European visions: The La Pérouse affair in Samoan history', *The Journal of Pacific History*, vol. xxvi, no. 1, June 1991, p. 7.

4 Dunmore, 'Appendix III', in *The Voyage of . . . la Perouse*, pp. 564–69.

5 *The Voyage of Governor Phillip to Botany Bay*, John Stockdale, London, 1789, reprinted Angus & Robertson in association with the Royal Australian Historical Society, Sydney, 1970, p. 68.

6 David Collins, *An Account of the English Colony in New South Wales*, Australiana Facsimile Editions no. 76, reproduced by the Libraries Board of South Australia, Adelaide, 1971, p. 17.

7 In respect to spelling the French navigator's name, Dunmore notes that 'anyone writing on La Pérouse is forced to make a choice between two widely used forms of the name: Lapérouse and La Pérouse' (p. xi). I use

the former in order to minimise confusion between La Perouse (the place) and Lapérouse (the man).

8   Carter, *The Road to Botany Bay*, p. 2, surveys Captain Cook's naming practices and describes some appellations as 'straightforwardly descriptive' and others as 'more fancifully evocative'.

9   See 'The Frenchmans Garden still flourishes', *Ports of New South Wales*, March 1982, pp. 12–13.

10 Translation from *Voyage Autour du monde sur la Corvette la* Coquille, par. Rene Primevere Lesson, P. Pourrat Fréres, Paris, 1838, in Henry Selkirk, 'La Perouse and the French monuments at Botany Bay', *JRAHS*, vol. 4, part 7, 1918, p. 350.

11 ibid., pp. 349–50.

12 Greg Dening, *Mr Bligh's Bad Language: Passion, Power and Theatre on the Bounty*, Cambridge University Press, Melbourne, 1992, p. 96.

13 Collins, *An Account of the English Colony in New South Wales*, p. 21. Watkin Tench, *1788: Comprising a Narrative of the Expedition to Botany Bay and a Complete Account of the Settlement at Port Jackson*, ed. Tim Flannery, Text Publishing, Melbourne, 1996, p. 62, acknowledged that Phillip's gesture reciprocated Lapérouse's restoration of the grave belonging to a crew member on Cook's third voyage: 'This mark of respectful attention was more particularly due from M. La Perouse having, when in Kamchatka, paid a similar tribute of gratitude to the memory of Captain Clarke, whose tomb was found in nearly as ruinous a state as that of the Abbe.'

14 Cited in Selkirk, 'La Perouse and the French monuments', p. 350.

15 ibid.

16 Obed West, *Old and New Sydney*, reprinted from the *Sydney Morning Herald* by Edward Hordern and Sons, Sydney, 1882, vol. 6, p. 22.

17 Healy, *From the Ruins of Colonialism*, p. 22.

18 Cited in Selkirk, 'La Perouse and the French monuments', p. 350.

19 ibid., pp. 351–52; *The Governor's Noble Guest: Hyacinthe de Bougainville's Account of Port Jackson, 1825*, trans. and ed. Marc Serge Rivière, The Miegunyah Press, Melbourne, 1999, p. 110.

20 Antoine Prost, 'Monuments to the dead', in *Realms of Memory*, p. 310.

21 *The Voyage of Jean-François de Galaup de la Perouse, 1785–1788*, p. 448.

22 Healy, *From the Ruins of Colonialism,* p. 25.

23 While the *NSW Calendar and General Post Office Directory*, Stephens & Stokes, Sydney, 1833–1837 mentioned the La Perouse monument, the

entire northern headland was referred to as Cape Banks, the name which Captain Cook had given the site. By 1879, the *Sand's Sydney and NSW Directory* lists La Perouse as a place of residence.

24 Images of the monument held by the Mitchell Library in Sydney include ones by Isabella Louisa Parry, Conrad Martens, Robert Russell, J. Austin, Robert Marsh Westmacott, William Leigh, Samuel Thomas Gill, Helena Forde, and Benjamin Warwick.

25 Candice Bruce, 'The prodigal tree stump', *Art and Australia*, vol. 25, no. 4, Winter 1988, pp. 496–99.

26 The comment is recorded in the 'The Journal of Governor King', in John Hunter, *An Historical Journal of Events at Sydney and at Sea, 1787–1792*, John Stockdale, London, 1793, reprinted Angus & Robertson in association with the Royal Australian Historical Society, Sydney, 1968, and in Tench, *1788*. It is cited in Ernest Scott, *Laperouse*, Angus & Robertson, Sydney, 1912, p. 76.

27 Advertisement placed by the Randwick Municipal Council in a local newspaper in 1930, RMC, press cuttings book, Bowen Library.

28 David Malouf, *The Spirit of Play*, ABC Books, Sydney, 1998, p. 27. The exhibition 'Terre Napoleon: Australia Through French Eyes' at the Museum of Sydney in 1999 provided an occasion for playing this game. While at the exhibition, I overheard a father tell his two young sons that Australia could have been French. In a slightly different mode, Ghassan Hage suggested at the 'Turning the Soil' conference, Canberra School of Art, May 1998, that some European migrants to Australia identified more strongly with Lapérouse than with Captain Cook.

29 *A Randwick Ramble, Part 3, La Perouse to Maroubra, A Guide to Historic Places from La Perouse to Maroubra*, 4th edn, Randwick and District Historical Society, Sydney, 1989, p. 3.

30 Ann Curthoys, 'Entangled histories: Conflict and ambivalence in non-Aboriginal Australia', in *The Resurgence of Racism: Howard, Hanson and the Race Debate*, eds G. Gray and C. Winter, Monash Publications in History, Melbourne, 1997, p. 121.

31 'Elders call for suburb name change', *Southern Courier*, 15 July 1997, p. 1.

32 'La Perouse. Historic ceremony. Land dedicated to France', *Sydney Morning Herald*, 16 July 1917; 'French land at Botany', *Daily Telegraph*, 17 July 1917.

33   As evidence of the way in which La Perouse (the place) was used for the expression of a national alliance between France and Australia, in 1919 a painting of the Lapérouse monument was presented by the Australian Prime Minister, William Hughes, to the French President, Puniere. See 'La pérouse monument', *Sydney Morning Herald*, 1 July 1919; Adrian Ashton, 'The La Perouse monument: A link with France', *B.P. Magazine*, 1 June 1934.

34   Selkirk, 'La Perouse and the French monuments', p. 330.

35   See 'Notes for Hon. R. J. Heffron, Minister for Education at ceremony at La Perouse Monument', 14 July 1945, Lapérouse Museum Archives, BBNP; 'Sir Samuel Walder's Speech', 14 July 1945, Lapérouse Museum Archives, BBNP.

36   'La Perouse anniversary. French ship recalls past', *Daily Telegraph*, 14 January 1959, p. 13.

37   'French connection', *Sydney Morning Herald*, 15 July 1975.

38   Lapérouse Museum, Sydney District National Parks and Wildlife Service, Sydney, 1988, p. 1.

39   Jacques Arago, *Narrative of a Voyage Around the World: In the* Uranie *and* Physcienne *Corvettes commanded by Captain Freycinet . . . 1817, 1818, 1819 and 1820*, Truettel, London, 1823.

40   These types of views were aired at a community consultation meeting convened by the NSW Premier's Department at the Lapérouse Museum in May 1998. See Maria Nugent, 'La Perouse versus Larpa: Contesting histories of place', *Public History Review*, vol. 5/6, 1996, pp. 192–9.

Chapter 5

1   See Charles H. Bertie, 'Captain Arthur Phillip's first landing place in Botany Bay', *JRAHS*, vol. 38, part 3, 1952, pp. 107–26; Royal Australian Historical Society, *Annual Report, 1954*, History House, Sydney. For a more recent inquiry into the landing place of Captain Phillip in Botany Bay, which challenges Bertie's findings, see Brian McDonald, *The Landing Place of Captain Arthur Phillip at Botany Bay*, Popinjay Publications' Australian Historical Monographs Series, no. 10, n.p., 1990.

2   Interview, Bob Wysocki, MN 3. For reference to unemployed families living in the Yarra Bay Pleasure Ground weekenders, see: 'Illegal

occupation Happy Valley—La Perouse 1931–40', Report, Metropolitan District Surveyor, 17 February 1931, NSW Department of Lands, Metropolitan Land Board, Special Bundle, SRNSW, 3/2417.4.

3 Heather Goodall, *Invasion to Embassy: Land in Aboriginal Politics in New South Wales, 1770–1972*, Allen & Unwin in association with Blackbooks, Sydney, 1996, p. 183.

4 Interview, Gladys Ardler, NSW Bicentennial Oral History Project, National Library of Australia.

5 'Governor's visit to La Perouse Camp', *Sydney Morning Herald*, 10 June 1931, p. 12.

6 For a debate about the historiography of the Depression, see: David Potts, 'A positive culture of poverty represented in memories of the 1930s Depression', *Journal of Australian Studies*, no. 26, May 1990, pp. 3–14; Joanne Scott and Kay Saunders, 'Happy days are here again? A reply to David Potts', *Journal of Australian Studies*, no. 36, March 1993, pp. 10–22. See also Peter Spearritt, 'Mythology of the Depression', in *The Wasted Years? Australia's Great Depression*, ed. J. Mackinolty, Allen & Unwin, Sydney, 1981, pp. 1–9.

7 For evidence of conflict within the camps see: 'Illegal occupation Happy Valley—La Perouse 1931–40', Report nos 31.214, 31.332, 32.104 and Letter & petition, Residents of Yarra Bay camp to Mr Wilson, Crown Lands Department, 24 October 1932, SRNSW, 3/2417.4; 'Police Courts, Disturbance at unemployed camp', *Sydney Morning Herald*, 20 October 1931; '"Happy Valley". 35 stitches in face', *Sun*, 26 December 1931.

8 Pamela Nixon, 'The integration of a half-caste community at La Perouse, NSW', MA thesis, University of Sydney, 1948, p. 21.

9 Interview, Lucy Porter and Shirley Murphy, MN 4.

10 See Allen Foster, Talking Lapa Oral History Collection, Office of Board of Studies, NSW; Cyril Cooley, 'Happy Valley', *La Perouse: The Place, the People and the Sea*, Aboriginal Studies Press, Canberra, 1988, p. 52.

11 'Mayor supports camp evictions', *Daily Telegraph*, 15 July 1938.

12 Interview, Allen Foster, Talking Lapa Oral History Collection, Office of Board of Studies, NSW.

13 'Illegal occupation Happy Valley—La Perouse 1931–40', Letter from Frances Goldreck to the Secretary, the Advisory Board of NSW, 12 March 1937, SRNSW, 3/2417.4.

14   Department of Education, Schools Files, La Perouse Public School (Botany
     Heads School), Memorandum, 26 May 1932, SRNSW, 5/16561.2.

15   Gloria Ardler, 'When we were children', *La Perouse: The Place, the People
     and the Sea*, Aboriginal Studies Press, Canberra, 1988, pp. 64–5.

16   'Illegal occupation Happy Valley—La Perouse 1931–40', Report, Metro-
     politan District Surveyor, 1953, SRNSW.

17   '£600 paid for shacks at Yarra Bay', *Sunday Sun*, 9 March 1952.

18   Interview, Gladys Ardler, NSW Bicentennial Oral History Collection,
     National Library of Australia.

19   Interview, Pam Koeneman, Talking Lapa Oral History Collection, Office
     of Board of Studies NSW.

20   Nixon, 'Integration of a half-caste community at La Perouse', p. 23;
     Ardler, 'When we were children', p. 63.

21   NSWAWB, 'Daily Diaries, La Perouse', SRNSW, 4/10746.4.

22   'Meeting place of many races', *Sydney Morning Herald*, c. 1954.

23   A film made by the Department of Education in 1954 entitled *Proud
     Heritage* represented La Perouse Public School as a model school in terms
     of addressing cultural diversity. See also Alice Beauchamp, 'The social
     relationship of white and coloured children in the sixth class at La
     Perouse Public School'. BA (Hons) thesis, University of Sydney, 1953;
     NSW Parliamentary Debates, 16 June 1951, p. 3594.

24   W.E. Champion, 'The state school and the colour bar', *New Horizons*,
     no. 3, Spring, 1949, pp. 8–11.

25   'Half-caste problem', *Pix*, 8 April 1950, pp. 17–23.

26   NSW Parliamentary Debates, 16 October 1951, p. 3591; 'Aborigines
     "neglected"', *Sunday Sun*, 14 October 1951; '"Not wanted" claim by
     aborigines', *Sun*, 15 October 1951; 'Defence of conditions at La
     Perouse', *Sydney Morning Herald*, 17 October 1951; 'Minister to inspect
     "shanties": A state minister is to inspect living conditions of aborigines
     and whites at La Perouse "shanty town"', *Daily Telegraph*, 17 October
     1951; 'Aborigines can't find other homes', *Sun*, 15 October 1951.

27   James Harle Bell, 'Some demographic and cultural characteristics of the
     La Perouse Aborigines', *Mankind*, vol. 5, no. 10, June, 1961, pp. 428–29.

28   'Tidying the "cradle of the nation"', *Sydney Morning Herald (Sun-Herald)*,
     13 September 1959. See also 'Letter to the editor', *Sydney Morning
     Herald*, 30 April 1952, p. 2; 'Neglected state of historic spot', *Sydney
     Morning Herald*, 30 April 1952; Randwick Municipal Council, Mayor's

Minute, 2 February 1954, no. 4/1954, Bowen Library; 'Letter to the editor', *Sun*, 12 December 1955, p. 2; 'Historic La Perouse: A finger slowly withering', *Sydney Morning Herald*, 4 October 1958.

29 'Squalid living conditions at "Hill 60"', *Sydney Morning Herald*, 24 February 1952; "Shanty town" camps in Yarra Bay—La Perouse area. Mr Renshaw proposes to "clean them up"', *Sydney Morning Herald*, 8 March 1952; 'Protests against proposed demolition, real estate market in houses', *Sun*, 9 March 1952; 'Shantytown to be demolished', *Daily Mirror*, 4 April 1952; 'Early steps to be taken to demolish—Randwick Council to co-operate with Lands Dept (Mr Renshaw)', *Mirror*, 4 April 1952; 'Comment by residents—no clean up wanted', *Sun*, 2 May 1952; 'Reply—Alderman LA Walsh', *Sydney Morning Herald*, 3 May 1952.

30 James Harle Bell, 'The La Perouse Aborigines', PhD thesis, University of Sydney, 1959, p. 23.

31 George Cann, 'Hill 60', in *Talking Lapa: A Local Aboriginal Community History of La Perouse*, NSW Board of Studies, Sydney, 1995, p. 30.

32 Kathleen Stewart, *A Space on the Side of the Road: Cultural Poetics in an 'Other' America*, Princeton University Press, Princeton, NJ, 1996, p. 44.

33 *The Voyage of Governor Phillip to Botany Bay*, John Stockdale, London, 1789, facsimile edition, Hutchinson, Melbourne, 1982, p. 44.

34 Royal Australian Historical Society, Minutes, 10 June 1955, History House, Sydney. The parentheses and question mark nicely encapsulate the ambiguity that characterised the monument project.

35 'Phillip's landing at Botany re-enacted', p. 2. See also *Dawn*, 1 April 1956, p. 2, in which the caption to a photograph reads 'Joe Timberry [*sic*] a great-great-great grandson of the original king of the tribe at the time of the landing at Yarra Bay presents a boomerang to the Governor'. The ascription of Joe Timbery, rather than Robert Timbery, is an error.

36 'Phillip's landing at Botany re-enacted', *Sydney Morning Herald*, 19 January 1956, p. 2; Randwick Municipal Council, Mayoral Minute, 17 January 1956, Bowen Library. It seems that the presentation of an 'historical' boomerang had become a tradition of sorts. A boomerang held in the National Library of Australia, which pictures a sailing ship, presumably the *Endeavour*, was made by Aboriginal people at the Lake Tyers settlement on the occasion of the 1951 jubilee anniversary of Federation. It was presented to the then prime minister of Australia.

37 'As it was in the beginning', *Daily Telegraph*, 19 January 1956.

38 *Dawn,* 1 April 1956, p. 2.

39 'Racial antagonism: A hatred in early flower', *Sydney Morning Herald,* 8 October 1958.

40 Bell, 'The La Perouse Aborigines', p. 379.

41 Nixon, 'The integration of a half-caste community at La Perouse, NSW', MA thesis, University of Sydney, 1948, pp. 41, 44–8.

42 'Racial antagonism: A hatred in early flower', 1958.

43 ibid.

44 Locally, the name Yarra Bay is still widely used. So, while Yarra Bay does not appear in the list of suburbs in the *Gregory's Sydney Street Directory,* Yarra Junction is listed in italics, indicating that it is a 'local name not shown on the maps'. The bay is still known as Yarra Bay and the beach as Yarra Beach. There is also a road called Yarra Road.

45 Interview, George Cann Jnr, MN 1.

46 In the 1970s, when the Aboriginal settlement was remodelled, the local council authority asked residents what they wanted to call the street. They nominated the surnames of prominent local Aboriginal families. That suggestion was rejected. However, the surnames of some well-known Aboriginal identities were used instead, such as Goolagong after the tennis player, Yvonne Goolagong.

47 Randwick Municipal Council, Minute, 19 May 1959, Bowen Library.

48 Ann Curthoys, 'Immigration and colonisation: New Histories', *UTS Review,* vol. 7, no. 1, May 2001, pp. 170–79.

Chapter 6

1 Randwick Municipal Council, Correspondence, National Trust of Australia to RMC, 21 April 1965, Bowen Library. In 1974, the National Trust of Australia listed the 'Botany Bay Entrance' on its register of heritage places.

2 Denis Mahoney, *Botany Bay: Environment Under Stress,* Charden Publications, Sydney, 1979, p. 61.

3 Noel Butlin, 'Port Botany and its users', in N.G. Butlin (ed.), *The Impact of Port Botany,* The Consultative Committee of the Academy of Social Sciences in Australia, The Australian Academy of the Humanities and the Australian Academy of Science in association with ANU Press, Canberra, 1976, p. 6.

4 John Morton and Nicholas Smith, 'Planting indigenous species: A sub-version of Australian eco-nationalism', *Quicksands: Foundational Histories in Australia and Aeotearoa New Zealand*, eds K. Neumann, N. Thomas and H. Ericksen, UNSW Press, Sydney, 1999, p. 165.

5 Maritime Services Board of NSW, 'Submission to the Botany Bay Port and Environment Inquiry', MSBNSW, Sydney, 1976, S188.

6 *Birth of a Port* (motion picture), Cinesound Movietone Productions, Sydney, c. 1974.

7 L.A. Punch, *The Port Botany Project: A Policy Statement by the Government of NSW*, Parliament House, Sydney, 1976, p. 1.

8 *Botany Bay Port and Environment Inquiry: Report of the Inquiry*, 25 November 1976.

9 *Botany Bay Port and Environment Inquiry*, transcripts of evidence and written submissions, Nos S148, S159, S173.

10 *City in Peril: A Review of the Botany Bay Port and Environment Inquiry*, Total Environment Centre, Sydney, 1977, p. 6.

11 The reports produced by the Botany Bay Project edited by N.G. Butlin and published by ANU Press, Canberra are: *Sydney's Environmental Amenity 1970–1975*, 1976; *Factory Waste Potential in Sydney*, 1977; *The Impact of Port Botany*, 1976. The project also produced a number of working papers.

12 *Environmental Policy in Australia: The Botany Bay Project*, Australian Academy of Science, Australian Academy of the Humanities, Academy of the Social Sciences in Australia, Canberra, 1972.

13 ibid., p. 2.

14 ibid.

15 ibid., p. 3.

16 Hugh Stretton, 'The Botany Bay Project: Historians and the study of cities', *Historical Studies*, vol. 19, April 1981, pp. 430–39.

17 ibid., p. 437.

18 Noel Butlin, *Our Original Aggression: Aboriginal Populations of South-eastern Australia, 1788–1850*, Allen & Unwin, Sydney, 1983.

19 National Trust of Australia, 'Just do nothing and watch it die: who cares?', c. 1970.

20 Paul Carter, *The Road to Botany Bay: An Essay in Spatial History*, Faber & Faber, London, 1987, p. xiii.

21 Nicholas Thomas, *Discoveries: The Voyages of Captain Cook*, Allen Lane, London, p. 112.

22 ibid.
23 See: RMC, Correspondence, I.M. Sim to Randwick Municipal Council, 'Aboriginal rock carvings at La Perouse', 25 January 1965, Bowen Library.
24 R.H. Mathews, 'Gravures & peintures sur roches par les Aborigènes d'Australie', *Extrait des Bulletins de la Societe d'Anthropologie de Paris*, tome IX, IV serie, Paris, 1898, p. 426. I am indebted to Martin Thomas for an English translation of this article. According to his diary, R.H. Mathews 'went to Rock carvings at head of Botany Bay' on 18 February 1894, R.H. Mathews Diary, 1893–1908, NLA 8006/1/2.
25 W.D. Campbell, *Aboriginal Carvings of Port Jackson and Broken Bay*, Government Printer, Sydney, 1899, p. 6.
26 E.W. O'Sullivan, 'Where three histories meet', *Daily Telegraph*, 28 March 1906, p. 13. The article was also published in a collection of writing by E.W. O'Sullivan entitled *Under the Southern Cross: Australian Sketches, Stories and Speeches*, William Brooks & Co., Sydney, 1906.
27 ibid.
28 NSW Joint Committee of the Legislative Council and Legislative Assembly upon Aborigines Welfare, Minutes of evidence and report, 2 February 1966, 1967, p. 5.
29 See for example NSW Aborigines Welfare Board, Annual Reports, JNSWLC, 1960–1966.
30 NSW Joint Committee of the Legislative Council and Legislative Assembly upon Aborigines Welfare, p. 41.
31 'The forgotten families of La Perouse', *Daily Mirror*, 6 April 1966, p. 4.
32 NSW Joint Committee of the Legislative Council and Legislative Assembly upon Aborigines Welfare, p. 149.
33 ibid., p. 67.
34 'The old king (and his people) nobody wants', *Daily Telegraph*, 10 February 1966.
35 'Aborigines at La Perouse', *Sydney Morning Herald*, 14 March 1928, p. 14.
36 'La Perouse. Aborigines protest against removal', *Sydney Morning Herald*, 4 April 1928, p. 24.
37 'La Perouse transformed. Neat Aborigines greet committee', *Sun*, 8 March 1966.
38 Interview, Iris Williams, MN 12.
39 'Why should we leave?', *Sydney Morning Herald*, 4 February 1966, p. 10.
40 Interview, Stan Sharkey, MN 5.

41 ibid. This primarily economic formulation of Aboriginal people's struggles to claim rights to land, not only at Botany Bay but elsewhere, was
typical of the time.

42 Dolores Hayden, *The Power of Place: Urban Landscapes as Public History*,
MIT Press, Cambridge, MA, 1995, p. 9.

43 'The passing of King Billy', *New South Wales Aborigines Advocate*, no. 61,
31 July 1906, p. 3; Iris Williams, 'Dreaming trees', *La Perouse: The Place,
the People and the Sea*, Aboriginal Studies Press, Canberra, 1988, p. 3; Iris
Williams and Beryl Beller, 'Wandering and trees', *La Perouse: The Place,
the People and the Sea*, p. 27.

44 'Relic of King Billy coming down', *Sydney Morning Herald*, 13 July 1974,
p. 4.

45 Williams, 'Dreaming trees', *La Perouse: The Place, the People and the Sea*,
p. 3.

46 NSW Joint Committee of the Legislative Council and Legislative Assembly upon Aborigines Welfare, Report. The late 1960s was a period of
significant change in policy direction relating to Aborigines. As a result
of the 1967 referendum, the Commonwealth assumed responsibility
from the states for Aboriginal affairs.

47 NSW Department of Youth and Community Services, Special Bundle,
'Endeavour Project', 1969–70, SRNSW, 7/8965; 'Integrated village at
La Perouse urged', *Sydney Morning Herald*, 7 May 1969; 'Plan for La
Perouse', *Sydney Morning Herald*, 8 May 1969.

48 La Perouse Society, The Endeavour Project, unpublished draft report,
January 1969; 'Integrated village at La Perouse urged', *Sydney Morning
Herald*, 7 May 1969, p. 4; 'Sydney's "Siberia" says resident', *Sydney
Morning Herald*, 7 May 1969, p. 4.

49 Iris Williams, 'Housing on the reserve', *La Perouse: The Place, the People
and the Sea*, Aboriginal Studies Press, Canberra, 1998, p. 8.

50 Geoffrey Moorhouse, *Sydney*, Allen & Unwin, Sydney, 1995,
pp. 98–100.

Chapter 7

1 For a transcript of the oration, see: 'Mourning for some . . .', *Sydney
Morning Herald*, 30 April 1970, p. 6. This newspaper report had a sting

in its tail. It described how an attempt to 'send smoke signals across the bay . . . had failed for lack of expertise' and concluded by saying that 'some residents of the reserve lay asleep in the sun, oblivious of the Cook landing, the day of mourning, and the struggle towards the rebirth of their race'. It made, in other words, that enduring charge of apathy on the part of Aborigines that had long characterised reportage of Cook's landing commemorations.

2   Margaret Jones, 'At La Perouse, a new drive for land rights', *Sydney Morning Herald*, 25 April 1970, p. 2.

3   'Aborigines mourn Cook's landing', *Daily Telegraph*, 30 April 1970, and 'Aboriginals in mourning', *Australian*, 30 April 1970. The matter of whether there was actually a tribe called Illawarra is disputed. According to Iris Williams and Beryl Beller, 'Wandering and trees', *La Perouse: The Place, the People and the Sea*, Aboriginal Studies Press, Canberra, 1988, p. 27: 'Illawarra was the district, not the tribe'. Regardless of the accuracy or otherwise of the historical details, the purpose of highlighting Trudy Longbottom's genealogical claims was the same: La Perouse on Botany Bay was represented as a site of continuous Aboriginal occupation since the time of Cook.

4   'Landmark for local Aborigines', *Maroubra Magazine*, 19 September 1984, p. 3. A short while later, the Land Council was given control of Yarra Bay House and the land around it, previously owned by the Department of Youth and Community Services. Yarra Bay House became the hub of the local Aboriginal community: 'Aborigines win land', *Eastern Herald*, 15 August 1985, p. 1.

5   'Aborigines get the deeds to their land', *Southern Courier*, 26 September 1984, p. 4.

6   Iris Williams, 'Housing on the reserve', *La Perouse: The Place, the People and the Sea*, p. 8.

7   See W.E.H. Stanner, *After the Dreaming*, 1968 Boyer Lectures, Sydney, 1969, for a discussion of the creation of the Great Australian Silence, and Henry Reynolds, *The Breaking of the Great Australian Silence: Aborigines in Australian Historiography, 1955–1983*, Sir Robert Menzies Centre for Australian Studies, University of London, 1984, for a discussion of its dismantling.

8   The photograph was taken by Juno Gemes. It was used on the front cover of an edition of *Meanjin* (no. 2, 1992) edited by Dipesh Chakrabarty and

devoted to post-colonial history. The photograph was likewise used on the cover of *We Have Survived: Images and Language '88: Aboriginal Perspectives on a Celebration*, a joint project between the Inner City Education Centre and the NSW Teachers' Federation, compiled by Jenni Stocks, Inner City Education Centre, Sydney, c. 1988.

9 Heather Goodall, *Invasion to Embassy: Land in Aboriginal Politics in New South Wales 1770–1972*, Allen & Unwin, Sydney, pp. 359–60

10 Chris Healy, *From the Ruins of Colonialism: History as Social Memory*, Cambridge University Press, Melbourne, 1997, p. 10.

11 Elisabeth Wynhausen, 'Changing face of Australia Day', *Sun-Herald*, 31 January 1993, p. 35.

12 Lucy Macken and Chips Mackinolty, 'For Aborigines, it was Survival '92', *Sydney Morning Herald*, 27 January 1992, p. 5.

13 *Survival* (videorecording), SBS, 26 January 1997.

14 ibid.

15 Bob Evans, 'Invasion party', *Sydney Morning Herald (Good Weekend)*, 25 January 1992, p. 9.

16 Mitchell & Clouston Inc., 'Heritage festival—Yarra Bay environs. National bicentennial project. Preliminary report', unpublished report to Bicentennial Committee, Randwick Municipal Council, 1985, p. 1.

17 Land Systems Pty Ltd, Phillips Landing bicentennial project, unpublished report to Randwick Municipal Council, February 1986, p. 2.

18 ibid., p. 1.

19 Paul Carter, *Lie of the Land*, Faber & Faber, London, 1996, p. 4.

20 'La Perouse bushtucker walkway opens', *Koori Mail*, 16 July 1997, p. 9.

21 *The Opal that Turned into Fire*, compiled by Janet Mathews, Magabala Books, Broome, 1994, pp. 10–12.

22 In a slightly different way, in a paper to the *Extrait des Bulletin de la Societe d'Anthropologie de Paris* in 1898, R.H. Mathews used the proximity of the French monuments to the rock carvings at La Perouse as a device for presenting his research on Aboriginal rock paintings and carvings to a French audience. See 'Gravures & peintures sur rochers par les Aborigènes d'Australie', *Extrait des Bulletin de la Societe d'Anthropologie de Paris*, tome IX, IV serie, 1898.

23 'Original touch for Botany Bay', *Sydney Morning Herald*, 4 March 2000, p. 1.

24 The art historian Bernard Smith used the metaphor of the locked cupboard to describe how white Australians tried to forget 'crimes perpetrated upon Australia's first inhabitants'. Bernard Smith, *The Spectre of Truganini*, Australian Broadcasting Commission, Sydney, 1980, p. 10.

25 Margot Nash (director), *Vacant Possession* (videorecording), Wintertime Films and As If Productions, Australia, 1994.

26 Bob Debus, 'Foreword', Botany Bay National Park Plan of Management, NSW National Parks and Wildlife Service, May 2002.

27 ibid., p. 25.

28 ibid., p. 27.

29 E.W. O'Sullivan, 'Where Histories Meet', *Daily Telegraph*, 28 March 1906, p. 13.

BIBLIOGRAPHY

Parliamentary papers and reports

Captain Cook's Landing Place Trust, *Reports*, JNSWLC, 1942–1953

Homes for Unemployed Trust, *Annual Reports*, JNSWLC, 1935–1942

La Perouse Monuments Trust, *Reports*, JNSWLC, 1950–1953

NSW Aborigines Protection Board, *Annual Reports*, JNSWLC, 1884–1939

NSW Aborigines Welfare Board, *Annual Reports*, JNSWLC, 1940–1969

NSW Board of Health, *Report of the Board of Health upon the Late Epidemic of Smallpox, 1881–2*, JNSWLC, 1883

NSW Board of Health, *Coast Hospital, Little Bay: Annual Reports*, JNSWLC, 1884–1930

NSW Protector of Aborigines, *Reports*, JNSWLC, 1882–1883

NSW Joint Committee of the Legislative Council and Legislative Assembly on Aboriginal Welfare, *Minutes of Evidence and Report*, 1967

Select Committee on the Aborigines, *Report with Appendix, Minutes of Evidence and Replies to a Circular Letter*, 1845

Archival collections

Botany Bay National Park (BBNP), Papers and Reports, NSW National Parks and Wildlife Service, Sydney

Botany Bay Port and Environment Inquiry, transcripts of evidence and written submissions, Nos. S148, S159, S173, Sydney, 1976

La Perouse Aboriginal Community Archive, Social History Section, Museum of Applied Arts and Sciences (MAAS), Sydney

Lapérouse Museum Archives, Botany Bay National Park (BBNP), Cable Station, La Perouse

Mathews, R.H., Papers, Manuscript Collection, National Library of Australia

Matthews, D., Papers, Mitchell Library, Sydney

NSW Aborigines Protection Board (NSWAPB), Minutes 1890–1939, State Records Authority of New South Wales (SRNSW)

NSW Aborigines Welfare Board (NSWAWB), Minutes and correspondence 1940–1969, SRNSW

NSW Board of Health, Minutes 1881–1883, SRNSW

NSW Colonial Secretary, Register of Aboriginal Reserves 1875–1904, SRNSW

NSW Department of Education, Schools Files, La Perouse Public School (Botany Heads School), SRNSW

NSW Department of Lands, Metropolitan Land Board, Special bundle: 'Illegal occupation Happy Valley—La Perouse' 1931–40, SRNSW

NSW Department of Youth and Community Services, Special bundle: 'Endeavour Project' 1969–70, SRNSW

Piper, J., Correspondence, Mitchell Library

Randwick and District Historical Society, Research files, Randwick Council Town Hall, Randwick

Randwick Municipal Council, (RMC) Minutes and correspondence 1880–1980, Bowen Library, Maroubra

Royal Australian Historical Society, Minutes and correspondence 1950–1957, History House, Sydney

Oral history collections

Individual Heritage Group Oral History Collection, Sydney, 1985–1987 (in possession of author)

La Perouse Aboriginal Community Oral History Collection, Museum of Applied Arts and Sciences (MAAS), Sydney, 1986, MRS 278/1–9

Botany Bay Oral History Collection, Maria Nugent, Sydney, 1996–1997, MN 1–17 (in possession of author)

New South Wales Bicentennial Oral History Project, National Library of Australia, 1987, ORAL TRC 2310 INT 71 and 163

Talking Lapa Oral History Collection, 1993–1994, Office of the Board of Studies, NSW

Film and video

Proud Heritage (film), NSW Department of Education, 1954

Survival (videorecording), SBS television, 26 January 1997

Botany Bay: Two Centuries After Cook (videorecording), New South Wales Film and Television Office, Sydney, 1989

Birth of a Port (film), Cinesound Movietone Productions, Sydney, 1974

Vacant Possession (videorecording), Wintertime Films and As If Productions, 1994

Unpublished theses and papers

Beauchamp, A., 'The social relationship of white and coloured children in the sixth class at La Perouse Public School', BA Hons thesis, University of Sydney, Sydney, 1953

Bell, J.H., 'The La Perouse Aborigines', PhD thesis, University of Sydney, Sydney, 1959

Burden, T., 'Governor Phillip's landing in Botany Bay: An analysis of the charts', paper presented to the Randwick and District Historical Society, Randwick, Sydney, 1992

Curthoys, A., 'Race and ethnicity: A study of the response of British Colonists to Aborigines and Chinese and non-British Europeans in New South Wales', 1856–1881, PhD thesis, Macquarie University, Sydney, 1973

Hage, G., 'Familiar colonialisms', paper presented at 'Turning the Soil' conference, Canberra School of Art, Canberra, May 1998

Nixon, P., 'The integration of a half-caste community at La Perouse', NSW, MA thesis, University of Sydney, Sydney, 1948

Nugent, M., 'Revisiting La Perouse: A post-colonial history', PhD thesis, University of Technology, Sydney, 2001

Vanni, I., '"When Jimmy Cook arrived": The production of artefacts at La Perouse', paper presented at 'Symbolic Souvenirs', a one-day conference on cultural tourism, Centre for Cross Cultural Research, ANU, April, 1998

Heritage and historical studies

Botany Bay National Park: Draft Plan of Management, NSW National Parks
    and Wildlife Service (NPWS), Sydney, 1995
Botany Bay National Park Plan of Management, NSW NPWS, Sydney, May
    2002
Elmowy, R., *Happy Valley*, Report to NSW NPWS, Sydney, 1991
Gojak, D., La Perouse Headland Conservation Plan, NSW NPWS, Sydney,
    n.d.
Kass, T., *The Bare Island and La Perouse Monuments Historic Sites: An Histor-
    ical Investigation*, Report to NSW NPWS, Sydney, 1989
—— 'Long Bay Complex 1896–1994: A History', unpublished final report
    for NSW Department of Public Works, Sydney, March 1995
Land Systems Pty Ltd, *Phillips Landing Bicentennial Project, Yarra Bay*, Design
    Report to Randwick Municipal Council, Sydney, 1986
Mitchell & Clouston Inc., 'Heritage festival—Yarra Bay Environs, National
    Bicentennial Project, Preliminary report', unpublished report to Bicen-
    tennial Committee, Randwick Municipal Council, 1985
O'Brien, C., *Phillips' Landing Bicentennial Project, Yarra Bay, Heritage*, Report
    to Randwick Municipal Council, Sydney, 1986

Ephemera, pamphlets and tourist guides

Birthplace of Australia, Pamphlet No. 4, Randwick Historical Society, Sydney,
    1967
*Ceremony of the Unveiling of the Sir Joseph Banks Memorial . . . at Captain
    Cook's Landing Place, Kurnell, on Saturday 6th September, 1947*, Captain
    Cook's Landing Place Trust, Sydney, 1947
Dymocks Illustrated Guide to Sydney, 8th edn, Dymocks Book Arcade Ltd,
    Sydney, 1922
Gregory's Sydney Street Directory (various editions)
Guide to the City of Sydney and Pleasure Resorts of New South Wales, NSW
    Bookstall Company, Sydney, 1921
The Hotel Metropole Visitors' Guide to Sydney and NSW, Hotel Metropole Ltd,
    Sydney, 1899

Kurnell: The Birthplace of Australian History, 2nd edn, Immigration and Tourist Bureau, Sydney, 1909

Laperouse Museum Guide, Sydney District NSW NPWS, Sydney, 1988

Laperouse Museum & Botany Bay National Park: Discovery tour, NSW NPWS, Sydney, 1991

The Laperouse Museum, flyer prepared by NSW NPWS, n.d.

NSW Calendar and General Post Office Directory, Stephens & Stokes, Sydney, 1833–1837

A Randwick Ramble, Part 3, La Perouse to Maroubra, A Guide to Historic Places from La Perouse to Maroubra, 4th edn, Randwick and District Historical Society, Randwick, 1989

Sand's Sydney and NSW Directory

Sydney Wants to See You! Issued for the Railway Commissioner for NSW, NSW Tramways, Sydney, 1928

Trips around Sydney, NSW, Issued by the NSW Government Tourist Bureau, Government Printer, Sydney, 1912

Visitors Guide to Sydney, Issued by the NSW Government Tourist Bureau, Government Printer, Sydney, 1919

Newspapers, magazines and periodicals

Australian

Australian Aborigines' Advocate

B.P. Magazine

Daily Mirror

Daily Telegraph

Daily Telegraph Pictorial

Dawn

Eastern Herald

Globe Pictorial

Illustrated Sydney News

Koori Mail

Maroubra Magazine

Meanjin

New Dawn

New South Wales Aborigines' Advocate

People
Pix
Southern Courier
Sun
Sun-Herald
Sydney Mail
Sydney Morning Herald
United Aborigines' Messenger
Wentworth Courier

Books and journal articles

Arago, J., *Narrative of a Voyage Around the World: In the* Uranie *and* Physcienne *Corvettes commanded by Captain Freycinet . . .1817, 1818, 1819 and 1820*, Truettel, London, 1823

Attenbrow, V., *Sydney's Aboriginal Past: Investigating the Archaelogical and Historical Records*, UNSW Press, Sydney, 2002

Attwood, B., *The Making of the Aborigines*, Allen & Unwin, Sydney, 1989

—— ed., *In the Age of Mabo: History, Aborigines and Australia*, Allen & Unwin, Sydney, 1996

—— *Rights for Aborigines*, Allen & Unwin, Sydney, 2003

Attwood, B. and Arnold, J., eds, *Power, Knowledge and Aborigines*, special edition of the *Journal of Australian Studies*, no. 35, La Trobe University Press in association with the National Centre for Australian Studies, Monash University, Bundoora, Victoria, 1992

Attwood, B. and Magowan, F., *Telling Stories: Indigenous History and Memory in Australia and New Zealand*, Allen & Unwin, Sydney, 2001

Attwood, B. and Markus, A., *The Struggle for Aboriginal Rights: A Documentary History*, Allen & Unwin, Sydney, 1999

Barwick, D., 'Writing Aboriginal history: Comments on a book and its reviewers', *Canberra Anthropology*, vol. 4, no. 2, 1981, pp. 74–86

Bashford, A., 'Epidemic and governmentality: Smallpox in Sydney 1881', *Critical Public Health*, vol. 9, no. 4, 1999, pp. 301–16

Bayley, G., *Sea-Life Sixty Years Ago: A Record of Adventures which Led to the Discovery of Relics of the Long-missing Expedition Commanded by the Comte de la Perouse*, Kegan Paul, Trench & Co., London, 1885

Beaglehole, J.C., *Cook The Writer*, Sixth Arnold Wood Memorial Lecture, Sydney University Press, Sydney, 1970

—— 'Textual introduction' in *The Journals of Captain James Cook, Volume 1, The Voyage of the Endeavour, 1768–1771*, ed. J.C. Beaglehole, Hakluyt Society at Cambridge University Press, Cambridge, 1968

Beasley, P., 'The Aboriginal household in Sydney', in *Attitudes and Social Conditions*, eds R. Taft, J. Dawson and P. Beasley, ANU Press, Canberra, 1970, pp. 137–86.

Beckett, J., ed., *Past and Present: The Construction of Aboriginality*, Aboriginal Studies Press, Canberra, 1988

—— 'The past in the present; the present in the past: Constructing a national Aboriginality', in *Past and Present: The Construction of Aboriginality*, ed. J. Beckett, Aboriginal Studies Press, Canberra, 1988, pp. 191–217

—— 'Aboriginality in a nation-state: The Australian case', in *Ethnicity and Nation-Building in the Pacific*, ed. M.C. Howard, United Nations University, Tokyo, 1989

—— 'Walter Newton's history of the world—or Australia', *American Ethnologist*, vol. 20, no. 4, 1993, pp. 675–95

Bell, J.H., 'The economic life of mixed blood Aborigines', *Oceania*, no. 26, 1956, pp. 181–99

—— 'Some aspects of the New South Wales situation: Some factors hindering the assimilation policy in NSW with special reference to the South Coast and La Perouse', *Proceedings of Conference on Welfare Policies for Australian Aborigines, University of New England*, Armidale, 1960, pp. 71–87

—— 'Some demographic and cultural characteristics of the La Perouse Aborigines', *Mankind*, no. 5, 1961, pp. 425–38

—— 'Aborigines in Sydney', *Australian Aboriginal Studies: A Symposium of Papers Presented at 1961 Research Conference*, Oxford University Press, Melbourne, 1963, pp. 429–33

—— 'The part-Aborigines of New South Wales: Three contemporary social situations', in *Aboriginal Man in Australia: Essays in Honour of Emeritus Professor A.P. Elkin*, eds R.M. Berndt and C.H. Berndt, Angus & Robertson, Sydney, 1965, pp. 369–419

Bennett, T., ed., *Celebrating the Nation: A Critical Study of Australia's Bicentenary*, Allen & Unwin, Sydney, 1992

Bertie, C.H. 'Captain Cook and Botany Bay', *The Royal Australian Historical Society Journal and Proceedings*, vol. x, part v, 1924, pp. 233–78

—— 'Captain Arthur Phillip's first landing place in Botany Bay', *JRAHS*, vol. 38, part 3, 1952, pp. 107–26

Bonyhady, T. and Griffiths, T., eds, *Words for Country: Landscape and Language in Australia*, UNSW Press, Sydney, 2002

Boughton, C.R., *A Coast Chronicle: The History of the Prince Henry Hospital 1881–1981*, n.p., c.1981

Brooks, J., *Shut Out from the World: The Hawkesbury Aborigines Reserve and Mission, 1889–1946*, 2nd edn, rev., Deerubbin Press, Sydney, 1999

Broome, R. with Jackamos, A., *Sideshow Alley*, Allen & Unwin, Sydney, 1998

Bruce, C., 'The prodigal tree stump', *Art and Australia*, vol. 25, no. 4, Winter 1988, pp. 496–99

Bruce, C. and Callaway, A., 'Dancing in the dark: Black corroboree or white spectacle?', *Australian Journal of Art*, vol. 9, 1991, pp. 78–104

Butlin, N.G., ed., *The Impact of Port Botany*, The Consultative Committee of the Academy of Social Sciences in Australia, The Australian Academy of the Humanities and the Australian Academy of Science in association with ANU Press, Canberra, 1976

—— ed., *Sydney's Environmental Amenity 1970–1975*, The Consultative Committee of the Academy of Social Sciences in Australia, The Australian Academy of the Humanities and the Australian Academy of Science in association with ANU Press, Canberra, 1976

—— ed., *Factory Waste Potential in Sydney*, The Consultative Committee of the Academy of Social Sciences in Australia, The Australian Academy of the Humanities and the Australian Academy of Science in association with ANU Press, Canberra, 1977

—— *Our Original Aggression: Aboriginal Populations of Southeastern Australia, 1788–1850*, Allen & Unwin, Sydney, 1983

Byrne, D., 'Deep nation: Australia's acquisition of an indigenous past', *Aboriginal History*, no. 20, 1996, pp. 82–107

Campbell, W.D., *Aboriginal Carvings of Port Jackson and Broken Bay*, Government Printer, Sydney, 1899

Carleton, F., *Terre de France a La Perouse? A Study of the Historical Foundations of a Local Myth 1788–1950*, Pere Receveur Commemoration Committee, Occasional Publications, no. 1, 1995

Carter, P., *The Road to Botany Bay: An Essay in Spatial History*, Faber & Faber, London, 1987

—— *Living in a New Country: History, Travelling and Language*, Faber & Faber, London, 1992

—— *The Lie of the Land*, Faber & Faber, London, 1996

Champion, W.E., 'The state school and the colour bar', *New Horizons*, no. 3, Spring, 1949, pp. 8–11

City in Peril: A Review of the Botany Bay Port and Environment Inquiry, Total Environment Centre, Sydney, 1977

Clark, M., 'The choice of Botany Bay', *Historical Studies*, vol. 9, no. 35, November 1960, pp. 221–30

Clendinnen, I., *Dancing with Strangers*, Text Publishing, Melbourne, 2003

Clifford, J., *The Predicament of Culture: Twentieth Century Ethnography, Literature and Art*, Harvard University Press, Cambridge, MA, 1988

—— *Routes: Travel and Translation in the Late Twentieth Century*, Harvard University Press, Cambridge, MA, 1997

Cochrane, P., ed., *Remarkable Occurrences: The National Library of Australia's First 100 Years 1901–2001*, National Library of Australia, Canberra, 2001

Collins, D., *An Account of the English Colony in New South Wales*, David Collins, London, 1798, reprinted A.H. & A.W. Reed in association with the Royal Australian Historical Society, Sydney, 1974

Coltheart, L., 'The moment of Aboriginal history', in *Past and Present: The Construction of Aboriginality*, ed. J. Beckett, Aboriginal Studies Press, Canberra, 1988, pp. 179–90

Cooper, D.M., *Randwick 1859–1909*, Randwick Municipal Council, Sydney, 1909

Cowlishaw, G., *Blackfellas, Whitefellas, and the Hidden Injuries of Race*, Blackwell Publishers, Malden, 2004

Curson, P., *Times of Crisis: Epidemics in Sydney 1788–1900*, Sydney University Press, Sydney, 1985

Curthoys, A., 'Good Christians and useful workers: Aborigines, Church and State in NSW 1870–1883', in *What Rough Beast? The State and Social Order in Australian History*, ed. Sydney Labour Group, Allen & Unwin, Sydney, 1982, pp. 31–56

—— 'Entangled histories: Conflict and ambivalence in non-Aboriginal Australia', in *The Resurgence of Racism: Howard, Hanson and the Race Debate*, eds. G. Gray and C. Winter, Monash Publications in History, Department of History, Monash University, Melbourne, 1997, pp. 117–28

—— 'Immigration and colonisation: New Histories', *UTS Review*, vol. 7, no. 1, May 2001, pp. 170–79

Darian-Smith, K. and Hamilton, P., eds, *Memory and History in Twentieth-century Australia*, Oxford University Press, Melbourne, 1994

Davison, G., *The Use and Abuse of Australian History*, Allen & Unwin, Sydney, 2000

Dening, G., *Mr Bligh's Bad Language: Passion, Power and Theatre on the Bounty*, Cambridge University Press, Melbourne, 1992

—— 'MS1 Cook, J. Holograph Journal' in *Remarkable Occurrences: The National Library of Australia's First 100 Years 1901–2001*, ed. P. Cochrane, National Library of Australia, Canberra, 2001, pp. 1–19

A Documentary History of the Illawarra and South Coast Aborigines 1770–1850, comp. by M. Organ, Aboriginal Education Unit, Wollongong University, Wollongong, 1990

Driver, F. and Samuel, R., 'Rethinking the idea of place', *History Workshop Journal*, no. 39, Spring, 1995, pp. v–vii

Dunmore, J., *Pacific Explorer: The Life of Jean-François de la Perouse, 1741–1788*, Dunmore Press, Palmerston North, New Zealand, 1985

The Endeavour Journal of Joseph Banks: 1768–1771, ed. J.C. Beaglehole, The Trustees of the Public Library of New South Wales in association with Angus & Robertson, Sydney, 1962

Environmental Policy in Australia: The Botany Bay Project, Australian Academy of Science, Australian Academy of the Humanities, Academy of the Social Sciences in Australia, Canberra, 1972

Etherington, N., 'Myths of local history', in *Bridging the Gap: National Issues in Local History, Proceedings of the Royal Australian Historical Society's Annual Conference with Affiliated Societies*, Macquarie University, Sydney, 1988, pp. 6–19

Fitzgerald, S., *Rising Damp: Sydney 1870–90*, Oxford University Press, Melbourne, 1985

Foucault, M., 'Of other spaces', *Diacritics*, Spring, 1986, pp. 22–27

—— 'Questions on geography', in *Power/Knowledge: Select Interviews and Other Writing 1972–1977*, ed. C. Gordon, Harvester Press, Brighton, Sussex, 1980, pp. 63–77.

Frost, A., *Botany Bay Mirages: Illusions of Australia's Convict Beginnings*, Melbourne University Press, Melbourne, 1994

Gammage, B., 'Places and peoples: Local and regional, national and international', *Australian Studies*, no. 9, 1988, pp. 5–9

Garton, S., *Medicine & Madness: A Social History of Insanity in NSW 1880–1940*, UNSW Press, Sydney, 1988

Gille, D., 'Maceration and purification', *Zone*, 1/2, 1986, pp. 227–83

Gillis, J., ed., *Commemorations: The Politics of National Identity*, Princeton University Press, Princeton, New Jersey, 1994

Goodall, H. 'King Burraga and local history: Writing Aborigines back into the story', in *Bridging the Gap: National Issues in Local History, Proceedings of the Royal Australian Historical Society's Annual Conference with Affiliated Societies*, Macquarie University, Sydney, 1988, pp. 40–48

—— *Invasion to Embassy: Land in Aboriginal Politics in New South Wales, 1770–1972*, Allen & Unwin in association with Blackbooks, Sydney, 1996

—— 'Too early yet or not soon enough? Reflections on sharing histories as process', in *Challenging Histories: Reflections on Australian History*, special edition of *Australian Historical Studies*, no. 118, ed. K. Darian-Smith, 2002, pp. 7–24

The Governor's Noble Guest: Hyacinthe de Bougainville's Account of Port Jackson, 1825, trans. and ed. Marc Serge Rivière, Miegunyah Press, Melbourne, 1999

Griffiths, T., *Hunters and Collectors: The Antiquarian Imagination in Australia*, Cambridge University Press, Melbourne, 1996

Grosz, E., 'Bodies-cities' in *Sexuality and Space*, ed. Beatriz Columina, Princeton Papers on Architecture, Princeton, New Jersey, 1992, pp. 241–54

Halbwachs, M., *The Collective Memory*, trans. F.J. Ditter, Harper and Row, New York, 1980

Hallam, S., 'A view from the other side of the western frontier: or "I met a man who wasn't there . . ."', *Aboriginal History*, vol. 7, no. 2, 1983, pp. 134–56

Harris, J., *One Blood: 200 Years of Aboriginal Encounters with Christianity*, Albatross, Sydney, 1990

Hayden, D., *The Power of Place: Urban Landscapes as Public History*, MIT Press, Cambridge, MA, 1995

Healy, C., *From the Ruins of Colonialism: History as Social Memory*, Cambridge University Press, Melbourne, 1997

Hirst, J.B., *Convict Society and its Enemies: A History of Early New South Wales*, Allen & Unwin, Sydney, 1983

History of Randwick, Comp. D.M. Cooper, Randwick Municipal Council, Randwick, 1909

Holden, R., *Bunyips: Australia's Folklore of Fear*, National Library of Australia, Canberra, 2001

Horner, F., *Looking for La Perouse: D'Entrecasteaux in Australia and the South Pacific, 1792–1793*, Miegunyah Press, Melbourne, 1995

Hunter, J., *An Historical Journal of Events at Sydney and at Sea, 1787–1792*, John Stockdale, London, 1793, reprinted Angus & Robertson in association with the Royal Australian Historical Society, Sydney, 1968

Hutton, P.H., *History as an Art of Memory*, University Press of New England, Hanover and London, 1993

Jacobs, J.M., *Edge of Empire: Postcolonialism and the City*, Routledge, London and New York, 1996

Janson, S. and Macintyre, S., eds, *Making the Bicentenary*, Melbourne University Press, Melbourne, 1988

Jervis, J. and Flack, L.R., *A Jubilee History of the Municipality of Botany 1888–1938*, W.C. Penfold, Sydney, 1938

The Journals of Captain James Cook, Volume 1, The Voyage of the Endeavour, 1768–1771, ed. J.C. Beaglehole, Hakluyt Society at Cambridge University Press, Cambridge, 1968

The Journal of Governor King, in J. Hunter, *An Historical Journal of Events at Sydney and at Sea, 1787–1792*, John Stockdale, London, 1793, reprinted Angus & Robertson in association with the Royal Australian Historical Society, Sydney, 1968

Kelly, M., ed., *Sydney—City of Suburbs*, UNSW Press, Sydney, 1987

Kennedy, K., 'Aboriginal display at La Perouse', *Mankind*, vol. 1, no. 4, 1932, pp. 86–87

Kerr, J., 'Strange objects: A special kind of identity', in *Remarkable Occurrences*, ed. P. Cochrane, National Library of Australia, Canberra, 2001, pp. 87–103

La Perouse, Jean-François de Galaup de, *The Voyage of Jean-François de Galaup de la Perouse, 1785–1788*, trans. and ed. John Dunmore, Hakluyt Society, London, 1995

La Perouse: The Place, the People and the Sea, Aboriginal Studies Press, Canberra, 1988

Larcombe, F.A., *The History of Botany 1788–1970*, rev. 2nd edn, Council of the Municipality of Botany, Botany, 1970

Larkin, M., *Sutherland Shire: A History to 1938*, Sutherland History Press, Sydney, 1998

Linnekin, J., 'Ignoble savages and other European visions: The La Perouse affair in Samoan History', *Journal of Pacific History*, vol. 26, no. 1, June 1991, pp. 3–26

Long, R., *Providential Channels*, Australian Inland Mission, Sydney, 1935

Lowenstein, W., *Weevils in the Flour: An Oral History of the Depression*, Scribe, Melbourne, 1981

Lynch, W.B. and Larcombe, F.A., *Randwick 1859–1959*, Produced for the Council of the Municipality of Randwick NSW by O. Zielger Publications, Sydney, 1959

—— *Randwick 1859–1976*, Produced for the Council of the Municipality of Randwick NSW by O. Zielger Publications, Sydney, 1976

Maddock, K., 'Myth, history and a sense of oneself', in *Past and Present: The Construction of Aboriginality*, ed. J. Beckett, Aboriginal Studies Press, Canberra, 1988, pp. 11–30

Mahoney, D., *Botany Bay: Environment Under Stress*, Charden Publications, Sydney, 1979

Malouf, D., *The Spirit of Play*, ABC Books, Sydney, 1998

Marcus, J., *A Dark Smudge upon the Sand: Essays on Race, Guilt and the National Consciousness*, LhR Press, Sydney, 1999

Martin, J., *The Australian Sketch Book*, James Tegg, Sydney, 1838

Massey, D., 'Places and their pasts', *History Workshop Journal*, no. 39, Spring, 1995, pp. 182–92

Mathews R.H. and Enright, W.J., 'Rock paintings and carvings of the Aborigines of New South Wales', *Australasian Association for the Advancement of Science*, Brisbane, 1895

Mathews, R.H., 'Gravures & peintures sur rochers par lese Aborigenes d'Australia', *Extrait des Bulletins de la Societe d'Anthropologie de Paris*, Paris, 1898, pp. 425–32

McCarthy, F.D., *New South Wales Aboriginal Place Names and Euphonious Words, with their Meanings*, Australian Museum, Sydney, 1946

McDonald, B., *The Landing Place of Captain Arthur Phillip at Botany Bay*, Popinjay Publications' Australian Historical Monographs Series, no. 10, 1990

McIntyre, L.R., 'Botany Bay' in *Some Australians Take Stock*, ed. J.C.G. Kevin Longmans, Green and Co., London, 1939, pp. 39–67

Miller, D.P. and Reill, P.H., *Voyages, Botany, and Representations of Nature*, Cambridge University Press, Cambridge, 1996

Milo, D., 'Street names', in *Realms of Memory: The Construction of the French Past, Vol. 2*, ed. Pierre Nora, trans. Arthur Goldhammer, Eng. lang. edn, Columbia University Press, New York, 1997, pp. 363–89

Moorhouse, G., *Sydney*, Allen & Unwin, Sydney, 1995

Morris, B., 'Making histories/living history', *Social Analysis*, no. 27, April 1990, pp. 83–92

Morris, J., *Sydney*, Viking, London, 1992

Morton, J. and Smith, N., 'Planting indigenous species: A subversion of Australian eco-nationalism', in *Quicksands: Foundational Histories in Australia and Aotearoa New Zealand*, eds K. Neumann, N. Thomas and H. Ericksen, UNSW Press, Sydney, 1999, pp. 153–75

Muecke, S., 'Discourse, history, fiction: Language and Aboriginal history', *Australian Journal of Cultural Studies*, vol. 1, no. 1, May 1983, pp. 71–79

—— *Textual Spaces: Aboriginality and Cultural Studies*, UNSW Press, Sydney, 1992

—— 'Towards an Aboriginal philosophy of place', in *Speaking Positions: Aboriginality, Gender and Ethnicity in Australian Cultural Studies*, eds P. van Toorn and D. English, Department of Humanities, Victoria University of Technology, Melbourne, 1995, pp. 167–79

Mulholland, G., *The Heritage of Botany*, MMA Production, Sefton, 1989

Myers, F., *Botany: Past and Present*, John Woods, Sydney, 1885

Neumann, K., Thomas, N. and Ericksen, H., eds, *Quicksands: Foundation Histories in Australia and Aotearoa New Zealand*, UNSW Press, Sydney, 1999

Neville, R., *A Rage for Curiosity: Visualising Australia 1788–1830*, State Library of New South Wales Press, Sydney, 1997

Nora, P., ed., *Realms of Memory: The Construction of the French Past*, Vols 1–3, trans. Arthur Goldhammer, Eng. lang. edn, Columbia University Press, New York, 1996–1998

Nugent, M., 'La Perouse versus Larpa: Contesting histories of place', *Public History Review*, vols 5/6, 1996–97, pp. 192–99

—— 'Botany Bay: Voyages, Aborigines and history', *Journal of Australian Studies*, no. 76, 2003, pp. 27–33

The Opal that Turned into Fire, Comp. by Janet Mathews, Magabala Books, Broome, 1994

O'Sullivan, E.W., *Under the Southern Cross: Australian Sketches, Stories and Speeches*, William Brooks & Co., Sydney, 1906

Park, R., *Ruth Park's Sydney*, rev. by Ruth Park & Rafe Champion, Duffy & Snellgrove, Sydney, 1999

—— *The Companion Guide to Sydney*, Collins, Sydney, 1973

Parsons, M., 'The tourist corroboree in South Australia to 1911', *Aboriginal History*, vol. 21, 1997, pp. 46–75

Phillips, R.B., 'Why not tourist art? Significant silences in Native American museum representations', in *After Colonialism: Imperial Histories and Postcolonial Displacements*, ed. Gyan Prakash, Princeton University Press, Princeton, New Jersey, 1995, pp. 98–125

Pilger, J., *A Secret Country*, Vintage, London, 1990

Potts, D., 'A positive culture of poverty represented in memories of the 1930s Depression', *Journal of Australian Studies*, no. 26, May 1990, pp. 3–14

—— '"There's nothing squashed about me": A Reply to Scott and Saunders', *Journal of Australian Studies*, no. 41, 1994, pp. 50–55

—— 'Tales of suffering in the 1930s Depression', *Journal of Australian Studies*, no. 41, 1994, pp. 56–66

Prost, A., 'Monuments to the dead', in *Realms of Memory: The Construction of the French Past, Vol. 2*, ed. P. Nora, trans. Arthur Goldhammer, Eng. lang. edn, Columbia University Press, New York, 1997, pp. 309–30

Reynolds, H., *The Breaking of the Great Australian Silence: Aborigines in Australian Historiography, 1955–1983*, Sir Robert Menzies Centre for Australian Studies, University of London, 1984

—— *Frontier: Aborigines, Settlers and Land*, Allen & Unwin, Sydney, 1987

The Road to Botany Bay: The Story of Frenchmans Road Randwick through the Journals of Lapérouse and the First Fleet Writers, comp. and introd. Alec Protos, Randwick and District Historical Society, Randwick, 1988

Robinson, P., *The Women of Botany Bay: A Reinterpretation of the Role of Women in the Origins of Australian Society*, Macquarie Library, Sydney, 1988

Robson, L.L., *The Convict Settlers of Australia: An Enquiry into the Origin and Character of the Convicts Transported to New South Wales and Van Diemen's Land 1787–1852*, Melbourne University Press, Melbourne, 1965

Rose, D.B., 'Remembrance', *Aboriginal History*, vol. 13, nos 1–2, 1989, pp. 135–48

—— *Hidden Histories: Black Stories from Victoria River Downs, Humbert River and Wave Hill*, Aboriginal Studies Press, Canberra, 1991

—— 'Hard times: An Australian study', in *Quicksands: Foundational Histories in Australia and Aotearoa New Zealand*, eds K. Neumann, N. Thomas and H. Ericksen, UNSW Press, Sydney, 1999, pp. 2–19

Salt, D., *Kurnell—Birthplace of Modern Australia: A Pictorial History*, Clarion House, Sydney, 2000

Scott, E., *Laperouse*, Angus & Robertson, Sydney, 1912

—— *A Short History of Australia*, Oxford University Press, Melbourne, 1916

—— 'Some notes on Laperouse', *JRAHS*, vol. 13, no. 5, 1927, pp. 273–88

Scott, J. and Saunders, K., 'Happy days are here again? A reply to David Potts', *Journal of Australian Studies*, no. 36, March 1993, pp. 10–22

Selkirk, H., 'La Perouse and the French Monuments at Botany Bay', *JRAHS*, vol. 4, 1918, pp. 329–61

Shelton, R.C., *From Hudson Bay to Botany Bay: The Lost Frigates of Lapérouse*, NC Press, Toronto, 1987

Sim, I.M., 'Records of the rock engravings of the Sydney district: Nos 111–137, part 2', *Mankind*, vol. 6, no. 2, November 1963

Smith, B., *European Vision and the South Pacific 1768–1850*, Oxford University Press, London, 1960

Spearritt, P., 'Mythology of the Depression', in *The Wasted Years? Australia's Great Depression*, ed. Judy Mackinolty, Allen & Unwin, Sydney, 1981, pp. 1–9

Stallybrass, P. and White, A., *The Politics and Poetics of Transgression*, Cornell University Press, New York, 1986

Stanner, W.E.H., 'The Aborigines', in *Some Australians Take Stock*, ed. J.C.G. Kevin, Longmans, Green & Co., London, 1939

—— *After the Dreaming*, 1968 Boyer Lecture, Sydney, 1969

Stewart, K., *A Space on the Side of the Road: Cultural Poetics in an 'Other' America*, Princeton University Press, Princeton, New Jersey, 1996

Stretton, H., 'The Botany Bay Project: Historians and the study of cities', *Historical Studies*, vol. 19, April 1981, pp. 430–39

Talking Lapa: A Local Aboriginal Community History of La Perouse, NSW Board of Studies, Sydney, 1995

Taussig, M., *Shamanism, Colonialism and the Wild Man: A Study in Terror and Healing*, University of Chicago Press, Chicago, 1986

Taylor, P., ed., *After 200 Years*, Aboriginal Studies Press, Canberra, 1988

Telfer, E.J., *Amongst Australian Aborigines: Forty Years of Missionary Work. The Story of The United Aborigines' Mission*, Fraser & Morphet, Sydney, 1939

Tench, W., *1788: Comprising a Narrative of the Expedition to Botany Bay and a Complete Account of the Settlement at Port Jackson*, ed. Tim Flannery, Text Publishing, Melbourne, 1996

Thomas, J., 'A history of beginnings', in *Quicksands: Foundational Histories in Australia and Aotearoa New Zealand*, eds K. Neumann, N. Thomas and H. Ericksen, UNSW Press, Sydney, 1999, pp. 115–31

Thomas, N., *Discoveries: The Voyages of Captain Cook*, Allen Lane, London, 2003

Torgovnick, M., *Gone Primitive: Savage Intellects, Modern Lives*, University of Chicago Press, Chicago, 1991

'"A trip to La Perouse and elsewhere in 1838", Extract from *The Voyage of the Venus* by A. Du Petit Thouras, Paris, 1841', trans. Sir William Dixson, *JRAHS*, vol. 28, 1942, pp. 119–22

United Aborigines Mission, *Challenging the Almighty: 100 Years of Trusting God in the Work of the UAM*, Box Hill, Victoria, 1994

The Voyage of Governor Phillip to Botany Bay, John Stockdale, London, 1789, reprinted Angus & Robertson in association with the Royal Australian Historical Society, Sydney, 1970

A Voyage to New South Wales, The Journal of Lieutenant William Bradley RN of HMS Sirius 1786–1792, The Trustees of the Public Library of New South Wales in association with Ure Smith, Sydney, 1969

Ward, L. and O.H.H., 'A Frenchman sees Sydney in 1819: Translated from the letters of Jacques Arago', *JRAHS*, vol. 53, 1967, pp. 277–94

West, O., *Old and New Sydney*, Reprinted from the *Sydney Morning Herald*, Edward Hordern and Sons, Sydney, 1882

White, J., *Journal of a Voyage to New South Wales*, J. Dabrett, London, 1790, reprinted Angus & Robertson in association with the Royal Australian Historical Society, Sydney

White, R., *Inventing Australia: Images and Identity, 1688–1980*, Allen & Unwin, Sydney, 1981

—— 'The shock of affluence: The fifties in Australia', *The Australian Dream: Design of the Fifties*, ed. J. O'Callaghan, Powerhouse Publishing, Sydney, 1993

Willey, K., *When the Sky Fell Down: The Destruction of the Tribes of the Sydney Region, 1788–1850s*, Collins, Sydney, 1979

Zelinka, S., *Tender Sympathies: A Social History of Botany Cemetery and the Eastern Suburbs Crematorium*, Hale & Iremonger, Sydney, 1991

INDEX

Aboriginal camps
  behaviour in 46–7
  creation of reserves 63–4
  see also La Perouse Aboriginal
    settlement
Aboriginal history-making
  1770 encounter 15
  alternative narrative 33
  Captain Cook stories 27–33,
    84–8
  from colonial collections 34–6
  Cook's arrival 28–3
  historical-event basis 85–6
  indigenous interpretation 35–6
  and landscape 182
  Lapérouse's deeds 117
  *La Perouse: The Place, the People
    and the Sea* (community
    history) 181–2
  reclaiming history 33–6
  relics as 89–90
  reposition starting point 56–7
  sense of continuity 56–7
  see also historiography; oral
    tradition
Aboriginality
  1950s images 138
  archetypal image of 76
  national sense of 187
  staged for tourists 76–9
Aboriginal Land Rights Act NSW
  1983 180, 183
Aboriginal–non-Aboriginal relations
  changing consciousness 175–6,
    182–3
  Depression camps 123–4
  see also racism

Aboriginal presence
  Botany Bay 29, 56, 64, 137–9,
    177
  conspicuous 46–7
  depicted in paintings *11, 23,*
    104–5
  in history writing 27–9
  ignored 54–7, 61, 63–4
  La Perouse 128, 137–9, 188–9
  Sydney 45–46
'Aboriginal Quarters' 53–4
Aborigines
  1770 encounter 9–16
  1788 encounter 15
  1845 parliamentary inquiry 48
  disruptive behaviour 46–7
  emerging national politics 175–9
  employment 46, 126, 127–8
  government control 121
  government policies 38–39
  as historical sources 28–31, 100
  inquiry into welfare 164–6
  as national community 186–9
  protocol for meeting strangers
    13–15
  relationship to the land 52–3,
    164–8
  relocation of 45–7, 48, 83
  social reformation 171–2
  tourists' perception of 75
  tourists' reactions to 71–3
  as tourist traders 72–3, 79–83
  treatment by historians 27–9,
    31–3, 54–7
  two-sided 'assault' 94–5
  Victoria Downs region 15–16
  violent encounters 93–4

243